Nanny Knows Best

Nanny Knows Best

How to bring up a happy child

NANNY SMITH AND NINA GRUNFELD

WITH PHOTOGRAPHS BY MARTYN J. ADELMAN

BBC BOOKS

The Authors

Nanny Smith is the daughter of a Yorkshire policeman. In 1938, when she was sixteen, she attended a one-year course to become a nursery nurse at St Monica's in Bradford, one of many homes around the country where unmarried girls came to have their babies. After she qualified, she stayed on as a member of staff until she left to go to her first family. Altogether Nanny has looked after ten children, the oldest of whom is now in her fifties, the youngest of whom is still at school.

Nina Grunfeld was one of Nanny Smith's 'children', and Nanny has since been a maternity nurse to Nina's three children. Nina Grunfeld has written nine books, including *Pregnancy Week By Week*, one of Mothercare's best-selling publications.

Designed by Simon Bell

© Jean Smith and Nina Grunfeld 1993

The moral rights of the authors have been asserted

Photographs by Martyn J. Adelman
© Martyn J. Adelman 1993

Photographic paper and film kindly supplied by Kodak Ltd.

The photographs of Nina as a baby, on pages 53, 61, 66, 73, 77, 128, 131, 133, 176, 178, 179, 185, 202, 212 and 215, were taken by Gitta Grunfeld, and are © Gitta Grunfeld 1993

ISBN 0 563 36966 3 (paperback)
ISBN 0 563 36987 6 (hardback)

First published in 1993
Published by BBC Books, a division of BBC Enterprises Limited, Woodlands, 80 Wood Lane, London W12 0TT

Set in Janson by Ace Filmsetting Limited, Frome
Printed and bound in Great Britain by Butler & Tanner Ltd, Frome and London
Jacket and cover printed by Richard Clay Limited, St Ives plc

Author's note

Each time one of my three children was born I received different advice from the doctors, midwives and nurses in charge. I am sure that they believed that the advice they were giving was in my and my baby's best interest, and that it was based on the latest research, but it was often confusing. I came home to Nanny who always said the same thing. Both she and I feel that if something has worked once, in anything but the most exceptional circumstances it is likely to work again. I wanted parents to be able to be guided by her confidence in the same way that I was. Throughout the book we have mentioned current government recommendations if they differ considerably from Nanny's, but we both feel that in a few years they may change, whereas Nanny's views will probably have stayed the same.

Unless a specific child is being written about, throughout the book your baby is referred to as 'he', not because of any bias but to differentiate you, the mother or child carer, from your baby. The term husband has been used instead of partner because in all the families Nanny worked for the parents of the chidren were married.

Nina Grunfeld

Contents

to Johnny

Children Learn What They Live

If a child lives with criticism,
   He learns to condemn.

If a child lives with hostility,
   He learns to fight.

If a child lives with ridicule,
   He learns to be shy.

If a child lives with shame,
   He learns to feel guilty.

If a child lives with tolerance,
   He learns to be patient.

If a child lives with encouragement,
   He learns confidence.

If a child lives with praise,
   He learns to appreciate.

If a child lives with fairness,
   He learns justice.

If a child lives with security,
   He learns to have faith.

If a child lives with approval,
   He learns to like himself.

If a child lives with acceptance and friendship,
   He learns to find love in the world.

DOROTHY LAW NOLTE

Having a Nanny

For the last few years, whenever I told anyone I was writing a book with my childhood nanny, people were very interested.

'Is it a book for nannies to read?' they would ask.

'No,' I would say. 'For mothers, or for nannies of course, but mainly for mothers.'

'But what does a nanny's experience of children have to do with a mother's? After all, she doesn't have anything else to do. What has she got to say that would be useful for mothers?'

In a way they were right. What did Nanny know about juggling extreme tiredness with amusing a husband *and* running a home? And yet I knew that what Nanny had to say about looking after children could change every mother's life.

'Well . . . ' I would begin. 'You see Nanny has looked after children for over fifty years. In that time she has learnt that all children grow up in the end. She has learnt how *not* to worry about them and instead how to encourage them so they blossom. And, above all, having done it so often, she has learnt all the shortcuts. So, if you follow what Nanny says you will have happier, more confident children – *and* more time for yourself.'

I hated having to explain Nanny like that, but if I wanted people to listen and learn from her I had to do it. At the best of times it is difficult to describe one of your best friends in a few sentences, but when they are wearing a label saying 'Nanny', which to most people means either

OPPOSITE *Nanny with my daughter Ursula*

a young girl in search of a career or, worse still, a Victorian tyrant in a starched uniform, it is almost impossible.

Nanny is her own woman, a remarkable person who from a very early age decided she was going to devote her life to children – and did just that. In many ways extremely traditional and yet deep down highly unconventional, she vowed that she would *never* put a child down and would *never* make a child do anything because she wanted him to. It made her a very special nanny.

When I first met Nanny it seems I was a typical six-week-old baby. On her first night she was left in my room with an 'I'm afraid she wakes during the night' warning. But there was no need for any of that. With Nanny by my side I slept like a model baby that night, and every other one; and to this day, sleeping remains one of the things I am undeniably good at.

Nanny and I had a six-year love affair, which for the last four years was shared with my brother. The three of us did everything together – we shared our ordinary days, our high days and holidays. Nanny made up our routines and we all three lived and breathed by them and yet had more freedom than anyone could imagine. I'm sure we even stuck to her routines on her two afternoons a week off, and no doubt, during her holidays, although I can't remember her ever being away. She was our whole lives.

Once Nanny left and I was a little older I remember her occasionally coming to tea and feeling slightly desperate hearing all the stories about her 'beloved' next set of charges. Of course I was jealous. I was also bored – who wants to hear about other children? I was not remotely interested in any of the adventures Nanny was longing to tell me about, nor in the photos of her children she was so keen to share with me.

Then one day I found I was pregnant. I was immediately on the phone. For the last fifteen years her endless chatting about all her children and all the other nannies' children had not interested me in the least, yet now I wanted all that love, knowledge and experience for *my* child. I instinctively felt that there was no one else I would trust my child with – not even myself. So, with bated breath, I dialled Nanny's number.

'Nanny. What are you doing around the middle of September?' I asked (Nanny is always booked up for months ahead). 'You have to come and help – I'm going to have a baby'. From the moment that she said 'Yes of course, sweetie. I'll move in whilst you're in hospital', I was happy to listen to any stories about children she could tell me – and I learnt and learnt.

Nanny moved in. She put all the baby's clothes away, folding them beautifully into little piles in the drawers. She made up the crib so cosily that I could happily have snuggled down in it there and then. She double-checked that my husband took the right clothes with him when he collected me and the baby from hospital. But her practical skills were only a small part of the delight of having her with us. For six weeks my son and I were both her babies – me, her first (and favourite) and Michael, much loved for being mine – and from the moment we stepped through the front door we were treated as if we were the only beings left in the world.

Nanny knew what to do at all times. Her sense of timing was impeccable. Before I even knew I needed it, she brought me one drink after another and endless rounds of marmalade on toast. But, more importantly, she pointed out the joys of my baby to me. 'Look at him, sweetie . . .' she would say time and time again, 'isn't he wonderful?' Or, on other occasions 'He's so clever . . . I'm sure he's been here before'. She admired the top of his head peeping out of the blankets, the way he stretched, the way he stared, the way he sucked, the way he kicked. And slowly she helped bring me out of myself and into motherhood.

She worked her magic on Michael too. Night after night she held him in her arms if he was wakeful and brought him to me if he was hungry. She knew what each of his noises and cries meant and she slowly and carefully explained them to me. During the day she kept him calm, cosy and clean, and during the night she made him feel warm and secure. I could see the encouragement she gave him, the way she helped him develop. I noted the times she left him by himself, exploring a world of his own, and how she knew just when to scoop him up out of it and into her arms. And, on a simply practical level, by the time she left us at six weeks, he could take liquids from a teaspoon, he was very definitely smiling and he slept through the night.

Since then Nanny has returned twice to act as maternity nurse for my two daughters, Frances and Ursula. Each time I felt the same sense of calm that I must have felt on that first night we shared a room together all those many years ago. It spread itself around our home and worked its subtle magic on my children as it did on me.

As we were working on this book together I learnt a lot from Nanny, not only how to bring up children, but also how I was brought up. I found out a lot about myself and my past which a parent would probably rarely remember. In many ways it is a very personal book. The pictures in this book are of my children and their friends and they were taken in my home.

It took me five years – the entire time we were working on this book – to persuade Nanny that it should be published and not just go into my files. I was fortunate enough to have Nanny look after both me and my children and I wanted as many people who look after children as possible to be able to learn from her wisdom and experience in the same way that I have been lucky enough to do. I think this book has managed to capture some of that knowledge – and some of her magic too.

Nina Grunfeld

Being a Nanny

Up to the early 1930s a young girl who wanted to be a nanny would more often than not have been found a place with a family. As nursery maid she would clean the pram, the highchair and anything else that needed cleaning, would set the table, wash and iron the clothes and help with the older children; the new baby would always be looked after by nanny. In a grand house there would have been two under-nurses responsible for looking after the older children, so it could take a long, long time to become proper nanny and she might well have left that family and gone as nanny to another family rather than wait her turn.

By the time I began my training more would-be nannies trained in children's homes or colleges than in grand houses under nanny. I had always wanted to train and presumed I would go to a training place for nursery nurses although I did not know quite where.

I was on our annual holiday at the seaside with my parents in 1938 when I picked up the *Yorkshire Post* and saw: 'Girls wanted as probationers to train as nursery nurses.' I had only just left school and it seemed like the answer to a prayer. I applied straightaway.

Ever since I was twelve, still smarting from one of my mother's tellings-off, I had decided that when I grew up I would be involved with children; that I would always see their point of view and that I would look at each and every situation through their eyes. I had vowed never to put a child down and never to make him do what I wanted, just because I wanted it.

The eldest of three children, I came from a happy home and had a very secure childhood, but I felt strongly that my mother's way of dealing with me was too repressive; she never tried to understand my viewpoint. Later I came to appreciate how admirable she was in many ways, but the ideas I formed at that time remained and became the basis of my whole approach to child care.

My application was successful and at the age of sixteen I began the one-year course for nursery nurses in a place called St Monica's Home in Bradford – I was in fact on night duty when the Second World War broke out. It was a home run by a Church committee where unmarried girls came to have their babies in the days when it was a disgrace to give birth outside marriage; some girls came in as much as six months beforehand.

At any one time, St Monica's had between six and fifteen 'patients'. Before they had their babies, they worked as if they were in their own home, doing simple housework and helping in the laundry. After their babies were born they stayed firmly in bed for six days, and we brought them bed-pans because they were not allowed to leave their beds even to go to the lavatory, and they all breast fed their children. On the seventh day they only got up for supper, on the eighth day for tea as well, on the ninth day for lunch too and after ten days they would get out of bed for good and sit round the kitchen table talking. By today's standards, weren't these mothers spoilt? Just as it should be! When a mother left, she was given a complete layette, bought from a little shop near by, and a shawl, and off she went. It was a very cosy set-up and, of course, a haven for the unmarried mother, since in those days there was no social security.

As well as looking after new babies we had a dozen children in the nursery, aged from a month to three years, who had been born at the Home but not taken away by their mothers. The children had very nice toys and clothes and the same doctor came in the middle of every morning to look at them all. Each child's mother visited twice a week, often taking her child out for the day. If a mother still did not want – or could not take – her child once he was three he had to be fostered, because there were no provisions for children over three at St Monica's.

We probationers were being trained to work as children's nurses in private houses; it was an excellent training but hard work and very, very strict. We were called at 6.15 a.m. and worked until 8 p.m. every day, with two hours off-duty (four on Sunday) at some time during the day. We also took our turn doing the night shift from 8 p.m. to 8 a.m.

As well as our practical experience we had lectures once a week. By the end of our year we had to have made two sets of babies' clothes, one knitted and one sewn. When we had completed the course we got a certificate to say that we had been trained to care for children up to three years old.

I got my first job in 1940 through my father who knew somebody who knew somebody who wanted somebody for her two children. They were the first children I was to look after. I was there for seven years, then I went back home and began looking for a temporary job because I planned to get married. I was offered a six-month-old baby by a local agency; at the interview I told the mother that I could only stay for a few months but they wanted to have me. When it came to the crunch I decided not to get married: I had become so attached to the baby I did not want to leave. So I stayed on until she was six and starting school.

We have to make choices in life and often a choice made early on directs you to the path that you will follow for the rest of your days.

People have often asked me why, loving children as I do, I never did get married and have babies of my own. Yet for someone who values above all else the company of the very young, marriage is not necessarily the right choice. Your own babies grow up all too soon and before you know it they will have flown the nest. A nanny can continue to do what she does best – and loves best – look after little children, for the whole of her working life.

For all us nannies our children were the centre of our interest and they were (and still are) discussed all the time. We all thought our own children were the best. Our children's lives were our lives, because we were with them all the time until we left them. We would sometimes ask advice from the older nannies over supper and talk over problems or get ideas. We very, very often went on our own holidays with a nanny friend, because it really was our whole life. We cared so much because we were the person entrusted by the child's mother to take care of her child and obviously a good nurse would never do anything that the mother would not approve of. We were so proud of our children.

We took a pride in our appearance too. As children's nurses our outdoor uniform was a grey costume or grey coat and a grey or navy blue felt hat – smart and simple. Indoors I wore a dress in strawberry pink (the colour of where I was trained) which was my working kit. It had long sleeves which I usually rolled up and then I put what we called 'pie frills' on either arm. They were white cotton and looked neat and tidy and kept the sleeves from slipping down. When I was no longer busy with my chores I put the sleeves down and attached stiff, white cuffs. I also wore a stiffly starched white belt, fastened with mother-of-pearl studs and a white cotton apron and either a soft white detachable 'Peter Pan' collar which I had to tack on every time I washed it or the stiff collar which attached with studs that I had worn when training.

Even today when working as a maternity nurse I wear a white overall when working. I would not have worked anywhere unless I could have worn a uniform. It was smart and clean and in a way it was a status symbol. All us nannies were pleased to be dressed as a child's nurse and on our days off we wore what we wanted, whatever the fashion was.

A nanny's work included caring for the children's nursery, their toys and their clothes. I also looked after my own room and things. The children and I had a separate life from the rest of the household – it was a little world on its own. Our food arrived at the nursery on trays which were prepared by the cook or, in some cases, the mother. Nursery food was simple; the only cooking nannies ever did was for the first two years of a child's life when we were very fussy about what the baby ate and would do all the steaming and sieving, either in the kitchen or on a tiny stove that we had in the nursery. I also made the children's 5 p.m. tea, so I kept jam, honey and yeast spread in the nursery, and every day I fetched fresh bread, milk and butter from the kitchen. To make my own hot drinks or to heat up the new baby's bottle, I had an electric kettle which I kept on a table on the landing, just outside the nursery.

The first year in a new family was the easiest as there was only the first baby so there was just washing, ironing, knitting and cooking for one little person. Of course I was up in the night as well, very often, and the day always started at 6 a.m. with the early morning feed and change. As time went on there would be a school child to get off to school as well as a toddler and baby.

Being a nanny of the old school was not so much a job as a way of life. We worked twenty-four hours a day with one day off each week and a weekend off each month. We were always together with our children until they went to school and even then we were together all the time before they went and when they came home. When children were ill we were very busy keeping them in bed and looking after them. If it was the kind of weather when you couldn't go out we stayed in and made things and played games. When the child went to bed we were still responsible if the child was sad or ill or anything. Sometimes if I had a party dress or something special to iron, then I would stay up until midnight.

Naturally, in the fifty or so years since I trained as a nanny, a lot has changed in the way people live, in the standard of comfort and convenience in the home and in the way children are brought up.

I realize, of course, that there is a tendency for someone of an older generation to see all change as change for the worse, yet I want to say what I honestly believe: that most of the improvements in what they call 'the quality of life' in the last twenty years have benefited the parent rather than the child. It seems to me that many parents today expect their children to fit into their lives rather than to adapt their way of living to their children's needs.

Although ours was thought of as a more repressive era, within their boundaries I think children had more freedom. The child who lived in a nursery or playpen had his own safe world to develop in without anyone telling him not to touch things or treading on his toys or toes. Today a child may be given the run of the home but with it a whole set of rules to make him fit in with what adults want, or for his safety, when there are better ways of protecting him than orders and reprimands.

Playpens are rarely used so small children climb and fall and are constantly scolded for opening cupboards. Safety gates are less commonly seen though stairs are as much a danger to crawlers and toddlers as ever they were. You see small children heading for the road with someone shouting 'Stop' or 'Wait' – with reins children have a certain freedom and yet are protected. You do not need to say 'No' to them and as they are with you they feel safe and, paradoxically, free.

People think they are becoming more relaxed with their children because they have removed these 'restrictions' and yet the ways in which they are relaxed only leads to the child's needs being less well provided for. Instead of a warm, comfortable pram, little children, and indeed babies, are put into pushchairs with no springs and no possibility of tucking up against the cold and certainly no room for a comfortable mattress. The person who benefits is the adult – a pushchair can thread through a crowded high street, be wheeled into small shops and carried on to a bus or folded away in the car.

To be fair, a change like the pushchair ousting the pram, which is clearly not for the child's sake, has taken place in response to the requirements of millions of mothers who need to go out to work and who could not cope with their complicated lives without them.

Today, on top of the pressures of the working mother's life, she so often has the burden of guilt about not looking after her own children. It is difficult for me to understand why these mothers feel guilty. If you are not looking after your child because you go to work, then someone else is doing it for you. In my day, when people employed a nurse to look after the children, they certainly didn't feel guilty; it would never occur to them not to do so. They might have been brought up by a nurse themselves and, after all, to make a good job of bringing up a child is a full-time occupation; they wanted to look after their husbands and continue to lead their own lives knowing the children were well cared for. A child is a person in his own right and childhood is a time when he develops his *own* life, so a mother should never feel guilty if she is not looking after her child, so long as there is someone there who is doing the job and doing it well.

Sadly, the vocation of the children's nurse is disappearing and it is more and more looked upon as a well-paid job. Young women often no longer live in, but go daily to their jobs, so the round-the-clock continuity that spelt security for the child has gone. Children now often have to fit in with whatever their parents want or the whims of whoever can be found to look after them. It seems so irresponsible that girls leave their employ just when the child has got fond of them. What does that do for the child's feeling of security? No wonder mothers say their baby cries when they leave for work – the baby may well be being left with the third different 'nanny' that year.

We always felt that the longer a nanny could stay the better; that if you are someone who has always been there and then one day you are

not, it must be very strange for the child. Many nannies used to leave a family once the youngest child started school at five but if she was able to stay on there was always plenty to do, the child's clothes, the child's room, knitting and then meeting them from school. It is very sad when it is time to leave. It is a life that has been very happy and it is suddenly finished. It is a very, very sad time indeed.

In the really old days nannies didn't leave. They would still live upstairs in the nursery and their food would still come up on a tray and if nanny wasn't that old she would go on to the next generation. A few nannies I know do still live in their old houses and lend a hand, a little ironing or something to help out, although they are retired. But times have changed and not many still live in the old nursery – it must have been quite lonely for the ones who did, although they would be very, very pleased when the children came to see them.

When I look around and think of my nanny friends I think the children were so safe and so happy and so well cared for. They all had an added bonus because they all had very good parents and they had a nanny as well. So if the parents were not there they had a third person and were always safe. They had three people with their best interests at heart. Of course, even if they have a nanny, all children love their mother best of all, but if they feel ill they may want nanny because nanny is their best friend. Mothers also never felt jealous if their child loved nanny more, or sometimes appeared to. After all, if a mother loves her child and he loves his nanny then the mother should be pleased that he has such a loving nanny and is being so well cared for.

Nina, who pushed me into writing this book, was the fourth of the ten children I looked after until my retirement in 1983 when I settled into my little flat. At first I didn't like my new life at all, it seemed so empty, but very gradually I began to enjoy myself having plenty of time to see exhibitions, to visit places and friends, to do all things that there had been very little time for in my career of full-time nannying. I still help with children on an occasional basis and, of course, I have been maternity nurse to all three of Nina's children. I also see all my children very often and at Christmas I have a tea-party for them: it is such a joy to see them all together. I look round the table and think of measles and birthdays and tonsils and starting school and here they are – grown up.

What I keep in my handbag

Even though I no longer work full time with children, I am still prepared for most emergencies. If you stopped me in the street tomorrow you would find in my handbag, as well as my purse, bus pass and keys, everything mentioned below:

A thermometer

Folding scissors

A few plasters

Plastic spoon and knife

2 combs (one for me and one clean spare one)

Wipes

A book of soap leaves (often public basins do not have soap)

Spare clean handkerchief

Packet of tissues

Sugar lumps – in case I meet a horse

Nuts – for squirrels

Little bits of bread crust – for feeding the birds

My folding umbrella and a plastic rainhat (in case it's too windy for my umbrella)

A tape measure

A folding clothes brush

A 'hussif' – a travelling sewing kit

A pen and notebook

A packet of throat lozenges (in case I have my tickly cough)

Diary

Lavender pouch made by one of my girls – it makes my handbag smell nice.

View from the Pram

I find it a treat to be able to share a child's childhood. I see it as my work to get each child used to being in this world, to help him or her to enjoy and understand life. It's an attitude that has given me patience and fulfilment. I have always looked at my children as people who simply have not been here very long. I try and look at life through their eyes. I try and see their point of view. I am on their side – I am there for them.

People often do not realize how much children are taking in. From a very, very early age you can notice how much a child can understand. A child of eight to nine months sitting up at the end of his pram often knows exactly what you are talking about and you can see it in his face and movements. If you say to your companion that you got the baby's coat from a particular shop, the child will touch his coat, showing that he knows perfectly well what you are talking about. Consequently it is so important never to say anything horrid or negative about a young child in his or her presence.

You so often hear people wanting to put children into categories and boxes and somehow to demean them. 'Oh, doesn't he like doing that?' they will ask, amazed. Never give in to them and put the child down or start apologizing for him – stick up for your child. I just look at them and simply say: 'No, I don't think he does.' I can never understand why people always try and find fault with children. 'Doesn't he want to come to me?' they will ask. I just answer calmly: 'No. I don't think he does.'

> *'I am my child's rock'*

15

Always support your child, showing that you are on his side and want him to do what he wants to do. It is so important.

It is also important to praise your child constantly, they can never have enough approval. I have frequently said in a child's hearing 'I think he's wonderful'. People may think I'm soppy, but it boosts a child's morale no end. Just as I am always on the side of my child, I would expect the person in charge of another child to be on her child's side in case of any dispute. I am my child's rock. Provided their actions don't harm or distress other people, I think children should be able to do what they please, when they please, with as much support, encouragement and protection as I can give them. As life gives them more and more experiences, their horizons will move further and further away and on their own they will be able to cope with more and more situations. Until then I want them to be able to count on me.

I can never understand people who tease their children. It is a form of mental torture and quite diabolical. It abuses the trust they have in you. Of course teasing comes in any shape or form, from putting pretend spiders down children's backs to publicly humiliating them about their fears, dislikes or anything else. Teasing is a form of aggression and I would never, ever tease anyone, especially not a child. I would never, ever tickle a child either. Why do people do it I always wonder? I think it is very unkind. Then there are people who blow raspberries on their children's stomachs but I think it's a rather peculiar thing to do. Of course if the children enjoy it, that's fine, but if you think *you* might not enjoy it being done to you, then why are you doing it to them?

Making your child feel safe

I always try and make my children feel secure. The means to achieve this is through love. Love really is the most important thing, not cuddling, kissing, presents and treats, but instilling in the child the knowledge that all is well induces a feeling of security and trust of never having to question life. One of my children wrote to me saying 'I shall always remember you for your great kindness'; I think that's another way of saying that the child felt secure.

Children are born with trust and without fear. They accept they are

safe and secure in every way until a thought is put into their head that maybe they aren't. If, for example, you have to leave the room in which your child is playing, they will always assume you are coming back. If for any reason I have to leave the room for a long time, I just leave the child in a playpen or, if older, drawing with a book at the table, and walk out. I wouldn't say 'You'll be all right, I won't be long', I'd just leave him to it and not draw his attention to the fact that I am leaving the room. If you are always seen to come and go the child will assume you are coming back even if you go away for a slightly longer time than usual. I would never say to a child 'I won't be long' or 'I'm coming back', I would just go in and out of the room and it never worried them, they just went on playing. If you want to leave the room and your child starts crying just carry on going, don't worry them by returning. Keep your actions consistent and keep things as casual as possible. Don't come back and make a big thing out of your child's cries. If you keep calm your child will too.

After I retired I once looked after a seven-year-old girl whose mother had gone out, saying she would be back by a certain time. When the mother wasn't home one and a half hours after she'd said she would be, the little girl asked me if I thought her mother had been killed. That's a very sophisticated worry for a seven-year-old. I would think it had been put there by a previous baby-sitter who must have asked her 'What's happened to your mother? Do you think she's been killed?' on another evening when Mummy was late coming home. Children don't worry. When people say 'It won't hurt you', it's unnecessary. A child never thought it would. It's just like saying 'Don't worry, Mummy will be back soon' when they had never imagined Mummy wouldn't come back. It's only adults who make children insecure.

Calm and consistency

A calm atmosphere helps greatly to foster a sense of security. I always tried to create one. When I first took one of my children on she was eight weeks old and her mother said to me, 'I'm afraid she wakes in the night' (as of course many children do). But from the first night we slept together in the same room she slept right through until 7 a.m., when her mother came to wake us up. Whether we had a great rapport or whether she just felt a calm presence I shall never know, but she slept through the night from then on.

One way of ensuring calm is to have as few changes as possible. I know several children who have had a great many changes. One little boy always used to ask his nanny on her day off whether she would come back; he had never had a nanny who had stayed very long, there was always someone different and he was feeling a little insecure. Children like the security of one person to look after them; someone who has built up their trust and confidence.

Children will always accept what you tell them and so you must never betray them. Their life is the life you show them, they take their pattern of life from you but in return they like and need consistency. If you start by doing something with them, like taking them into bed with you in the morning, that's what they think life is. But if you have gone into their room and fed them and then put them back into their own bed, then that's what they think life is.

You must just make up your mind what suits you and your lifestyle and then introduce it positively into your child's routine. Just try not to change your mind too often – children like routine. They also need the truth from you and consistency of thought and action. One thing you must always do is to keep your promises, and if you can't, don't make them. It can be most hurtful to the child if you promise something but don't remember to keep that promise. For you it may be something you said casually, but for the child it can be quite harmful. If it only happens occasionally that's normal, anyone can forget, but if it happens all the time, the child will lose his trust.

Today so much emphasis is put on keeping your child in close contact with you, which as much as anything else wears the parent out. I see mothers with babies on their backs walking around the house with them because they have heard somewhere that the baby needs constant physical contact to feel secure. It's ridiculous. There's not just you and the baby on a desert island, you have to fit in with the household and the needs of the rest of your family as well as those of the baby. Of course you have to have contact with the baby but I really don't think it is necessary to have him always hitched to your front or back. I'm sure the baby enjoys it, but I think he will be just as happy tucked up

peacefully in his crib so long as he has some physical contact with people during the day. You see, in orphanages or children's homes, for instance, such as where I was trained, the staff have rows of babies. They couldn't all be fed on one's knee as there were too many of them. They had their bottles tucked up very carefully in their cribs and then when the feed was finished they were settled down nicely and cosily. When they were bathed and dressed they were in contact with people. Anyone coping with twins also has to cuddle first one and then the other. Nannies of twins will have fed one twin in their arms and propped the other one with the bottle and then next feed turned them the other way round. You have to have reason in all things. You don't want neglect, but then you don't want obsession either.

Often people confuse making their children feel loved with hugging them. I found a secure child really only needed cuddling when he wasn't well. Otherwise life was fun – when he was awake there were games to be played and when he was tired he went to bed. But nowadays people are always scooping their children up and hugging them. It is important to cuddle a child when he is ill, sad or very tired, and wants to climb on your knee and feel safe and be made a fuss of, but otherwise let a child get on with living. You hear people saying 'Come and let me give you a cuddle!' and 'Do you love me?', but why are they doing it? Probably because they feel insecure themselves.

I have had a child on my knee all day wrapped up in a blanket when he has not been well and I think that is fine, but I believe that when children are well and running about they should be encouraged, not smothered with a hug. You will often notice children pushing adults away and wanting to get on. Let them. You should always be available for a cuddle but do not try and soak up their personality out of them. Of course, if you are with a small child who wants to be picked up all the time, then pick them up. I always do. It worries me though. I feel there must be a hidden fear there and they need more than cuddling, they need to feel secure. And I never ever use that awful sentence 'You're a big boy now, you don't need cuddling.' You certainly do need cuddling.

Let a child develop his own life in his own time, knowing you are there, right behind him. Childhood should be golden – it is so short and so precious and the foundation of all the years ahead. It is up to us to

> '*Childhood should be golden*'

make sure children in our care have the assurance that all is well and that they are safe, happy and loved. I have often noticed that neglected children seem to love their mothers much more than a child who is safe. But it is a tortured, not a happy love. A safe child does not have to question his love. He does not need constant hugs and kisses. He just accepts. A safe child can do things that a repressed child cannot. He knows he can say what he thinks and no one will disapprove. Quite often children who are continually put down carry on doing 'naughty' things in order to assert themselves. Because everything a safe child does is accepted he does not have to push barriers so far.

Praise, rather than criticize

As your child develops don't worry about whether somebody is pleased with him or not. Your role is to be positive rather than negative. To praise him as he attempts to do different things, to admire his persistence and his experiments, not to crush him by saying 'No!' Children should be respected. Try to see their point of view before saying 'No' or getting angry. Once you have realized why they are doing something you may find you can understand and do not need to get angry but just simply distract them without a struggle.

Once a child's cord is cut he is a separate person and should be treated as one. I have always behaved with children in the same way as I have with adults. It is up to you to let children develop their own lives and not to lean on you. Do not expect them to behave the way you want them to. Let them behave the way they want to, as long as it doesn't hurt others. Life, for them, is one big experiment and you should try and create an atmosphere in which they can be experimental. I remember one of my children's cousins coming for tea in my nursery with his rather bossy nanny who insisted he ate every last crumb of sandwich before he was allowed a biscuit. When some of his sandwich fell on the floor, his nanny got angry. My little girl, age three, turned to him and said: 'It doesn't matter, you can do anything you like in this nursery.' That was the atmosphere I always tried to create. In their own room or area children should be allowed to do and say what they like, providing the room is child-proof; it is up to you to see that it is.

'Always be available for a cuddle'

I sometimes feel parents are never happy with their children. They want them to be different, to develop quicker and in different directions from the way they are going. They compare them to other toddlers they see and feel disappointed. I think this is so sad. A child will have quite enough pressure on him later. From his home he needs love, security and praise. Only this way will he be able to shine.

Children should be constantly encouraged, but to do this effectively you too need to use your imagination. I never use the words 'good' or 'bad' with children. Who is to say what's good or bad? When people use the word 'good' with children they mean he is conforming. When people say 'Isn't he a good baby?' they mean he hasn't cried and woken them up in the night. When people use the word 'bad' they mean the child is doing something that he wants to do and not what you want him to do. To me bad is being evil and killing people and good is being kind and helpful. I would never apply those words to children. Instead I think about what the child has actually done. I tell them they are 'clever', 'imaginative', 'bright', 'kind' or whatever adjective fits and I say 'Well done, sweetie!' continually. I might say 'that's very unkind' with a smaller child or 'that's rather mean' with a larger one if I was upset.

'The words "good" and "bad" are too subjective'

23

The words 'good' and 'bad' are too subjective. One of the fathers I worked for asked me every day whether his children had been 'good'. For years I always answered: 'They've been happy.' Good is what *you* would want a child to be. Happy is what they ought to be.

When a child is small, everything they do is special and they should be told so. As they get older you might occasionally secretly think they could have worked harder or been more imaginative, for example with a school essay. In that case I might sometimes say 'Well, maybe that could have been different' or 'Why don't you try it this way next time?', but I always try to be positive rather than negative. It is important to encourage them, to go along with what they are doing. I do always tell children they are wonderful, I would never dream of criticizing them. When one of my girls was four, I found a little boy who was staying with us sitting on top of her and hitting her very hard. I took him off and told him off. 'You're not to do that to my little girl,' I said. 'Why?' he replied. 'Well, she's very special . . . and you're very special too.' 'I'm not,' he said. 'All I can do is shovel up the leaves.' I thought that was very sad. I always tell my children they are very special. No-one had ever told him how special he was.

There should not be a lot of unhappiness in the lives of small children. Obviously if they are cold or hungry that will make them unhappy, but they should never be left to get that cold or hungry. It is really only when children step out over the threshold and meet a lot of different circumstances that they become unhappy. But that is when they are older and with more expectations which will sometimes lead to disappointment and, in turn, unhappiness. When children are younger you ought to be so much on their side that they need not be unhappy or angry.

It is so important for a child to have a safe feeling of trust and security. I knew of a little boy whose father said: 'You are a naughty little boy and I don't love you.' The child looked straight up into his father's eyes and replied 'Nanny loves me. She doesn't like the naughty things I do, but she still loves me.' That child was secure – he had a unique relationship with his nanny, especially as he knew his nanny would always stay with him. Although children always love their mothers best, if they have a nanny they can feel extra-specially safe. As a nanny I was my children's ally against the world. I was my children's best friend.

Golden rules

Show your child how much fun life can be

1   Try and help your child enjoy life.

2   Never push him into doing something he doesn't want to do or stop him doing something he does – unless it will cause someone else harm.

3   Don't do anything to your child that you would not want done to you.

4   Let your child develop in his own time and in his own way.

5   Never put your child down. Accept and enjoy everything he does.

6   Let your child experiment.

Support, encourage and protect your child

1   Always try to understand what your child must be thinking. Try and see every situation from his point of view.

2   Never talk about your child in his presence unless you are going to praise him.

3   Always be on your child's side. Never apologize for anything he wants to do. He is an individual – be proud of that.

4   Praise your child constantly. He can never have enough approval.

5   Never compare your child to anyone else's.

6   Be your child's rock.

Help your child feel secure

1   Never, ever tease your child.

2   Never let your child down. Always keep your promises – if you can't, don't make them.

3   Show him how much you love him – not by kissing him or giving him treats but by making him feel secure.

4   Show him you respect him.

5   Don't try and make him do things he is not yet ready for.

Create a calm atmosphere

1   Avoid unnecessary changes in your child's life.

2   Keep your actions consistent.

3   Give your child a routine and stick to it.

4   Never put ideas of fear or insecurity into a child's head.

5   Be as casual and relaxed as possible.

I

Feeding

Where I was trained, everyone breast fed their babies. If the mother is in a relaxed frame of mind and has someone to encourage her, breast feeding should be possible. But it is not the end of the world if the baby has to have a bottle. In my experience, when babies had to be bottle fed, they did very well and there were never any problems. Only two of my mothers breast fed their children and none of the others have suffered because of being bottle fed. But there is absolutely no need for a mother to breast feed her baby if she does not want to or feels she is not able to. It is just that a baby has to have some food and as a mother has food in her breasts, that is obviously the food that is meant for a baby. Not all animals automatically want to feed their young – some do reject them. Many sheep walk away from their lambs, for instance, especially first-time mothers.

Breast feeding is so handy and the milk the right temperature but I always tried to give my bottle-fed children warm milk, a cosy hug and a quiet time, so that they felt as close as possible to the feeling one must have when being breast fed. I never left a baby to hold his own bottle; I always fed him in my arms. If he is breast fed he is in his mother's arms, so why shouldn't he be if he is bottle fed? I suppose if you had several children and were desperately busy and the child was screaming for milk you would let him feed himself, but if possible I would keep the baby in my arms. I always liked it to be as peaceful as possible during a feed, so the baby was more relaxed and so was I.

OPPOSITE *Wrapping the bottle in a muslin nappy keeps the milk warm – it's like having a cover on a hot-water bottle*

Weight gain

Testing that the milk is the right temperature by dropping a little on the back of my hand (see question 31)

1 · What does the average newborn baby weigh and measure?

The average weight of a baby at birth is 3.2 kg (7 lb) and the average length 51cm (20in). Of course, some are heavier and others lighter and some longer and some shorter. A new baby almost always loses around 100 g (3–4oz) or so of weight during the first week. I'm not sure why that is. I believe it is because he doesn't take in as much liquid as he loses through urinating and sweating.

Feeding a newborn baby

'Routine makes life much easier'

2 · Is a new baby hungry the moment he is born?

We never fed a baby the first twenty-four hours of his life, we just gave him boiled water with a little glucose when he cried; we were told it took a while for the milk to be established. Our babies certainly didn't scream and scream to be fed. On day two we put them on the breast or bottle; now they put them on the breast as soon as they are born, and I hear mothers talking about the importance of 'bonding'. What nonsense, I say, you've got the rest of your lives together.

3 · How will I know when to feed my new baby?

There is a vogue for feeding babies at any old time – whenever they cry for food – but in a busy life surely it is better to have a routine, which will need to be a little flexible, of course. If, for example, a brand-new baby is fed at 6 a.m. he can then be tucked up until 10 a.m. while older children are dressed and given breakfast in peace and various chores done. Then, when the older children are either settled with toys or have gone to school, the little one can be bathed and fed again in peace.

I know of many young mothers who demand feed their babies, that is they feed them whenever they want food, and their lives are ruled by this little baby. And it becomes especially difficult to demand feed baby number two or three because you have the other children to look after. For example, if you demand feed your baby and he wants feeding at 8.30 a.m. in the morning, when the other children need getting ready for school, it is complete chaos. Routine makes life much easier and children feel safe.

Routine or demand feeding?

4 · What is your daily routine?

I follow the same routine with both breast- and bottle-fed babies. It's a good idea because you know where you are. I gave all my brand-new babies, except one who was very tiny, six feeds a day, one every four hours. They were given at 6 a.m., 10 a.m., 2 p.m., 6 p.m., 10 p.m. and whenever they woke at night – unless they slept through the night and missed their night-time feed, in which case they only had five feeds that day. I wouldn't as a rule wake a normal-sized baby in the night after his 10 p.m. feed, though. If he sleeps through the night, he sleeps.

There are babies who sleep all night and babies who do not. Most babies first sleep through the night by three months, some do not. There is no general rule. I had one baby who woke and shouted at 3 a.m. for a long time. I think food is the only answer, for after food they sleep. Ignoring the baby, scolding him, offering water is to no avail; the child continues to shout and no one can sleep.

If the baby wakes up in the middle of the night, then I would always feed him (see SLEEPING, questions 24–28).

5 · How did your routine change with an underweight baby?

I have cared for one underweight baby and she was fed when she cried – on 'demand' if you like. It worked out that for the first six weeks I was feeding her more or less every three hours. Underweight babies obviously need to be fed more often than normal-sized babies as they have smaller tummies. They will cry when they need a feed but I would always wake an underweight baby for a feed if he slept over three hours. Where I was trained we found that underweight babies soon gained weight and got on very well. Once that happens, probably at around six weeks, they will settle down to a four-hourly feeding routine with each feed at roughly the right time. Premature babies are, of course, a special case and your doctor will advise you.

6 · Do you stick to a routine no matter what?

I always used to be fairly rigid about my routines. As a rule I fed children at the correct time. I even woke a child up, if it was necessary, so that he got all his day-time feeds. At the 10 p.m. feed particularly they very often didn't open their eyes and appeared to be fast asleep but they would still suck the bottle right down to the very end. Of course, if there are dire circumstances – such as your being stuck in a traffic jam without the bottle with you – then there is nothing you can do about your routine. However, I would certainly always aim to feed the child on schedule, unless there were exceptional circumstances such as that we were going on a journey or something, when I would feed him a little earlier. Or if the baby woke up fifteen minutes, or even half an hour, before his feed was due and started crying I would give him his feed a bit sooner. If a baby is hungry he should always be fed. At night I am also more flexible. If the baby was due to be fed at 10 p.m. and was still fast asleep and I am busy, or taking my bath, I wouldn't rush to wake him up but I would wait until 11.00 or 11.30 p.m. I noticed last year when I was looking after a brand-new baby that I never woke her at all but left her in the night to wake me – somehow I just couldn't bring myself to disturb her – but I never used to be like that. Of course, if you have a schedule that your baby has to fit into then you cannot afford to be so flexible and you must wake him.

7 · What if the baby is always hungry after three or three and a half hours?

A bottle-fed baby who regularly cries for another feed after three or three and a half hours should have his feed increased by 30 ml (1 fl oz) so that he can last

'Food is the only answer, for after food they sleep'

the four hours.

The trouble about feeding a baby when he cries is that quite often babies cry even when they are not hungry and you find people thinking they are hungry and so feeding them or trying to. With breast-fed babies I have noticed that there must be a temptation for the mother to feed them at each cry because I have known mothers who seem to spend almost all day putting the baby on and off the breast. Babies just do like sucking, which is why they will suck empty bottles and dummies as well as their fingers and thumbs.

Of course bottle-fed babies enjoy sucking and filling the tummy just as breast-fed babies do and are also cosy in someone's arms, but breast-fed babies smell breast milk and it is available, so they cry, and mothers are tempted to offer the baby a little suck – indeed, why not, if it soothes a fractious baby? But this should not be encouraged at every shout or the result will be an exhausted and depressed mother. I think as a mother you must be firm and keep to ten minutes on each side or you will spend all night nursing him. If a breast-fed baby does seem to be genuinely hungry between feeds try giving him a bottle after each feed for a top up. You will then be able to see how hungry he really is (see questions 49 and 51).

8 · But I don't want my baby to be fed using a schedule. Do you think it matters?

Not at all. If you are determined to do demand feeding and feed your baby whenever he cries, you will most probably find that by six weeks the feeds have established themselves every four hours anyway – although they might all be at inconvenient times. I suppose when the five/six feeds a day schedule was originally formulated it must have been because child health experts had observed that every four hours the baby's tummy needs feeding, or every three hours for a small baby.

The feed

9 · Do you think it matters where you feed a baby?

No. The child must always come first and if he has not been fed for four hours and is hungry he has to be fed wherever. I have seen babies breast fed on long train journeys, for example, and the mothers have always managed it very successfully – and discreetly. Of course, feeding in a public place is not as peaceful as sitting at home.

Wherever you are, whether a baby is breast or bottle fed, it is essential to be as peaceful and comfortable as possible. I have never allowed any visitors in the room when I was feeding a new baby and the same applied to a breast-fed baby. I would bring the baby to the mother and she would either be in bed or on a special chair or wherever she felt comfortable. I would also bring a feeding mother a jug of water or a mug of tea so she could drink when she felt like it. I wouldn't read or put the wireless on either when the baby was feeding although I am not sure the baby cared. If you want to hear *The Archers* I don't think it matters, but new babies do look round if there are other people there and they do get stimulated, so visitors were always forbidden in the nursery at feed times.

10 · How long does a feed last?

I always reckon the feed will last for approximately half an hour including the nappy change and the sitting on the knee to get rid of the bubble in the tummy (see question 13). It may be longer, but certainly not shorter. If it is child number two and the night time feed, that is when I cuddle him – when the elder child has gone to bed and we are all alone, so the feed may take a bit longer.

11 · What if my baby falls asleep during his feed?

If a baby falls asleep when he has finished his bottle (or after twenty minutes breast feeding) it is usually a sign that he has had enough. Sometimes you get a baby that falls asleep halfway through his feed, or after ten to fifteen minutes on the breast. He could be a very sleepy baby. I always encourage him to have a little more, I try and wake him up so that he can finish his feed. I just gently pull the bottle in and out of his mouth to wake him up. If breast feeding try pulling your breast slightly so the nipple moves out of his mouth a little, that might wake him; otherwise try stimulating his mouth again by gently squeezing his cheeks a few times, or blow on his face so the cold air wakes him up.

When I'm bottle feeding him and it takes a long time to wake him up, I put the bottle in a jug of hot water until he is awake and then I offer it again. I think when babies are new, although nature tells them to suck, it requires quite an effort and quite often they do fall asleep in the middle of their feed. Usually when they are very small they don't need to be wide awake to suck again, so I do persevere. If the baby will not waken to take more I just wait until the next feed and offer him the correct amount for that feed. I would never offer him the milk he was not able to drink the last time as well as the new feed; that would be too much for him.

With breast feeding it is more difficult to tell whether a sleepy baby has had enough or is tired. You should judge it by how long ago the last feed was and whether or not he sucked last time for the full twenty minutes. I would still try to wake him up and help him suck, although I am not sure if it is really necessary because by the next feed he will be really hungry and will make up for the last half-eaten feed by taking the whole feed he is offered.

'I have never allowed any visitors in the room when I was feeding a new baby'

12 · Does a small baby drink only milk?

After the first day of a baby's life, when we were trained to give him boiled water (see question 2), I seldom give new babies water except on very hot days. The reason I don't is because they are fed a minimum of five times a day and in between they sleep or just gaze. There doesn't seem to be any reason for heaving them out of their peace to give them water. If they were terribly hot I might sponge them down and give them a little drink of boiled water, but normally I wouldn't disturb them. When they are one month old I introduce fruit juice – greatly, greatly diluted fruit juice – just a pleasant little drink from a spoon. It was thought those few extra vitamins were helpful to a baby and, more importantly, would teach them how to drink from a spoon. If you don't want your child to drink fruit juice you could always give them plain boiled water instead. (See WEANING TO EATING, question 1.)

After the feed

13 · Is it necessary to help my baby bring up wind?

The extraordinary banging and thumping on a baby's back which I have seen people do is quite unnecessary. If you were simply to put a baby in his cot he would expel wind and there is no need to make a great fuss about it.

I always give the baby the entire bottle first unless I notice he has some wind, in which case I sit him up. I feel sorry for babies who are given half a feed and then rubbed and banged on the back before being allowed to have the second half. Then, after the feed I always just sit quietly with the baby upright on my lap, with one hand firmly, but not pressing, on his back and another on his front so any wind can come up – or down. I sit with him for no longer than five minutes; if anything is going to come up it will probably have done so by then. I then put the baby down to sleep and either any remaining wind will go up or down or maybe he hasn't got very much.

Sometimes a baby, it seems especially a breast-fed baby, does have a windy tummy. It could be anytime, not just after his feed. You sometimes notice his upper lip is blueish and he will stretch out his body and draw his knees up and his little tummy will go all hard. When this happens with my babies I sit them up or lie them on their tummies on my lap or put them over my shoulder; sometimes you have to walk around with them like this. They are little tyrants – they can always tell when you sit down.

14 · Do all babies posset?

OPPOSITE *The end of the feed*

No. My proud boast is that I do not have what they call posseting. Posset is just excess food coming out. It has no smell but it may look curdled because it is partly

'Banging and thumping on a baby's back is quite unnecessary'

digested and it may contain some mucus if the baby has a cold. It can happen for one of several reasons. If a baby does bring up his food it may be because he has had a little bit more than he needs – it is like a sort of overflow. The baby is saying that he has had enough food, so if he has just posseted, never top him up with more food. I think another reason babies posset is because they are jiggled about and patted and banged and rubbed and squeezed after their feed (see question 13, above). I remember one mother I know giving her six-month-old daughter such an affectionately hard hug that quite a lot of her dinner came out of the top. But even then I would not have given that baby any more food. Let a baby's tummy rest until the next meal.

Even though I have not had a baby that possets, I always put a little towelling bib on my babies for their feed whether they are breast or bottle fed. I think it is essential as sometimes the milk does run out and the bib can just soak it up.

15 · What should I do if my baby is sick?

Unlike posset, vomit smells sour. If your baby is vomiting it is a sign of trouble. It may indicate an infection, it could be that there is a bug going round the household, in which case give the baby only boiled water to drink and seek advice immediately from your doctor. It is more serious if the baby has diarrhoea and vomiting at the same time, because these symptoms are often combined in gastroenteritis, which used to kill many babies as it caused dehydration. Today it can be treated and medical advice must be sought immediately; any vessel connected with milk bottles, spoons, cups, etc. must be sterilized (see CHANGING AND TOILET TRAINING, question 27).

16 · My baby consistently brings up his entire meal, what should I do?

I have come across a few babies who brought their entire feed up time after time. I did hear of a Swiss powder which just thickened the milk so it could not come up. You should consult your doctor.

17 · What if the vomit shoots out of his mouth across the room?

If your baby shoots food out of his mouth soon after you have fed him ('projectile vomiting'), you must take him to the doctor. It is a condition that must not be ignored and can have serious consequences for the child. I met it where I was trained and I have come across it since.

18 · Why might my baby cry after a feed?

Sometimes a baby will scream and scream and scream immediately after each feed and possibly for quite a long time between feeds and you will not know why. It may well be that he is allergic to milk and you should certainly go and see your doctor about it. I've never had a baby who was allergic to formula or cow's milk, though it certainly happens. I know of two babies who were allergic to breast milk – the first to the protein in her mother's milk, the second to the dairy products that his mother ate – and both screamed continually after their feed. The first mother was told to stop breast feeding and give her baby soya milk. The second mother gave up eating all dairy products and continued breast feeding her baby. In both cases the babies did stop screaming.

A crying baby may just not be well, so you should look into that, or it could be that he is still hungry. If you are breast feeding you may be unsure if he is hungry or just wanting to suck (see question 7). You may find it a good idea to test weigh him (see question 49). If you are bottle feeding see question 28.

If your baby cries at the beginning of his feed it may be that he has either thrush or laryngitis or some other problem. Talk to your doctor about it.

19 · Might my baby have colic?

Colic is very much a mystery and it is a great nuisance if your baby has it. I once held a colicky baby for someone I was visiting and I found holding him upright in my arms and pressing his tummy against my chest seemed to help (see SLEEPING, question 29).

20 · What will I need to buy if I want to bottle feed my baby?

If you are going to bottle feed your baby you need six bottles and two teats, with different sized holes depending on the child. I always started by using a teat with a medium-sized hole and saw how my baby sucked. Then, after a while, I would change the teat accordingly. If the baby was entirely bottle fed and a very, very strong sucker I would change the teat to one with three tiny holes, because if you have big holes and the baby sucks hard the milk fills his mouth and he chokes. If a baby drinks his milk more slowly it is probably also better for the digestive system.

If you have a baby who is not a strong sucker then you use a teat with one bigger hole; we often used to enlarge holes with a red-hot needle. Of course you would buy more teats as and when you needed them, once you had found out what kind suits your baby.

When I started working there was only ever one hole in a teat – I think the later three-holed teat must have been produced to try to imitate the breast. We never had any funny-shaped teats like there are now either, there was no choice.

Bottle feeding
Equipment

39

I think you must buy what takes your fancy because whichever shape teat you buy, if a baby is hungry and something goes in his mouth he sucks it – whether it is his thumb or a teat.

The other difference was that when I first worked with children my bottles were always glass, so when I first came across plastic bottles I felt suspicious and thought that germs could lodge in the scratches in the plastic. Now you can even buy plastic ones with pictures and I believe glass ones are no longer obtainable.

21 · *What sterilizing equipment do I need to buy?*

To clean and sterilize bottles and teats you really only need to buy a bottle brush. You can of course buy lots of specialist pieces of equipment which you will only use for a few months, until the next baby. Chemists sell very neat little sterilizers – which get more and more sophisticated by the minute – that you can use, but I never did. All I ever needed was some liquid detergent, a jar of fine, pouring salt and a pan in which to boil the bottles and teats. Alternatively, if you want to use a sterilizing solution instead of boiling the bottles, you will need a plastic bowl and a clean tea towel or other piece of fabric and the sterilizing solution which can be bought from any chemist. You will also need a measuring jug or an empty milk bottle.

22 · *Do I really need to keep the feeding equipment spotlessly clean?*

Normal babies are not tender blossoms so a little bit of dirt is not going to hurt them too much. But I always sterilize feeding bottles as long as children have them which is nine months in my book. Milk is notorious for breeding germs and sterilizing is no great trouble.

23 · *How do I keep all the feeding equipment clean?*

There are two methods of sterilizing which I have used. One is by boiling (see question 24) and the other is by using a sterilizing solution which leaves the bottles and teats smelling a little of chlorine (see question 25). I have often wondered whether babies would mind the taste but apparently not as they have never refused a bottle. You can also sterilize by steaming, but I've never used that method.

No matter which sterilizing method you use you must always first rinse the bottles with cold water to remove the milk and then scrub them thoroughly with a tiny squirt of liquid detergent, some warm water and a bottle brush, rinsing them very, very well afterwards to make sure you have removed all the detergent.

You must also clean the teats. I was taught to turn teats inside out to clean them,

'Normal babies are not tender blossoms'

but I quickly discovered that if you poured salt into the teat you can rub the outsides of the teat together and the salt seems to make them perfectly clean inside. Turning a new teat inside out is terribly difficult and I don't think it cleans them any better. Rinse the teats very well afterwards with cold water and store them on a saucer with a cup over them until you have collected enough to sterilize. You can then either boil them with the bottles or drop them into the sterilizing solution, again with the bottles. But never keep them boiling for too long as they do eventually go all soft and sticky and perish. Once I had sterilized them I just put them back on a saucer, over which I had previously poured boiled water, with an upside-down cup over them until I needed to use them.

24 · *What do I do if I want to boil the bottles and teats rather than use a sterilizing solution?*

This is the old-fashioned method of sterilizing. You just put the bottles and teats in cold water once they have been washed and bring them to the boil, let them boil for at least ten minutes, then take them off the heat and carefully fish them out of the boiling hot water, preferably with tongs, one at a time. Alternatively, you can leave the bottles in the water until you need them, but you should remove the teats (see question 23). I either left the bottles in the water or took them out, filled them with milk and put the caps on top to seal them. I then put them in the fridge (see question 30).

25 · *How would I sterilize using a solution?*

Once a day you make a solution using a sterilizing tablet or liquid and lukewarm water, carefully following the manufacturer's instructions. When you have washed and rinsed the bottles until they are all lovely and sparkling (see question 23), you just put them into the sterilizing fluid and leave them there at least as long as the manufacturer recommends and until you need them (see question 30). The solution is changed at the same time daily. You can buy a proper sterilizing kit but I used to use an oblong plastic bowl for my sterilizing which I kept on the nursery bathroom windowsill. I just put a clean tea towel or gauze nappy on top of it to keep the dust off.

26 · *Nanny, what did you give a bottle-fed baby to drink?*

For the first month to six weeks of a baby's life I continued using whatever brand of formula milk he had been given in hospital, following the manufacturer's instructions; you can now buy formula milk pre-mixed which is very handy

Which milk and how much?

41

though much more expensive. I always made sure it was half-cream formula milk, rather than full cream, which can give children very rough skin on their faces and sore, red bottoms. It might be that there is too much fat for them to digest at first. Some adults cannot take cream, so why should children be able to?

If, after those first few weeks, the baby started waking a little early for his feed and showing signs of not being satisfied and always a little hungry I would put him onto full cream formula milk which he would be bottle-fed until he was nine months old and then given in a cup until he was one year old. Once a child is a year old he can then be given homogenized and pasteurized cow's milk straight from the milk bottle.

My very last full-time baby was fed like this – starting on half-cream formula milk and then graduating to full cream formula milk when she was a little older, but all the rest of my children, from when they were one month old, were given diluted, boiled cow's milk to drink, mixed together with various other things which made the milk more digestible. They now say cow's milk is meant for baby cows and not for baby children and that one should give the child formula milk for the first year of his life. They may be right but I'm inclined to think that not giving children cow's milk is a fashion – all my children were very healthy and I only fed the last child with formula milk because the ingredients I used became too difficult to obtain. After all, what is formula milk but skimmed cow's milk anyway? Of course, it is essential to boil any cow's milk the child is going to drink for the first year of his life and some milk, such as Devon milk, is so rich it is indigestible, so when we went to Devon I would use formula milk instead.

27 · How much milk will my bottle-fed baby need?

If a baby is born smaller than average (under 3.2 kg/7 lb at birth), I feed him every three hours or eight feeds a day until he has settled (see questions 4 and 5). If he is average size (over the above weight at birth), I feed him every four hours or five feeds a day (6 a.m., 10 a.m., 2 p.m., 6 p.m. and 10 p.m.) or six feeds if he wakes at 2 a.m. This soon becomes five feeds as he gets older and no longer needs the 2 a.m. feed.

To work out how much milk to give a baby at each feed we were taught this useful formula, which I am giving just as I was taught it, in Imperial, as giving two sets of measures make it look more complicated than it is: whatever the baby's body weight is, you reckon 2½ fl oz to each 1 lb of body weight per day. So if the baby weighed 8 lb 12 oz, I would reckon that as 9 lb; I would multiply 9 by 2½ which is 22½ fl oz – call that 22 fl oz.

You want to feed him with five feeds (just in case he does not wake for the night-time feed he should have all his nutrition during the day and since the baby is over 3.2 kg (7 lb) in weight he should have five, rather than six, day-time feeds) so at each feed you would give him approximately 135 ml (4½ fl oz). If the baby does wake during the night you would then make up an extra 135 ml (4½ fl oz) feed, or if you knew he was likely to wake up you could make it before you went to bed or in the morning with the other feeds (see question 30) so his total daily consumption would be 750 ml (26½ fl oz).

28 · Do babies ever need more milk than that?

I found that it was usually enough to give the baby just the amount I had worked out he needed and no more, but if he was still desperately hungry, I would give him more food. You have to make your own judgement. If he drained the last drop, even if he was not shouting for more, I would make him some more, not a lot, just 60 ml (2 fl oz) for one or two feeds in a row and see if that satisfied him. Sometimes a baby may cry out as if to say: 'Don't take the nipple/teat away' and this may be just a little annoyed sound. A more prolonged angry shout may well mean a hungry baby who should be given a little more.

You would use your judgement. If a baby is not gaining much weight then it is always worth trying to give him more milk (see questions 50–51). If he is gaining 100 g (4 oz) or more a week then I wouldn't give him any more. A baby who is gaining well will probably not cry if the bottle is removed, but if he does he may well be crying for extra comfort. Give him a few big cuddles (see question 18).

29 · What if my baby doesn't finish his feed?

If a child wants to leave a little milk in the bottom of the bottle I always let him. I never force a baby to drink every last drop; he may just bring it all up (see question 14).

30 · Nanny, when did you make the feeds up?

Whenever I used formula milk I made each feed when it was needed. I always kept a clean teaspoon and knife for measuring out the powdered milk and a spotless tea towel for drying utensils. I never made up five feeds of formula milk at once as it was quick and easy to make up each feed as needed, although of course it does save time in the long run to make them all up at once. I did find that it was easier to get the temperature of the milk right – making the freshly-made hot bottle cold, as opposed to the cold already-made bottle hot. However, once I knew a baby was likely to wake up during the night and demand an extra feed I always got a bottle ready for the middle of the night just before I went to bed. I kept it in the fridge until the baby woke (see question 32).

The feeding routine

If I was busy I would make all the feeds at once. I would give the baby his bath and the 10 a.m. feed and then, when he was tucked down for the morning, I would make the feeds so I had them all ready for the next twenty-four hours, including a night-time one which might or might not be used.

31 · How did you get the bottle ready for the feed?

Once the next feed was due I would take the bottle from the fridge and a sterilized teat from under the cup where it was placed (see question 23). I would put the teat in a cup and pour boiling water on it, leave it for a second or two, pour off the boiling water and then place the teat on the bottle, picking it up by the rim as carefully as possible. I would then put the bottle into a jug and pour boiling water into the jug all over the teat and the bottle, just to make sure the teat was really sterile. I would leave the bottle in the boiling water for a few minutes until the milk was the correct temperature for the feed, testing it by dropping a little on the back of my hand. When the milk felt neither hot nor cold I knew it was ready to be given to the baby.

32 · What do you do when a baby wakes and wants a feed in the middle of the night?

Some people give their babies water in the middle of the night but I think that is so mean (see SLEEPING, question 28). I used to make up a bottle before I went to bed, then, at 2 a.m. or whenever the baby woke, I would simply nip downstairs and get it out of the fridge and warm it up.

It is always terrible in the middle of the night when the baby's scream seems so loud. If I hadn't prepared a bottle I would have to leave him in bed to cry whilst I was getting the milk ready. There's nothing else you can do; he might be even angrier if you picked him up whilst the kettle was boiling and then put him down again to measure everything out. He wouldn't understand why he has suddenly been put down again to cry. I still remember one of my little boys watching me as I made up a very early feed for his little sister. As she was screaming he said to me 'Can't you love her until the kettle boils?' Wasn't that a sweet thought?

I have heard of people making the baby's feed beforehand and putting it into a Thermos to keep warm. I think it's a terrible thing to do. I would think the germs would multiply in the warm milk waiting for hours in the Thermos.

33 · How did you make a baby's feeds as cosy as possible?

Where I was trained we always tried to get the milk as close to mother's milk as possible. We even used to keep the bottles warm during the feed by keeping them in knitted bags whilst we were using them. I remember one nanny made some once out of the best bits of one of her client's woollen underpants with a little elastic at the top – what a clever idea.

Whenever I was at home I sat on a low feeding chair so my feet could be on the ground, with the baby's head in the crook of my left arm (I am right-handed) and the bottle in my right hand. But no matter where you sit, the only really important thing to remember when bottle feeding is always to make sure the teat is entirely filled with milk or water or whatever liquid is in the bottle. If you have twins you often have to feed one and prop the bottle up with a pillow for the other. But you should never rely on a baby to feed himself properly and you must also always keep an eye on any baby feeding himself in case he chokes.

(See also weight gain section, questions 47–52, at end of this chapter.)

34 · Do you think every mother should breast feed her baby?

A friend of mine found it difficult to feed her baby in hospital so they said she should give the baby a bottle instead. When she came home her doctor told her that everyone could breast feed and she should too. It took about two weeks for her to get her milk re-established but after that it was plain sailing.

I think if one is in a relaxed frame of mind and has someone to encourage one it should be possible to breast feed, but it can be very nerve-racking for a young mother whose baby is screaming his head off if her milk doesn't seem to be coming, or very painful indeed if her nipple is cracked. Indeed I have heard many mothers say that the beginning of breast feeding is much more painful than having the baby, but if you can persevere I think it must be worth it – breast feeding is just so handy and the milk the right temperature.

Don't expect things to work easily from the beginning. It can take six weeks or longer for the supply of breast milk to match the needs of the baby. I think one of the main worries at first for a breast-feeding mother is never being sure if her baby has had enough food or if she should let him keep sucking (see question 7). As you cannot weigh the milk you are giving a breast-fed baby, you have to weigh the baby himself. I always weigh a baby weekly, but you can of course do it more often if you are worried about your baby's progress (see question 49).

35 · Will there be any milk in my breasts immediately after the birth?

For the first two or three days after birth, as during the last few weeks of pregnancy, your breasts will be filled with a yellowish fluid called colostrum which the baby will drink at first. On the third or fourth day the milk comes into

Breast feeding

Getting it going

the breasts and makes the breasts engorged (full of milk). The entire breast area, up to the armpits, feels hard, painful and lumpy. It helps to remove a little milk by bathing the breasts in warm water, which you can do by lying in a bath and laying a wet flannel over each breast or gently stroking your breasts towards the nipple so that some milk flows into the bath. It is a good idea to apply cold compresses to your breasts between feeds as well.

I have heard some people suggest that the baby sucks each breast empty but this can make your nipples extremely sore and uncomfortable. Anyway, the breasts fill up again almost the moment they are emptied so let your baby suck but not for very long at first (see question 36). What is most important is that he should put as much of your areola (the dark area surrounding the nipple) into his mouth as possible, not just the nipple or it will be painful. You should also massage all over your breasts very gently during the feed, massaging out any hard areas so that your whole breast is floppy; keep doing this while feeding for the next few weeks. In a few days the worst fullness and pain will be over. By six weeks the fullness will have diminished more or less completely, except for at the start of each feed or if the baby has not fed for an unusually long time.

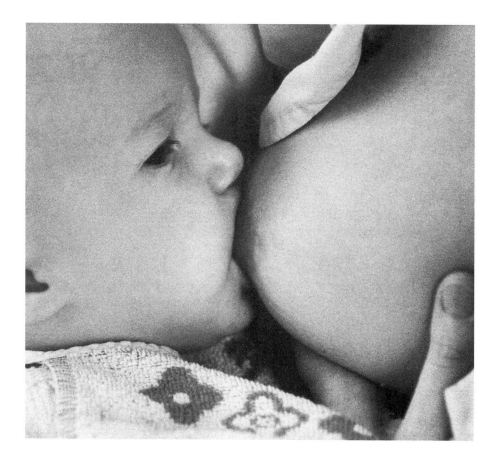

36 · *How long do I let my baby feed for?*

A new baby does not need food at once but you can start feeding your baby the moment he is born if you feel like it, although there is no rush. The most important thing is to get your nipples gradually used to being sucked, or they can become very sore. Your baby can always be given a top up from a bottle if he is very hungry after each feed, but once your nipples are cracked it can take a few days for them to stop hurting, so look after them first.

Each time you begin the feed you change the breast you start with. So, if at the 10 a.m. feed you started feeding the baby on the right breast, you start the next feed (2 p.m.) on the left breast. One of my mothers used a ribbon tied to her bra which she re-tied after each feed to remind her which side to start with at the next feed.

Let the baby suck for a minute or two only at each breast six times a day for the first day. On the second day let him suck for three or four minutes on each side, six times a day, on the third day for five or six minutes a side, building up very gradually so that by the end of the baby's first week you will have reached ten minutes of sucking at each breast five times a day. Even with sucking for only a few minutes at a time your baby will not go hungry, but if you are worried I would give him a top up of bottle milk (see question 7) after each feed from day two until day five. Then on the fifth day I would stop the bottle and just feed the baby from the breast. This way your nipples will be more gently broken into breast feeding.

37 · *If I am breast-feeding do I need to change my lifestyle?*

The care and attention breast-feeding mothers need at first often seems to be ignored these days. Where I trained we made sure they had three good meals a day, a lot of water to drink and plenty of rest – for the first ten days after childbirth they stayed in bed and we gave them bed baths and a bedpan. It has always seemed to me that the more calm and rested the mother, the more contented the baby.

38 · *How do I avoid hurting my back during the feed?*

A new mother must avoid straining her back so she needs always to take care how she stands and bends and holds the baby – whenever possible she should bend her legs so they take the strain. How she sits when feeding is important too. The baby should always be brought to the breast and not the breast to the baby. If a mother wants to feed in a chair she should use four pillows; one placed vertically behind her, one placed horizontally under each arm to support it and

'The more calm and rested the mother, the more contented the baby'

47

one on her lap on which the baby lies so she does not have to bend forward. She should then lift her legs so they are resting on a bed to bring the baby even higher up.

I have also seen many mothers feeding a baby when lying down, which must be very comfortable. I know a mother who had a cracked nipple for whom the only way to carry on feeding her baby without being in too much pain was if the baby lay flat on the bed and she lowered her nipple into his mouth. It made it easy for her to make sure as much of the areola was in his mouth as possible and it also made it impossible for the baby to pull at the nipple in any way. It was not very comfortable for her back, but it made feeding a baby bearable.

Feeding problems

39 · What can I do if my child won't suck?

Sucking is an instinct and you would have thought that when the baby was first put on the breast he would just latch on like kittens, but sometimes babies seem a little bit puzzled. With bottles, they do latch straight on so I don't know why they fuss about the breast at first, but they do (see question 41). Where I trained we often used to have to pull a baby's chin down to open his mouth so we could put the nipple and surrounding areola in it. Some babies had a good old suck, some of them were not so enthusiastic.

If a baby still didn't want to suck we were taught to try to keep him on the breast by pushing the back of his head to hold his face against the breast. We would then work his little face, manipulating his cheeks in a sucking manner to make him move his mouth. Or, instead of moving his cheeks we would try placing a finger under his lower jaw and carefully pushing it up and down. Once a little bit of the milk went in he would usually carry on himself. Sucking is terribly hard work for a new baby at first, especially if the breast is engorged so that his little mouth will keep slipping off. It may be a good idea to try and soften your breast by removing a little milk first with a breast pump or just by massaging your breasts gently with your fingers (see question 35).

If your baby is premature he will probably be too weak to suck at the breast and if he has jaundice he may feel too tired. Your doctor will advise you.

40 · Why does my baby choke at the beginning of each feed?

I have known babies start to feed at the breast and there has been such a lot of milk that they have choked slightly and you have to take them off for a bit. If your breasts are very full, after a long night for example, and your baby has a tendency to choke, it may be helpful to squeeze out a little milk from each breast before you start so the milk does not come into his mouth with such a gush.

41 · My baby squirms when I'm feeding him. Why do you think this is?

'Some babies had a good old suck, some of them were not so enthusiastic'

I have seen a lot of babies sort of wriggling about when they are feeding. I think this may be because when you begin feeding the milk always takes a bit of time to come into your breast. This is called 'letting down' and I believe it's slightly painful at first for the mother – it sort of stings. It may be that the milk is not being let down quickly enough and this is what is making the baby a little frustrated. I suppose all you can do is relax.

Before the next feed, try stopping whatever you are doing at least half an hour before the feed and spend that time with the baby. It may help you get into a calm mood. It could also be that the baby is not yet hungry or because he has some wind. If you think he's not hungry, take him off the breast and next time wait the full four hours before giving him his feed. Or if you think he is windy, try sitting him upright for five minutes or until he brings the wind up – or down (see question 13). Another reason a baby may keep removing his head from the breast is if he has a cold and it is difficult for him to breathe. Try feeding him in as upright a position as possible and make sure that his nostrils aren't pressing against your breast so he can't breathe.

Sometimes a baby may stop sucking because something has distracted him. I do remember two breast-fed babies I knew being fascinated by the dots on their mother's dressing gown. They would gaze at them for a short time rather than feed, but then they would carry on feeding.

42 · When the feed is over, how do I remove the baby from my breast?

If your baby wants to suck once his feed is over you should remove his mouth from your breast. I would never suggest doing this by putting your finger inside the baby's mouth to substitute it for the nipple as your finger may not be very clean. I would also not recommend just pulling the baby off your nipple as it can make the nipple rather sore. Instead I would pull the baby's chin down very gently which will open his mouth so you can remove your nipple.

43 · How should I look after my breasts?

Breast care

A breast-feeding mother needs to wear a good feeding bra which will support her breasts. I remember when feeding bras were first invented and mothers used to button in a little fabric square to catch any excess milk. Before then, they used to put a small square cut out of a towelling or muslin nappy inside the bra to catch the excess. It allowed the breasts to breathe, collected the milk and did not need to be bought especially. These days mothers wear those nursing pads inside their bras which absorb any excess milk.

49

When I was training antibiotics were not available so everyone was very fussy about breast hygiene. Before each feed the mothers washed their breasts to make sure they were absolutely clean and to remove any creams they had put on their nipples to toughen them. We would bring each of the mothers a bowl with warm water and a clean towel but no soap. Soap should not be used on breasts because they aren't dirty, they are just a little sweaty. I think even washing the breasts before a feed was probably one of those fussy things that is not really necessary, but we were very careful (see questions 36, 38 and 42).

44 · What should I do as my nipples are inverted?

If a mother had inverted nipples or no protruding nipple at all I was taught to place a rubber breast shield over her nipples and the baby would suck on that instead. Sometimes the sucking action even helped to pull out the nipple, but sometimes it did not (see question 46 for how to use the breast shield).

45 · What if my nipples hurt?

I think sore nipples occur for a number of reasons. It may be that your baby is a very, very strong sucker – either because of his nature or because he is very hungry and the milk isn't coming fast enough, which could be because the mother is a little tired or tense. It might also be because the baby has taken only the nipple in his mouth instead of taking the entire areola as well as your nipple, as he should be doing.

If you do feel your nipples becoming sore you should immediately take preventive action. I was taught to harden a mother's nipples so they did not crack and split by rubbing them with an ointment made of Friar's Balsam which was washed off very thoroughly before each feed. Today I have heard of special herbal creams being used very effectively. I think it is also a good idea for the mother's nipples to be exposed to the air between feeds as much as possible. If a nipple hurts I would discuss the problem with your doctor or midwife because if it is not treated it will probably become worse with each feed rather than better (see also question 46).

46 · What should I do if I have a cracked nipple?

I believe it is very uncomfortable to have a cracked nipple. The crack may sometimes be visible or the entire nipple may look red. A cracked nipple will give you a pain that lasts throughout the feed, not just at the beginning. If the pain is only at the start of the feed it is probably not a cracked nipple that is causing

OPPOSITE *Whether he is breast or bottle fed, your baby will enjoy a cuddle.*

it; the pain may just last for a few more days or until the milk is established, so try and find a new feeding position in which you are comfortable.

If a mother had a cracked nipple I would always make her rest it for a few days until it healed. She should do this in several different ways, depending on the baby and how co-operative he is. I would first try using a rubber breast shield over the cracked nipple at the next feed. This looks like a disc with a teat and it fits over the mother's nipple whilst the baby is feeding. The mother holds the shield over the breast forcing the milk out and down the teat. She would begin feeding the baby on the well breast and change to the sore breast after a minute or so, as soon as the milk started coming.

If the baby noticed something was different and refused to suck the shield I would try another approach. Just before the feed I would make the mother pump some milk from the sore breast, using a sterilized breast pump, and I would give the baby that milk from a bottle first, while he was hungry. Once he had finished the milk from the bottle I would then let him suck on the breast which was not sore. To know how many fluid ounces of breast milk to pump out I would use the same formula as for bottle milk and give him half the amount required for one of the feeds for someone of his weight (see question 27). It is all a bit of a nuisance but the breast should heal in a few days. It may help the mother to pump her milk out if she can hear her baby crying a little. Or you can persevere with feeding (see question 38). Always ask your doctor or midwife if the pain continues.

Weight gain

47 · How much weight does an average baby gain?

After the first week (see question 1) babies quickly start gaining, sometimes very little, sometimes a lot. Most babies gain on average 100 g (4 oz) a week for the first six months. I was always very happy with a gain of this amount. Of course, sometimes it was only 85 g (3 oz) and sometimes 170 g (6 oz). Some weeks a baby won't gain anything, and then the following week 50 g (2 oz) and then the next week 170 g (6 oz) or even more. You never know quite why because they are eating just the same.

By the end of six months your baby should weigh around double his birthweight and by the end of a year he should have trebled it. After babies are a year old I don't weigh them any more, unless they've been ill, because by then their whole behaviour pattern is more established. Some children have big appetites and some smaller and I would just follow on from there. The gains of a one-year-old child are much less than that of a child in the first twelve months of his life and by the time they are two years old they are usually around 12 kg (28 lb). As a rule of thumb, the height of a child at two years old is said to be half the height he will be when he is fully grown.

48 · Nanny, did you weigh your babies?

I always had a proper pair of scales with a basket and weights. I used to put the naked baby on the basket on a clean nappy once a week until he was a year old and could sit up in the scales. By then babies are very wriggly so you have to weigh them quickly.

There's a great fashion for not weighing babies now but I always did it for interest rather than to check his progress; you can tell quite easily if a baby is all right just by seeing if he is reasonably happy and contented. If he doesn't gain much, well, he will later on. But I still think it is useful to have a pair of scales because if a baby didn't gain anything for two to three weeks there might be something wrong that should be checked up on.

49 · What is test weighing?

Test weighing is sometimes done with a very small baby (under a month) if you are feeling a little worried that he is not getting enough milk. It is especially useful if you are breast feeding your baby. You weigh the baby before he is fed wearing his night clothes (or whatever he is dressed in) and then, when he has been fed ten minutes each side, you weigh him again wearing the same clothes and without changing his nappy.

Test weighing is quite different from ordinary weighing – you only do it because you are worried. You keep the baby's clothes on because you are going to weigh him twice in a short space of time (before and after a feed) and you wouldn't want to keep dressing and undressing him. You can see how much he has taken even with all his clothes on. I would always test weigh the baby for a day, weighing before and after each of the feeds. You would probably find that for some feeds he was not taking very much and other feeds he was taking more. Each feed would vary. I would leave it at that unless he was really taking very little compared to the quantities a bottle-fed baby would be drinking (see question 27).

50 · What if my baby isn't gaining weight?

Quite often a baby gains hardly any weight for a couple of weeks and there is nothing wrong with him. If the food was being offered to him and he was taking it and not being sick, I would not worry. However I would seek advice if the baby had not gained anything in two weeks, especially if they were the first two weeks of his life. If the baby was unhappy, crying, being restless or running a temperature I would worry and I would ask the doctor's advice immediately.

Test-weighing Nina

I always try seeing if a baby who has gained 50 g (2 oz) or less in a week would like a little more feed. If a breast-fed baby has not gained any weight I might test weigh him for a couple of weeks (see question 49). If he was still not gaining any weight I would supplement the feed with a bottle of milk, but I would not rush into doing this (see question 51 below).

51 · If I am breast feeding will it be necessary to top up any of the feeds with bottle milk?

Quite often people top up one or two breast feeds a day when the baby is not feeding so well with a bottle; this is called complementary feeding. Apart from during the first week when your nipples are getting used to being sucked (see question 36), I am not a great one for doing this because if one feed is not very good, the next one will make up for it and soon breast feeding will establish itself satisfactorily. There was a great vogue for complementary feeding when I was starting out, but sucking does stimulate the milk supply, so if your baby is happy and gaining weight then you should not worry.

52 · What if my baby is 'overweight'?

Some people, adults and children, eat very little and get very fat. Others eat a lot and remain thin. In my experience there is not much you can do if your baby or toddler is fat. I think often it is hereditary. Some babies are born into fat families, others into thin families and they will weigh more or less depending on which they come from. You should not worry about their weight, you will be able to see whether or not your child is healthy and progressing, and if it is obvious that they are not, you should then ask the doctor.

After all, what is overweight? Some babies put on weight quicker than others, but they are not necessarily overweight. I don't think that there is anything you can do if a baby who is fed the correct quantities of breast or bottle milk is overweight. I know a mother who cut down her baby's food intake when Nanny was off on holiday and the poor baby cried a great deal.

Sometimes you get very fat babies and as time goes on they become very thin. One of my children was quite a fatty as a baby. When he was about two or three months old there was a period in which he put on 500 g (1 lb) a week for quite a while. He was an enormous child, but he was only being breast fed, ten minutes on each side, with nothing at all extra except a drop of fruit juice. He had these tremendous gains. I never worried, it seemed to me that he had a big frame and needed lots of food. He was a big chap as a baby but by the time he was a little boy he was quite slender. Now, as an adult, he is thin. For feeding the older overweight child see WEANING TO EATING, question 22.

Golden rules

Aim for a peaceful feed

1 Don't have visitors in the room during a feed.

2 Make bottle feeding as cosy for the baby as breast feeding.

3 Remember to keep the teat of the bottle filled throughout the feed.

4 Don't jiggle and bang and squeeze and pat your baby after his feed. The wind will come up or go down of its own accord.

5 Demand feeding is fine so long as there are no other demands on your time.

Babies do like sucking

1 Sometimes babies cry even when they are not hungry.

2 A baby could probably suck all day – but how would that leave you feeling?

3 Treat a painful nipple immediately or the sucking will hurt.

4 It is not the end of the world if a baby has to have a bottle.

Babies come in all shapes and sizes

1 You can tell more from looking at your baby than weighing him.

2 You cannot give a baby less food because he is 'fat'. You really should not.

2

Growing and Learning

They say every child is born a genius and it is adults who make a mess of it. It is stretching a point of course, but adults do seem often to be the cause of so much of a child's feeling of frustration. Quite often children attempt things and are told not to: 'Don't do that, it's naughty.' For a baby the whole world is there for him to explore. It's his insatiable curiosity and thirst for knowledge that can be what causes most accidents around the home, but also that which will make him learn and grow. It is encouragement rather than frustration that children need.

It seems people want children to grow up. But I always call a child a baby until he's seven years old. When people say 'You're not a baby' or 'Don't do that, it's babyish', to a four-year-old, I just laugh. Of course he's a baby. Why force him to grow up now? He'll have quite enough pressure on him later. Why do people appear to despise little people who haven't lived very long?

I also notice children being pressurized into doing things they are not yet ready for. I have always liked children to do things themselves. I judge children by the things they have done entirely from their own motivation and some children do things better and quicker than others.

Learning should be a part of everyday life and not something special. When children haven't lived very long, their brains are fertile and soak up information quickly. Learning is so easy and should be fun. I taught all my children their numbers and the alphabet, colours, left and right and how to read and write, more or less just by slowly introducing them

'Learning is so easy and should be fun'

OPPOSITE *Holding a small baby before putting her in the bath – one hand under the buttocks, the other under the back of the head. A new baby's head must always be supported. Normally she would be held in the crook of my arm with her head supported by my upper arm*

into our conversation and our life. They could all read by the time they started school at five. The thing is to keep it casual and stop immediately if you feel that your child has had enough. That is how learning should be.

1 · What will my new baby be able to do?

Cry! When babies are born they usually cry very loudly, endlessly. But there's no pattern, some do and some don't. Some make a mewing sound like a kitten and some hiccup a lot.

Babies are also born with instincts, the most important of which is their ability to find the nipple and suck. It is how the human race has survived, it is part of the human make-up. They will suck anything. Sometimes they suck one of their thumbs immediately on being born. For the first month, a new baby will also cling with a very tight grip. People going in to see new babies used to give the baby a coin, usually a sixpence, and when the baby held it tightly the visitors would say that means good luck, but of course the child always held it tightly. Newborn babies also make walking movements automatically. If you hold a newborn upright with his toes touching a surface and move him forward he will move his feet forward as though he is walking. Both the walking and the clinging are lost in about three to four months. One of my little boys went to the doctor when he was already past this stage – she tried to make him walk and all he did was pee.

2 · How much can a new baby see and hear?

It is thought that a brand-new baby can see light because he will certainly turn his face towards any bright light. But he can't yet focus his eyes and so may appear to be squinting. Up to six months babies do seem to be able to sleep anywhere, no matter how much noise there is, but they do notice loud bangs from very early on and jump when they hear a loud noise. Other sounds like a radio or people talking do not seem to worry them. After six months they are disturbed more by sound, because their field of interest is getting wider and anything that they hear is fascinating. It is best to have them sleep in a quiet room.

3 · How should I look after a new baby?

Babies like a quiet atmosphere. Many people think they must stimulate babies or they won't learn, with the result that they are very often over-stimulated. I wouldn't overdo talking to a baby. People talk into their babies' faces non-stop or turn the radio on for them. I don't talk to small babies much and I would never read to a tiny baby or put the radio on either unless I wanted to listen to a programme. I always think babies respond well to being warm and quiet and to being spoken to gently with a quiet voice. If they are over-stimulated, they can't relax and then they cry.

You should treat a new baby as you would treat yourself. Keep him cosy – don't

'Treat a new baby as you would treat yourself'

put him in a draught – and keep him clean and well-fed. Matron used to say to us 'Babies are tough. They bounce', but she didn't mean that we had to drop them. She did mean that normal full-term babies are quite tough otherwise the human race wouldn't have survived. You must always just hold a newborn baby gently but firmly, making sure his buttocks and the back of his head are well supported. If he is in your arms, rest his head on the crook of your arm so it doesn't fall back – your hand will automatically be under his buttocks.

Physical dexterity

4 · How soon can I expect my new baby to start moving?

The first thing a baby will probably move will be his head, from one side to another, at around four to five weeks. You look at him lying on his tummy and find him one moment lying on his right cheek and the next moment lying on his left. It can give you quite a shock. Then, at around six weeks a baby will lift his head when he is lying on his front. At first he will lift it sort of briefly, then it will just flop down. Then slowly he will hold it up more and more. People always reckoned that if a baby was put flat on his tummy to lie it gave him a nice, strong back, it meant his back muscles were strengthened as he tried to look up. However opinions about the right position to put a new baby to lie in have changed (see SLEEPING, question 18).

After six weeks a baby's head will be becoming less floppy, although it will still need support. Otherwise babies will still do very little except in water. By six weeks they start splashing with their feet and hitting the water with their hands. Once they are dressed, fed and tucked up they do very little again until the next bathtime.

By about ten weeks babies begin playing with their fingers and clasping their hands. When they are about twelve weeks they begin to hold things and put their hands very near the face, about two or three inches away, and 'hand regard' is observed. It is enchanting to see them study their (or your) fingers and toes and watch their slow and intense concentration. They will also pick up anything they can lift that is within their reach. I have never found it necessary to place things deliberately within the baby's reach to encourage this. Why should you? If there is no toy or object available for him to touch he will pick up the hem of his dress or the edge of a little coat, hold it up and look at it. If anything, I would think this is a good argument for putting a baby in a dress or nightie rather than placing him in a babygrow (see photograph on page 108).

The next large movements will be from about three months, when a baby who has been put on his tummy will take the weight on his hands and lift the top part of his body up. It is wonderful because of course he can see so much more then. Babies also begin to wave their legs and arms about, particularly when they are naked. At three months I always put them in a playpen lying on their backs and

'It is enchanting to see them study their fingers'

they wave about a lot and can see a lot. I might briefly put them on their tummies but they can see more on their backs and look at a mobile (see question 8 below and PLAYING, question 23) and at the ceiling. At this age they are also beginning to move from lying on their sides to their backs.

5 · When do babies start rolling?

Some children are physical and others are not; they vary tremendously. Usually children roll from the tummy on to the back a few months before they roll from the back on to the tummy. I would think one of my girls was nine months before she rolled from her tummy to her back, whereas her sister was a very little baby, only weeks old. She was in her crib and I was amazed to find she had rolled round to her back. She was so wriggly and energetic. I kept finding her nappy around her ankles, she twisted around so much.

I remember one baby I knew lying on her tummy at about a year and bringing just one knee up at a time; she was very slow at doing things like that, but when she was nine months or possibly before as she was sitting on her pot she would pick up a toy she had dropped with her feet. I should think from six months she may have been using her feet in this way, putting toys between them and bringing them up to her hands. Later, when she first sat, she automatically put her legs in the lotus position. I'm not sure what her skill was called, I would call it double-jointed. I had not seen it with many other children and it was very interesting. Every child has his own merits and abilities. It is impossible to compare them.

6 · When do children begin using their hands?

Children usually begin clapping and waving their hands when they are about a year old. They don't really wave, they just clench and unclench and stretch their fingers. Again, children vary tremendously in manual dexterity. A little two-year-old boy I know cannot take his socks off and yet another friend who is not even two can already put her socks back on. For a long time she has been riding her elder brother's little motorcar and she has fed herself with a spoon for ages and ages, something which I don't usually expect children to be able to do properly until they are eighteen months. By the time a child is two he will probably start screwing things, such as turning a door knob to get out. He may also start putting lids on things.

7 · How do you help a baby to sit up?

I never prop a baby up in a sitting position with cushions, but always lie them flat and only when they can pull themselves up do I sit them up with a pillow

Nina, at four months, lifting her head and shoulders

'Every child
has his own
merits and
abilities'

behind them. I remember somebody saying when one of my girls aged about eleven months, was lying down, 'When is that child going to sit up?' and I just replied: 'When she is able to.' The earliest of my children to sit up was a girl who at the age of six months grabbed the side of the pram, heaved herself up and looked round. I remember we were right next to the ducks on the pond and her little eyes popped out like organ stops. She was so thrilled to see them. She had always been lying down on her back in the pram until then. Another of my girls was about ten months and a brother and sister were a year old before they pulled themselves up.

Very often I see babies propped up by impatient parents who cannot wait for the 'next stage' to happen naturally, but I have found that if a baby is propped up then sooner or later he will just slip back down again. There are also so many people these days putting their babies into those baby chair bouncers. I don't like them. I think they are so restraining. It's better for a child to lie flat on the floor, relaxing, stretching and rolling, than being contained in one of those scoop things. People are worried that their children won't be able to see what is going on in the room, but why should they want to? I also don't like to see an older baby sitting in one of those bouncers being fed. If the baby is too small for a high chair, I like feeding him when he is sitting on my knee. It is far cosier.

8 · When should I expect my baby to stand?

Normally children pull themselves up, holding on to a playpen or whatever, at about ten or eleven months. As a rule, I do not hold children's hands so they can walk along or pull them up. I have always left them entirely to their own devices so when they are able to do something, they do it. With one exception. Once they start standing, children can often get up and then will cry and cry because they cannot get down again. They soon learn to plonk down on to their bottoms, but if they are frustrated at being unable to sit down and are distressed, I take their hands and gently lower them on to their behinds.

I never use one of those bouncer things that fix on to a door frame – I once saw a baby sitting in one of those and bouncing up and down and all her food came up and ran down her little dress. It seems extraordinary to me to put a child in one of those things. What is it meant to do? Strengthen the child's legs or just get the child out of the way? I feel children should do what they are able to do. If they are on the floor they can grab hold of their feet, make archways; one of my girls used to straighten her arms and her legs and stick her bottom up in the air from six months. Stringing a child up in a doorway or dangling him on a chain hooked to the ceiling won't help him stand any quicker. If you want to get your child out of the way, put him in a playpen, not one of those bouncy things.

I always put a baby in a playpen the moment he is three months old. It is

OPPOSITE *Learning to stand with the help of a playpen*

essential for keeping a child out of harm when he is young and able to do a lot of damage to himself, especially in the few seconds one might be out of the room answering the doorbell or heating up his bottle. At first he will just lie on his back and peer through the bars or gaze upwards. He doesn't really need to be in there yet, but if you wait and start with a child who is much older – when he will need to be in there – he will resent the playpen very strongly, and who can blame the child for feeling (and being) restricted? If you use a playpen from the beginning a child can enjoy it and can use it differently as he reaches different stages. It is his area in which he can do what he pleases and in which his toys are safe from being stepped on and broken. In it he can lie, sit, crawl, stand and learn to walk, holding onto the top of the pen. Once the child is able to walk confidently I never put him in a pen again.

My playpens were always wooden and a very generous size. I never use the curious netting playpens one sees. How difficult and restrictive they must be for an energetic little person and I would have thought the netting might be a hazard for the small fingers of a tiny baby. Even the wooden ones of today are at least a foot narrower and shorter than the pens we used. I preferred playpens with a floor which I could cover with a blanket or a cotton candlewick rug, as the pens without floors tend to move about. When I did have one of these, I secured it to a heavy piece of furniture with stout string, and used a piece of specially cut thick foam rubber, which I then covered with a big bath towel or blanket, for the base. In the summer I often moved the playpen into the garden where it was also very useful. Of course you have to check your baby from time to time and see that he is not being left to roast.

After four months babies put everything they can reach into their mouths. I am enraged when I hear them scolded for doing so. Why shouldn't they? It is instinctive: taste is discovery. I suppose that is how millions of years ago the human race must have survived, picking up tiny bits of anything that might be food and eating them. It is up to you to make sure a child avoids accidents, there are lots of things that obviously should not be swallowed. If a baby is on the floor he will pick up the tiniest of things; bits of silver paper, fluff, screws, small pins, bits of cotton, marbles, anything. So one of the reasons for putting a baby in a playpen at three months is that you can make sure any objects in it are safe.

9 · When do you expect a baby to crawl?

Like everything else, the age at which a child first crawls varies from one child to another. Some children never crawl, they just shuffle on their bottoms. I have known children to start crawling when they were six or seven months and others who did not move until they were over a year. I can't remember whether one particular little boy ever moved at all until he walked, he was not very ambitious about moving, yet now in his thirties he walks almost everywhere. One of my girls was very small, about seven months, when she started crawling, and then she moved very, very fast. I think ten months is probably the most usual time to start crawling.

Don't bother comparing your baby with someone else's if he isn't moving about. As another nanny once said when asked why her child wasn't crawling, 'He's got too much to think about.'

10 · How can I help my child learn to walk?

The point is that you don't teach children to walk. If the human race had had to be taught to walk they would have vanished ages ago, we wouldn't have been able to run away from things. People put babies in those baby walkers to help 'teach' them to walk. I think baby walkers should be banned. They are dreadful things and I think they are very dangerous. I've heard of so many babies falling over in them and even of one who was killed after falling headlong over into an open fire.

Babies learn to walk at different times. A child learns to walk when they have a sense of balance and not before. African babies who live on their mothers' backs and have never seen a baby bouncer or baby walker walk very early. And I have known two children who took steps when they were nine months. They were sort of freaks. One of my babies waited until he was twenty-two months before he first took a step. He just got up, this beautiful child in his smock, and stomped right across the nursery. He had never taken a step before, he just could not be bothered. Most of my children have walked at about sixteen months; the earliest when he was one year old. Nobody had held his hand or pulled him up, he was just an early walker.

11 · When do you expect children to start climbing and jumping?

Children climb upstairs at varying ages. At two one of my girls could not yet climb upstairs and I have known children walk up the stairs one foot at a time until they were at least four, but some children do climb very early. I think if they are crawling at a year they may well climb at a year too, they find it very easy. You must stand behind them at all times, of course. Some children will run at eighteen months, once they are stabilized walkers, even if they tumble and trip over things. Others take much longer. Jumping takes much longer, real jumping with two legs together. Often they will only start at two, or even later. It just depends on the child.

Mental agility

12 · When do you think babies start understanding things around them?

Even little babies do watch your face very, very intently. By the time they are a month they search your face with their eyes, and at the same time they twitch their mouths. They no longer look blank or into the distance; I should think they must be beginning to focus and can see something. When they are a few weeks old they can copy things, like sticking their tongues out when you stick out yours or copying your voice pattern when you speak. Certainly when babies are very small they make a lot of sort of cooing noises, and if you make noises to them they imitate. It is quite extraordinary. I remember when one of my boys was very small, not older than three months, that I would make noises to him and he would imitate them. We could almost talk to each other.

Babies do not usually smile before six weeks, but quite often until then the corners of their mouths turn up and it looks like a smile, though people say it is a little grimace while making wind. I have never been sure, I sometimes think it is a smile, a feeling of pleasure, of well-being. Around approximately six weeks they do start smiling though and you will have no problems about knowing it.

In my experience children understand what you are saying much, much earlier than people think, so from when they are quite small you should never say anything critical about them in front of them. It is very important never to harass the child, not to talk about his problems when he is there as he will undoubtedly understand and be inhibited. You can sometimes notice quite a small child, looking worried because of something you are talking about, certainly by a year old if not younger. At nine months babies can tell familiar people from strangers. It has nothing to do with the relationship, whether it is the parent or nurse, the baby just knows the people who are normally there and as a general rule begins to protest if somebody who is not in the immediate family circle holds him.

It's amazing how quickly they understand things. But I would never test them on their knowledge by saying 'Where's your ears? Where's your nose?' and getting the child to touch them. I find it's rather degrading to the child, it is like putting him in a circus.

Some children have a vast knowledge in their favourite field at a very early age. They can tell makes of cars when they are two and recognize their parents' cars when they are even younger. It always amazes me, I still have no idea what car is what. Often children count up to ten and recite whole nursery rhymes by the time they are two, but that is just copying, it is not really understanding, so it does not count.

13 · When can I expect my child to start speaking?

In my experience the age at which children begin to speak varies tremendously.

Sharing a joke with Nina at ten weeks

Of course very little babies of perhaps a month make 'cooing' noises and there is a point when they like to shout, about six months I suppose, and make sounds and gurgle. But real speech, proper words, can begin as early as around nine to ten months or it can begin much, much later. A child's first recognizable sounds are usually 'Dada', 'Mama', 'Baba' and 'Gaga'. The 'ah' sound is the first. After that it can take them any length of time to talk properly. One of my girls spoke gobbledygook until she was three, you could not possibly understand her. Another child spoke well between one and two, sitting up in her pram, and her children did too. If your child does not speak fluently, you should not worry. Only worry if they do not make any sounds at all in which case they may be mute.

At about sixteen months children usually start saying 'No'. I suppose it is an easier word than 'Yes' but they do say it a great deal. By about a year and a half you might expect a child to put two words together: 'Simon's shoes', 'Bye, door' or whatever. By two and a half they may be saying whole sentences. Again it varies a lot. Often you will hear people saying the second child is slow to speak and that he does not need to speak properly as the first child translates for him. Whilst it is rather amusing and the first child usually can understand the younger child before adults can, it does not mean the younger one is lazy. If he could speak he would, he is just not yet ready for it. Some second children are excellent speakers.

14 · How can I help my child to speak?

You can't really help a child to speak, they somehow speak when they are able to. I never scold a child if he uses 'baby talk', but I would always use proper words – I wouldn't say 'pussy' and 'bow wow' to my child but instead 'cat' and 'dog', though it probably doesn't really matter in the long run. And I speak very clearly, as children learn by imitation, and I think there is nothing more attractive than if a child speaks properly. Remember whatever you say, that is what a child will learn. However I never correct children when they talk, I always encourage them. They will get there in their own time. You so often hear adults saying 'Say this . . . , not that . . .'. Don't confuse a child or worry him about minutiae, he will learn.

15 · How do you teach children about colours and right and left?

You will notice that toddlers given a choice of things will always pick up something red, this being the brightest colour of all. They also say 'red' more often when they are first asked what colour something is. It is the colour they pick up first and can talk about first. Usually when they are around the age of two I start mentioning colours more and more and by the time they are three they know

'Whatever you say, that is what a child will learn'

OPPOSITE *At about two I start mentioning colours, for instance, when I'm dressing the child*

about them. Coming home from the park I will talk about the different colours of the cars very casually, 'Oh look, that's a blue car.' I will also mention the colour when it is relevant. I always say 'Pass me the red pencil' or 'you shall wear your blue jersey' so they learn as a sort of game, but even if I did not do that they would still learn.

It's the same with right and left. When putting on a baby's shoes, slippers, socks, etc., I always say 'Lift up your right foot' or when drying them after a bath, 'Put up your left foot' and then I'd take the relevant foot. I am very much against saying 'What colour is that?', treating the child as a toy. It seems to be an insult to the child's intelligence to ask them. I think the child must think 'For goodness sake, shut up!'

Golden rules

Your child has been born a genius

1   You don't have to teach children to stand or crawl or walk or talk – these abilities are all instinctive.

2   Don't keep pushing your child to grow up – he's got the rest of his life to be pushed about.

3   Each child has his own merits – never compare one child with another. When your child is ready to do something, he will do it. Don't call him 'lazy' – he's just not yet ready.

4   Keep learning a part of everyday life. Make sure it's fun. Always stop if your child wants to. Try and grab *his* interest, don't expect him to share yours.

5   Don't ask your child to touch his nose or ears or show off – he's not a circus animal.

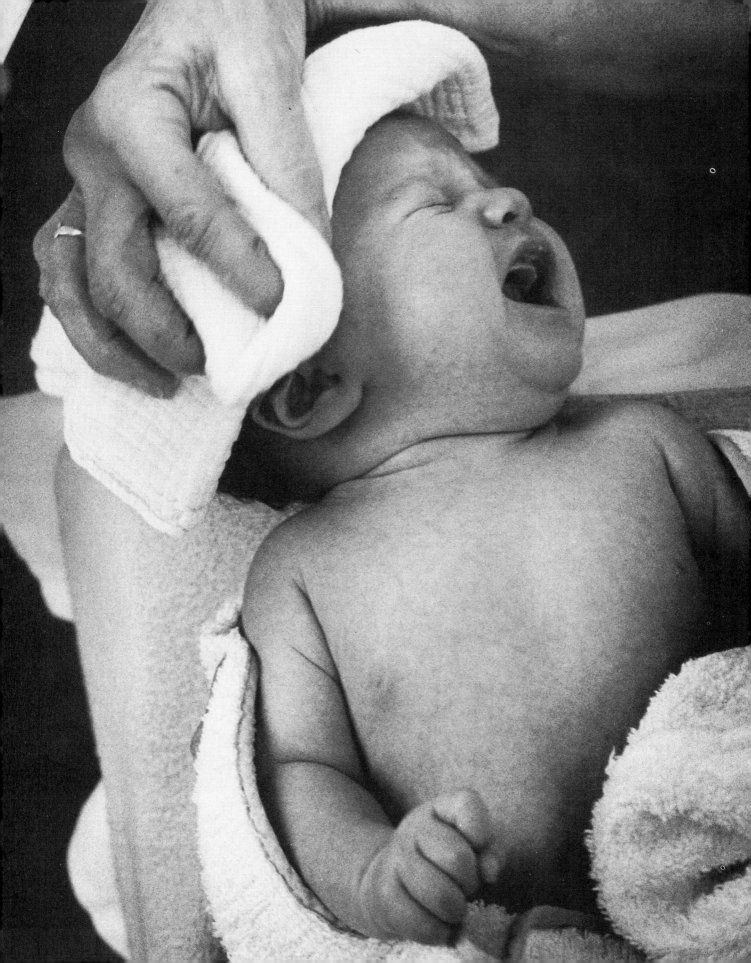

3

Bathing

There's nothing nicer than a clean, sweet-smelling baby but it's something one should never get obsessive about. I bath all babies every day, unless they are ill or we are travelling and nowhere near a bath. Even though they are obviously not exactly dirty it freshens them up and I think they enjoy being in the water – after all they've been floating in it for a while. Being in water is very relaxing even for a tiny baby. Bathing should be fun for both parties so don't hurry over it.

Bathing is normally a happy time even if the baby has not yet got to the kicking or splashing stage. Some small babies do scream and cry but I do not think it is because they are being bathed but perhaps because of the way they are being held. I have noticed that babies often cry more when being held tentatively and possibly a little loosely by people not used to handling babies. But two of my babies cried when they were being bathed and I bathed them all in the same way, so I really don't think one can ever know the reason why. Fortunately it happens very rarely and not for very long.

OPPOSITE *Drying a very young baby's head with a muslin towel*

Bathtime

1 · What time do you bath a baby?

I always find it a good plan to give a newborn baby a bath in the morning, usually at 9.30 a.m., just before their 10 a.m. feed. Water not only cleans them, and as they have been in nappies all night that's a good thing, it also relaxes them, which means they will take a better feed. An over-stimulated baby only takes just enough food to appease his hunger and needs food again in a very short time. I would never bath a baby after a feed, because I don't think it would be comfortable for him to have a bath with a full stomach.

2 · Do you wash babies at other times of the day as well?

Besides their daily morning bath, I also 'top and tail' my newborn baby every evening before his 6 p.m. feed until he is six months old when I first give him a bath in the evening. 'Top and tail' simply means washing both the baby's face and bottom. I also top and tail, rather than bath, a sick child, no matter how old he is.

Equipment

3 · Nanny, will I need to buy a baby bath?

I'm experienced enough to be able to bath a newborn baby in a basin, but it is a lot to ask a first-time mother to do what with hot taps and drips. So I think a baby bath is an essential purchase – you can always excuse the extravagance by using it afterwards for soaking clothes or other things.

Any baby bath you buy today will be made of plastic and you should buy one as large as you can because I think babies like to feel a floating movement as they are held. It is useful to have a place to put the soap, but not essential. A special stand is not necessary if you have a table or chest of drawers you can put the bath on. You need one or the other because to put the baby bath on the floor or inside a big bath is uncomfortable for your back. If the baby bath can rest on your bath you will be able to fill it with a shower attachment; otherwise you will need two buckets (see question 7).

The baby baths I always used were made of jaconet (a type of fabric sprayed with a very soft rubber) suspended on a low painted wooden frame. The bath folded away flat and there was a small metal tap underneath for draining. I would use a bucket to fill the bath and I would empty it by putting the bucket underneath. After use it needed to be dried very carefully with a soft cloth. It was lovely and soft to put a baby in and the right height for you to sit down to bath the baby.

Bathing Nina in an old-fashioned jaconet bath, with a wooden frame

4 · What else will I need for bathtime?

You will need a bath towel which you should keep just for baby's use and a muslin nappy or other soft, small towel which you use to dry his face, and later, hair. You will also need some soap. I always use simple, non-perfumed baby soap. If you like the smell of baby powder you can use that as well (see question 16). If your baby has dry skin you may want to buy some baby oil – I would either put a few drops of it in his bath water or rub a little gently into his body before putting him in the bath.

You should also buy a pair of fine, adult nail scissors. They are sharp so you must use them carefully when you cut his fingernails, but I find that those ones they sell especially for babies are rather thick and difficult. You probably won't have to cut your baby's toenails for the first six months of his life but just make sure they don't get too long or bent. To keep myself dry I wear a towelling apron (see CHANGING AND TOILET TRAINING, question 9).

5 · Will my new baby need any bath toys?

Even with a new baby it is fun to have something to play with in the bath. Babies love to have a sponge squeezed over them so the water trickles onto their tummies. This is the only time I use a sponge, but as it is used with soap and becomes a bit slimy, once a week I clean it. I just put it in cold, salt water and leave it for an hour or so.

Preparing for the bath

A small baby rolled in a towel for hair washing

6 · Does the room need to be a special temperature?

I always had a thermometer hanging on the wall in baby's room because we were taught that a small baby's room should normally be 16°C (60°F), and it should be made a good deal warmer when he was having a bath – not less than 18°C (65°F) and preferably several degrees higher. So I check the temperature and, if necessary, turn on the radiator. I also close all the windows, even in summer. The room should be nice and warm.

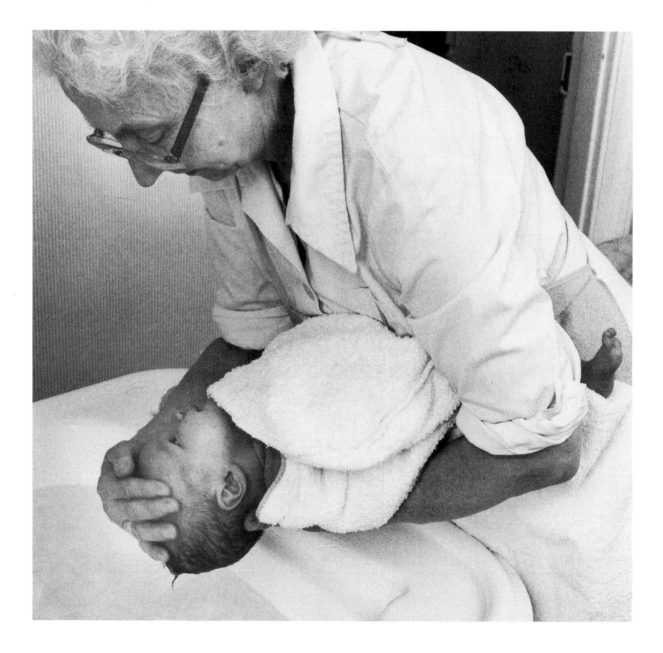

7 · What else do I need to do before I undress the baby?

Before I bath the baby I always place a collection on a small tray. It consists of all the things I need for the bath (see questions 3–5), everything I will need for the nappy change (see CHANGING AND TOILET TRAINING, question 10) and the baby's clean outfit (vest, nightie, jacket and bootees) which I warm on a nearby radiator in winter. I also have ready a small bowl of warm boiled water which I use to wash the baby's face (see question 10) and an empty bucket which I put the dirty clothes and nappies in.

I fill the bath with water a little hotter than I want to use – it will have cooled down a little by the time I have undressed the baby. I also have a bucket of cold water which I use to adjust the temperature of the bath the moment before I am about to put the baby in it (see question 8). I then put a chair near the bath for me to sit on and, if I was answering the telephone, I would put the answerphone on or take the receiver off the hook so I would not be disturbed. Bathtime should be relaxing. It is such a happy time.

8 · How do you ensure the bath water is the correct temperature?

A newborn baby's bath water should be body temperature. You can measure this by dipping your elbow or the side of your hand in the water, the water should feel neither hot nor cold, but the same temperature as your body.

I usually let cold water run in the bath first but it does not really matter when you are only filling a bucket to put into a baby bath. I suppose it is just a good habit to get into. But you must make sure you check the temperature of the water – and then double-check it the moment before you put baby in to make sure it is neither too hot nor has lost heat and become chilly.

9 · Nanny, now everything is ready, should I wash his hair first?

Yes, I always do. When I've taken off the baby's clothes and dropped them in the bucket ready to be washed, I lie him on a towel – preferably warmed – and then roll him up in it so he is wrapped up closely and can't get his arms out. That way he can't wriggle or slip when his hair is being washed.

Once the baby is swaddled in the towel I take him to the bath and hold his head over it, quite close to the water, holding him firmly all the time. I cup some water in my hand and pour it over his head, wash his scalp with the merest bit of baby soap (do not use too much or your baby will get dandruff) and then rinse the soap off thoroughly. I then lie the baby on my lap and gently dry his head by rubbing it softly with a muslin nappy. Remember to dry his ears and behind his ears very, very well.

'Babies love to have a sponge squeezed over their tummy'

Washing your baby

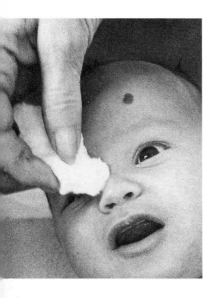

Washing a very young baby's eyes with warm boiled water and cotton wool, wiping towards the nose

'Bathtime is such a happy time'

10 · *What do you wash next?*

Keeping him still swaddled on my lap, again holding him firmly, I wash his face. For the first year of a baby's life I always wash his face with cool, boiled water only. I never put soap on a baby's face and all my children have wonderful complexions. I use three pieces of cotton wool, one for each eye, in case there is an infection in one eye which you do not want to pass to the other eye, and the third piece for the rest of the face.

I dip the cotton wool in the water, squeeze it out so that it is damp but not dripping, and then wipe one eye from the outside in, towards the nose. Then I take another piece and do the same with the other eye, again wiping from the outside in. After that I take another clean muslin nappy (not the one I used for drying the baby's hair) and very carefully dry one eye and then the other, using a different bit of the towel each time. They were very strict about eye infections where I was trained, so I have always been extremely careful. I then take the last piece of cotton wool and very gently wipe all over the rest of the baby's face and then dry it, again very gently, with the soft muslin nappy.

11 · *Now do I wash the rest of my baby's body?*

After I've washed the baby's face I unwrap the bath towel from around him so that it lies flat on my lap with the baby on top of it, lying on his back. I dip my hands into the bath, soap them and then with both my hands I lightly soap the baby's front ready for the bath. I use very little soap because babies' skins are so delicate, but I do soap them all over, taking special care to soap inside their hands, which are always full of fluff because they hang onto blankets, and under their chin. I used to feel sorry for my babies because I always have such cold hands so I would try and warm them up as much as possible with warm water. I dare say they did not mind as much as I thought they would and got used to me fairly quickly.

I do not clean the baby's navel. After all, when you bath him the navel gets a wash anyway, just by soaking in the bath. I never wash between a girl's labia with soap and I always clean a girl's bottom wiping backwards, away from her vagina and towards her anus. I only take special care to clean the tip of the penis if the baby has had a very dirty nappy. Otherwise I just wash the penis with a little soap in the bath. We were taught not to push back the foreskin to clean a baby's penis, so I have never done it.

12 · *Nanny, when do I put my baby in the bath?*

When soaping is done I rinse the soap off my hands so they are no longer slippery

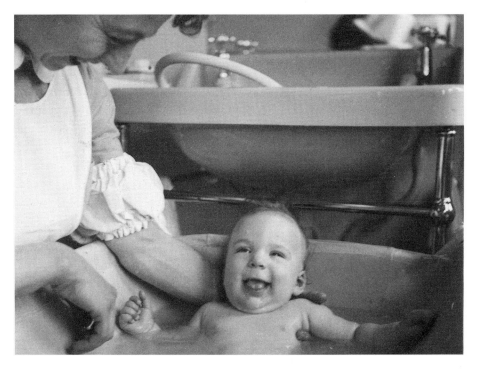

and lift the baby into the bath, putting my left arm under the baby's shoulders with my left hand holding the top of his left arm while my right hand holds both his ankles. I always take care to hold him *very* firmly. If you are left-handed you may want to swop my directions round.

Once the baby is in the bath I rinse the soap off him, using my right hand, – my left arm and hand still holding him firmly. Then I turn him over so that his chest is resting on my left forearm and my left hand is holding on to the top of his right arm. With my right hand I soap his back and bottom and then rinse the soap off and turn him over again so he is lying on his back supported by my left arm. For a few minutes we then have some gentle bath play. Newborn babies will normally love the water, especially if it is deep enough to cover the entire body, apart from head and shoulders, when they are stretched out in it. I scoop the water over his tummy with my right hand and squeeze the wet sponge over his tummy as well. Sometimes you will find he will grip the side of the bath like a vice and you will have to peel his fingers away gently.

13 · Couldn't I soap him in the bath instead of beforehand?

Once you are feeling confident it is just as easy to soap the front, as well as the back, of the baby in the bath rather than on your lap beforehand. You just hold him as before using whichever hand you have free to wash him and then to rinse the soap off.

Giving Nina a bath: I'm holding her firmly with my left hand under her shoulders, while I wash and rinse her with my right hand

14 · Do you clean a baby's ears and nose as well?

Once a week until my children are two or three I clean their ears with a fine, smooth cream at bathtime (or whenever it is convenient). I smear it all around the curly bits and behind the ears and then sort of clean it off with cotton wool, but never those cotton buds. You can put a little wisp of cotton wool inside a child's ears to wipe out the wax, but never poke anything into the ear as that can be painful and even dangerous.

I also clean the nose. I never ever poke up inside a child's nose. Instead, once a week for about the first year of life, I wipe around the edge of the nostrils and the outside of their nose with cotton wool dipped in baby oil. If there is anything stuck in their nose I massage it gently by stroking down from the bridge of the nose along the outside. That way you can ease whatever is inside down and out. I usually clean ears and nose on different days so I won't be wiping around their faces too much.

Drying your baby

15 · How do you dry the baby?

When the bath is finished I lift the baby up and out, my left arm under his back, holding his left arm firmly, and grasping his ankles with my right hand. I hold him over the bath for a second or two to let the drips roll off and then lie him on his back on the towel, quickly draping the other half of the towel over him. I then dry his front very carefully, turn him over and dry his back. I make sure I have dried him well under his chin, behind his knees, between his legs, in his elbows and under his arms. Try not to rub your baby dry roughly or pat him ineffectively, but give him a gentle wipe to dry him. Make sure he is always dried very, very thoroughly or he will become sore if continually left wet.

16 · Do you think I should use baby powder?

There are things to be said both for and against baby powder and I do know nannies who are violently against it. We were taught to use it only once the baby was absolutely dry, especially in all the creases. Baby powder must not be used like blotting paper. If you use powder when babies are not completely dry it goes like paste, causes irritation and makes the child very sore. I have always dried a baby very well and then used a little shake of powder on his chest, back, under his arms and just under his chin. I just shake a little out and spread it all around with my hand. There is nothing nicer and fresher than a child who smells of baby powder – but that's for my benefit. I'm sure the child wouldn't mind what he smelt of.

Golden rules

Bathing should be a relaxed, fun time

1   Never get obsessive about your baby's cleanliness.

2   Babies enjoy being in the water. It relaxes them.

3   Make sure your bath is at the right height for your back so you can relax too.

4   Keep the room warm and warm his towel and clothes in winter.

5   Even a tiny baby will enjoy 'playing' in the bath.

How to bath your baby confidently

1   Turn on the answerphone or take the 'phone off the hook so you don't get disturbed.

2   Hold your baby firmly.

3   Always check and double-check the temperature of the bath water.

4   Don't be put off by a screaming baby. Some babies just do – it won't last forever.

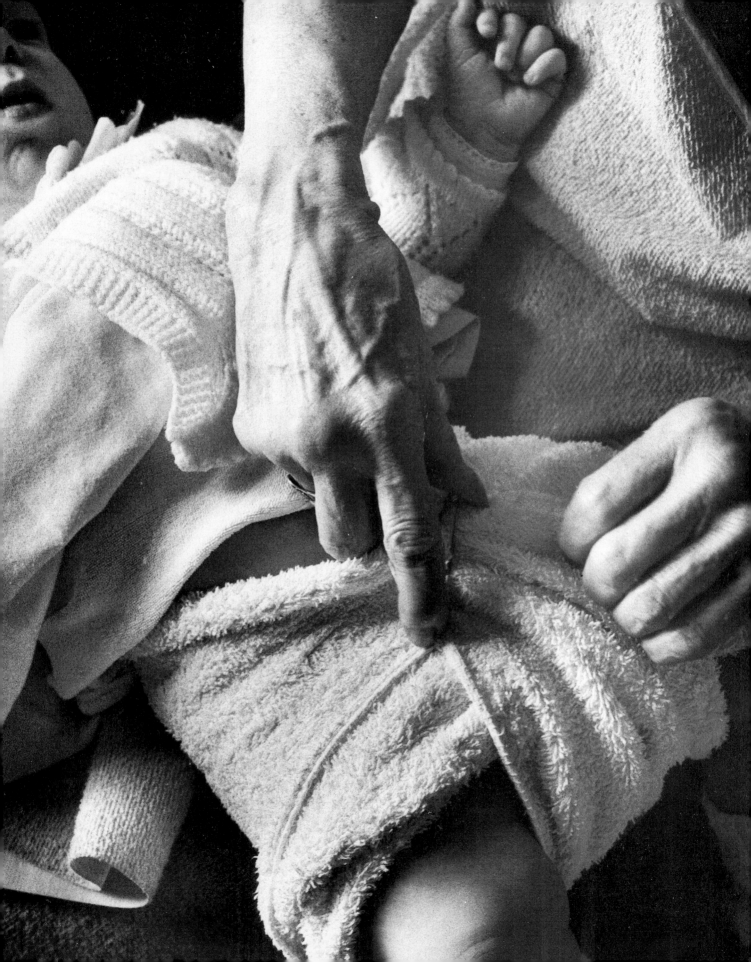

4

Changing and Toilet Training

A little boy I know who lived on a farm never wore a nappy, knickers or trousers, he was always naked from the waist down. His mother said it was no good putting trousers on him because he always wet them. She didn't have the inclination to potty-train him, but by the time he was three he would go to a corner of the farmyard, crouch down to defecate, then pick his stool up on a shovel and put it on the manure heap. The little boy did not just do it anywhere on the floor, he went somewhere special, like an animal. This story is just to show that children will 'toilet train' themselves. You are just there to help speed the process along.

Making a big fuss about toilet training has no justification, in fact the less fuss you make the quicker the desired results. Never ever be obsessive about putting children on the pot because you defeat your own ends. I always keep toilet training very casual. Don't worry about keeping their knickers clean. What does it matter if they dirty the odd pair of knickers? Sooner or later all children use a toilet, so don't worry about whether it is sooner or later. They all will by the time they are twenty-one.

'The less fuss you make, the quicker the desired results'

OPPOSITE *Putting a nappy on an older baby. After putting the towelling nappy under the baby's bottom, I bring the sides over. Then I secure all three points with a pin (see question 11 and the photos on page 87)*

1 · Do you talk to children about their poos and wees?

I find people talk far too much about their child's bodily functions. From a very early age they pick their child up, stick his bottom in their face and say 'Have you got a smelly nappy?', and once the child is older they talk in front of him about how his toilet training is progressing. Whether they have a prudish or prurient attitude to their own bodies I don't know. I am always totally relaxed about my body and bodily functions and those of my children. My children often saw me on the loo and they had no feeling of disgust about it at all. Disgust is something children only feel when other people suggest it to them, so don't.

Most children sometimes like to watch themselves defecating. They bend forward to look and then examine their stools afterwards. If *they* want to talk about what they have seen, don't discourage them, but just talk about it in a straightforward, matter of fact way. I have never known children make jokes about their genitals or defecating until they started school and even then they did not continue the joke at home with me. I suppose they knew I would be neither shocked nor amused by it. I do think it is somewhat unnatural if children make a special point of talking about their genitals or coming to watch you on the loo. Why should they want to watch? After all, everyone goes to the loo. Someone must have said something to them to make them feel that urinating was so interesting. In a relaxed home I would hope they would not get overly interested in peeing but would watch you do it and then want to imitate you. I think that children should see other people on the loo. They are great imitators and will always do what other people in the household do. So let them see them.

2 · What do I do if my child keeps laughing about 'poos'?

Many small children go through what we call a lavatorial stage. Obviously when a child is alone with adults who take a relaxed attitude he won't mention anything, because what's funny, but two children together will laugh and laugh about 'poo poo'. If I hear them I do say to them 'Do you want to go to the loo?' and if they don't then I say 'Why do you keep talking about poo? Why's it so funny? After all, if you didn't do poo you'd be very ill. You eat food to help you grow and there's always so much waste material which comes out in the loo and there's not really anything funny about it.' I wouldn't clamp down, I'd just explain what it is. Why, anyway, do so many adults find the ordinary bodily functions of urinating, defecating, copulating and so on, so comic? Why have the plain old words for these activities, like shit and fuck, become swear words? There shouldn't be any forbidden words, should there? I don't take any notice if a child says 'poo poo' or 'shit' or anything else. If they can't shock you they probably won't continue.

Keep it natural

'Disgust is something children only feel when other people suggest it to them'

83

I always say 'pee' for urinate and 'pee pee' for urine. Where I was trained they used to say 'B. O.' (bowels open) for defecating, but I've never used it. Although when children are small I sometimes call it 'poo' or 'poo poo' or 'big jobs' and say 'do a poo', when they are a little older and talking then I always say 'Number two'. It sounds better when they are four or five. You have to say something don't you? If they pass wind I say 'windy pop' which taken out of context sounds rather silly, but I didn't refer to it very often – perhaps only to a small child when talking about a baby.

3 · What do you call the sexual organs when speaking to young children?

I usually call a boy's penis a 'winkie' but I think that it is peculiar to me. These days you see 'willie' on 'rude' birthday cards and things, so I think I am unusual – sometimes I call it that, too. Certainly one wouldn't give it its right name, one wouldn't really say 'penis' to a small child. I find young children quite observant about their own and other people's bodies and they certainly never talk about the vagina so I find that there is no real need to have a word for this – I don't usually call it anything. I call their bottom and anus, 'botty'. Later on, some little girls say 'my front botty' for their vaginas, or even just call it 'botty' as well, because it's at the bottom.

Nappies

Changing equipment

4 · What kind of nappy should I use?

I don't think babies mind what kind of nappy you use although I do think to have soft muslin next to your skin must be nice. I know most people these days use disposables, but I have always used a terry towelling nappy and for the first six months of the baby's life a muslin nappy as well. I've sometimes been asked if the bulk of a towelling nappy will ever stop a baby walking. I've never noticed this happening – no nappy will ever make a child's legs become bow-legged, though an improper diet might. If a child wants to walk he will. Of course, if your child looks awkward you should see if you have arranged the nappy sensibly.

I used disposable nappies once, on holiday, and found them very useful. Disposables are, of course, very convenient and seem to be improving all the time (see question 6).

5 · How many towelling nappies will I need and what else will I need to buy if I use them?

If you decide to use terry towelling nappies you'll need twenty-four and you'll want the best quality really. A good thick towelling nappy will be much more absorbent than a thin one. It's also better to get them with hems rather than just stitched over as hemmed ones last longer and don't get ragged. I always boiled new nappies before using them for the first time, just to make sure they were quite clean. I remember there was a vogue for both shaped and coloured nappies but it didn't take off. I never used either. They used to make different sizes of terry and muslin nappies which you could use as the baby grew, and we all had them, but these days fabric nappies are all the same size; it is only disposable nappies that grow in size.

You will also need eighteen muslin squares, half a dozen pairs of plastic pants and half a dozen nappy pins. I like the plastic pants with elastic round the waist and the legs myself, although the elastic mustn't be tight or it could stop the baby's circulation. I always buy them big rather than small for the same reason. At each nappy change the pants should be changed too and washed and dried thoroughly before they are worn again. I always buy those curved nappy pins with a safety bit that you push down at the top. I never disinfect pins or sharpen them or put them in petroleum jelly to help them slide in or do any of those other things you hear about. I just stick them in a pin-cushion or in the corner of my apron, well out of the baby's reach when I change his nappy. If they get too blunt, which they will do, I buy new ones.

I never used nappy liners either until this year when I came across them in a house where I was looking after a new baby. They are not really necessary, but I did find them useful as they do keep the defecation away from the nappy so it remains cleaner. If you do use nappy liners you can sterilize and re-use them although that rather takes away the point of them.

6 · *If I use disposable nappies what will I need to buy?*

Disposable nappies nowadays seem to come in all sorts of shapes, colours and sizes as well as different types for boys and girls, so you will need to experiment a little until you find the right shape and size for your child. Some brands do seem to fit some children better than others. You will also need a large supply of plastic bags in which to put the soiled nappies or, better still, an incinerator. I don't believe in putting them in those special deodorizing bags – yet more waste and expense.

7 · *What should I use to clean my baby's bottom?*

Where I was trained we cleaned a new baby's bottom with olive oil and once they got bigger and their bottoms were not quite so delicate we used soap and water. I can't remember when or why I stopped using olive oil, but I did. For cleaning a baby's bottom, whatever his age, I now use either baby oil or a little very mild baby soap and water, on cotton wool. I use baby lotion when I am travelling as it is useful if I am somewhere where there is no water. Otherwise I am not sure how good it is for a baby's skin, although I know a lot of mothers do use it. Both baby oil and baby lotion are slightly oily so they do clean up a bottom beautifully. I rarely use baby wipes and when I do it is only on a larger baby's bottom. They are, of course, very useful for travelling. I might use baby wipes if a baby had a very soiled nappy, but I'd always wash his bottom afterwards with soap and water to make sure it was quite clean.

8 · What medicated creams do I need to use on my baby's bottom?

I always buy three kinds of botty cream: an ordinary zinc and castor oil cream (any brand will do) which I use at most nappy changes, a special botty cream which I use instead if the baby has a nappy rash and his bottom is a bit sore or red and a jar of petroleum jelly which is perfectly all right to use on a normal bottom as it makes the skin waterproof. If your baby is a little bit constipated I would put some petroleum jelly just inside the rectum, to help the baby pass stools. I have heard that with the latest kind of disposable nappies you shouldn't use any botty creams as it hinders the nappy's absorbency. When using these it does mean that you must take extra care washing the baby's bottom at each nappy change.

9 · Do I need to buy a special nappy changing table or mat?

When it comes to nappy changing, your back is the only consideration. You don't need anywhere special to change your baby, but you must protect your back. I think these special baby-changing chests you can buy now are just a very clever way of somebody making a lot of money. There's nothing wrong with using a bed or a chest of drawers although you can't leave the baby alone on any of these once he can roll. If you change the baby on a chest of drawers it must be quite high so you don't have to bend over too much, and of course padded so the baby isn't lying on a hard surface. And if you change a baby on a bed you should always kneel down next to the bed.

I've never owned a changing mat. It comes to the same as putting a towel on your bed and using a waterproof sheet underneath. If you are using a bed to change a baby on, of course you must have something waterproof underneath his bottom or you can get the bed wet, but even if I was using a changing mat I would always put a towel or towelling nappy on top of it to keep the baby warm. I don't like the idea of a baby lying on cold plastic.

I was taught to change a baby on my lap and have always done it – it means you can do it anywhere. I always wear a waterproof apron, of course, to protect

'When it comes to nappy changing . . . you must protect your back'

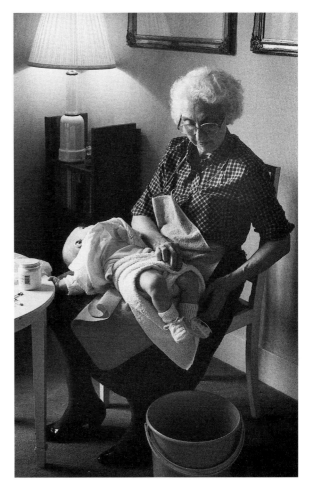

my clothing – usually one which is towelling on one side, so it is cosy for the baby to lie on, and plastic or rubber on the other, so if there is an accident my clothes won't get soiled. Changing them on the knee means they are in close contact with you, being held, rather than floating free on a changing mat.

10 · Where did you keep all your equipment to make nappy-changing as easy as possible?

At home, I always changed the baby's nappies sitting in a low nursing chair which had a drawer in the base in which I kept everything I would need. In the drawer was a baby basket or tray in which I kept all the creams, the baby oil and baby lotion (see questions 7 and 8); a roll of cotton wool; my nappy pins in a pin cushion and a small enamel kidney dish (or a little bowl) in which I put the cotton wool once it was soiled. I also kept a small bowl for water to wash the baby's bottom with, some baby soap and a towel.

Near the chair I had another smallish bowl to drop the soiled nappy in straightaway after taking it off. I find that if you are with babies all the time you

Changing a baby's nappy on your lap is very convenient for you and cosy for the baby. Hold their feet firmly by the ankles to stop them wriggling, and once they are older, give them something to hold to distract them.

don't notice how smelly they are, but as they are smelly, you really don't want to drop dirty nappies and bits of soiled cotton wool on the carpets or the smell will linger. In the bathroom I kept a lidded bucket filled with sterilizing solution into which I would put the soiled nappy once the baby had his new nappy on.

Within reach I also had the new nappies ready folded (see questions 12 and 13) and the clean plastic pants.

How to change

11 · What is your nappy-changing routine?

I first put on my waterproof apron and get out whatever I am going to need (see question 10), so it is all to hand and I tear some cotton wool off the roll into little pieces. I then lie the baby on his back on my lap with his head on my left knee

Putting a nappy on a newborn baby. Having put the baby onto a folded muslin nappy, I draw up the points of the nappy and secure them with a safety pin. Then I roll the baby in the towelling nappy and fasten it with another pin at the side, like a sarong (see question 12)

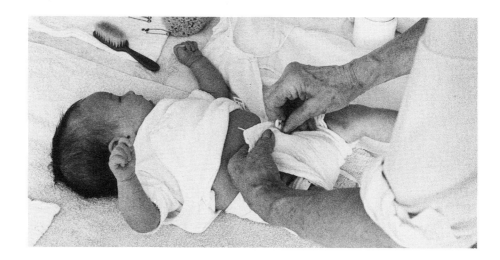

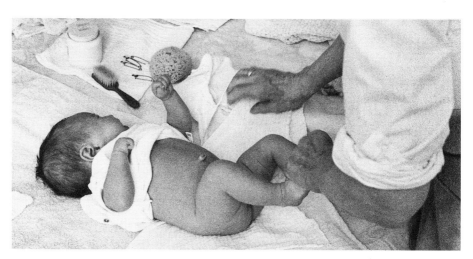

and his buttocks on my right (I am right-handed). This way my knees make a flat 'table'.

Once the baby is on my lap I remove the old nappy, putting the pins either in my apron or a pin cushion for safe keeping. Then I clean the baby's bottom. If the baby has done a poo I gently wipe as much of the poo as possible off his bottom with a clean bit of the old nappy. I then drop the soiled nappy into the bowl put out for the purpose where I leave it until the baby has his new nappy on. If his bottom is very soiled I always find it easiest to just pick him up and carry him over to the hand-basin, push his clothes up and wash his bottom with a little baby soap and water, then rinse it well making sure that the soap is absolutely rinsed off; I then dry it very carefully and thoroughly with a soft towel. If he has just got a wet nappy I clean his bottom either with a little soap and water that I have near me, again rinsing and drying thoroughly, or I use some cotton wool and baby oil (see question 7). When washing a girl's bottom I remember always to wipe away from her, towards her back, to avoid getting her vagina infected.

Next I take the clean, folded nappy and place it under the baby's buttocks and apply the zinc and castor oil cream or the special botty cream (see question 8), if he has a nappy rash. I always use a thickish layer of cream making sure that it completely covers the skin. I put cream on a girl's vagina as if I was filling a crack. I don't push it in, I just smear it over. I never put cream on the baby's tummy – it is unnecessary for girls and for boys, too, if the nappy is put on with the penis pointing down so he doesn't get urine going up to his uncreamed stomach and causing nappy rash. I never put cream on a penis either, it doesn't usually get sore. I then pin the nappy on using the old pins – I never stab my babies, I always put the fingers of my other hand (the one not pushing in the pin) between the nappy and the baby so that if I stick the pin into anything it will be my own finger. If the baby is over one month old I then put on his plastic knickers.

For folding and pinning instructions, see questions 12 and 13.

Once the baby has his nappy on I take the bowl containing the used nappy to the bathroom. For ways of dealing with used nappies, see question 15.

Using a disposable nappy is obviously much simpler. The only thing you have to remember with them is not to let any baby lotion or oil or botty cream get onto the sticky tags or any part of the outside where the tags are meant to be placed or they won't stick.

12 · *Nanny, how do I put a towelling nappy on a new baby?*

For the first month of a baby's life I use a muslin nappy which I fold in the same way as I will later fold a towelling nappy. I've always used what is called the 'triangle method' of folding a nappy, so I start by putting the square muslin nappy on the bed and folding it into four so it becomes a small square. I then fold it again into a triangle, and put it under the baby's bottom with the point of the triangle pointing downwards in between the legs and the top edge at the same height as the waist with one point either side of the baby. I then wrap the two points (left and right) around the waist and bring up the bottom point to meet them, remembering to point a boy's penis downward as explained in question 11. Then I fasten all three points together with a safety pin. Next I fold a towelling nappy in half and place the baby on top of it positioned directly in the middle of the nappy with the waist at the top edge of the nappy. Finally I bring over the two sides and fasten them with a safety pin, like a sarong. This is how I put a nappy on babies until they are one month old.

13 · What about putting a nappy on a child over one month old?

From one to six or seven months I put on the muslin nappy next to the baby's skin, either folded into four and then into a triangle (as above) or just folded into a triangle, depending on the size of your baby and the size of your muslin nappy. I then put on the towelling nappy in the same way as the muslin above only used singly, not folded into four. I use one pin for each nappy – I always find it fits very snugly. I then put plastic knickers on top. At six or seven months I stop using a muslin nappy and just put the towelling nappy directly next to the baby's skin. I still use plastic pants on top.

Once babies get older and begin to wriggle about a lot I give them something to hold – anything that's handy and preferably something they don't normally play with, such as the lid from the pot of petroleum jelly or their hairbrush or a piece of cloth. I would have to hold their legs very, very firmly as otherwise they would stretch backwards, touching the floor with their hands, and be difficult to hold. If your baby likes crawling away you just have to hang onto his legs with your left hand (if you are right-handed) and get on with it, working very, very quickly.

Another 'problem' is that most babies will go through a phase when they love being naked and kicking without their nappy on. I always let them do it for a minute or two when I change them if I have the time. But it isn't practical for them to be naked for any longer than a few minutes or they would get themselves and everything else around them wet. They can be naked and kicking in the bath.

14 · My baby's nappies always leak at night. What do I do about this?

Once a baby is sleeping through the night (from about nine months, when I stop waking them for the 10 p.m. feed) until they don't need to wear a nappy any more, I fold a second muslin square up into a pad, resembling a sanitary towel. I place this between the baby's legs going up to their tummy button at the front and up to the back of their anus at the back (always remember to point a boy baby's penis downwards). I use this instead of disposable nappy pads which are convenient but expensive. The muslin can even be used with disposable nappies. The next morning just rinse the muslin thoroughly in cold water (or soak it in a bucket of cold water for an hour) and then wash it with the rest of your washing. If your baby has defecated during the night, sluice the soiled nappy in the loo first.

15 · What do I do with my baby's dirty towelling nappy?

When I take off a baby's nappy, if it is just wet, I put it directly into a bucket of sterilizing solution. If there's a motion I tip the stool into the toilet first, rinse the nappy while flushing the toilet and then put it into the sterilizing solution. If the motion is soft or sticky and won't just drop off, I sluice the nappy about in the toilet bowl which seems to do the trick and then put it into the sterilizing solution. I would then leave the nappy, and the day's subsequent nappies, in the sterilizing solution until the next morning when I would wash them.

My routine was always the same. The first job of the day was to wash all the previous day's nappies. I took five, sometimes six of each kind out of the old sterilizing solution that they had been in overnight. I rinsed them well and then boiled them up in a mild soap or detergent solution, letting them boil for at least five minutes. It doesn't matter what you use to wash a nappy as long as you rinse it thoroughly afterwards, although I never use biological washing powders because even if they were rinsed very well I would always have a feeling they might not be safe for the baby's bottom. After rinsing them thoroughly, I hung them up to dry and made up a new bucket of sterilizing solution for the next day, following the instructions on the packet. Towelling nappies always remain soft, if you know how to look after them. Never iron them or dry them on a radiator as it hardens them. It's best if you can leave nappies to dry in the breeze outdoors. I do always iron muslin nappies – it makes them lovely and soft and also makes them easier to store.

Now I look back, I think that my nappy-cleaning routine was probably over-fussy. I think that once the nappies had been in the sterilizing solution for at least twelve hours it would probably have been enough just to rinse them and put them in the washing machine as normal. But my reward was that my nappies were always snow-white and as good as new by the time my children had finished with them. I would then embroider the towelling nappies with my children's initials and put little loops on them and they would use them for hand-towels and we would take the muslin nappies on picnics as large napkins.

16 · What nappy-changing equipment do you take when going out for tea?

If I am going to be away from home for a few hours I take a nappy bag with me

'I would then embroider the towelling nappies with my children's initials'

with a couple of clean nappies (two towelling and two muslin, if muslin is still being used), baby lotion and cotton wool (or baby wipes if they are a little older) and some nappy cream. I also take two pairs of plastic pants (one for each nappy change) and an old plastic bag for the soiled nappies. I just tie a tight knot in the top to keep the smell in and tackle them when we get home. You can buy a special bag for carrying all your nappies and creams in when you go out, but really any bag that is big enough will do.

When to change

17 · How often should I change my baby's nappy?

People do get obsessed with changing their baby's nappy. I quite often hear people saying 'Look! My baby's crying, he must have a dirty (or wet) nappy.' That's a fallacy. I don't think that babies cry when they have dirtied their nappies, at least not until they are six months old. For a child to empty his bowels and bladder is a perfectly normal thing. It would never occur to them to mind being wet or dirty. Urine is warm and so long as it's kept warm a baby won't notice. This doesn't mean that you should leave them that way for a long time but that you needn't be over-anxious. Babies do mind if they're left for a very long time and the nappy gets cold. They might also mind if they have a sore bottom – you shouldn't leave a child with a sore bottom in a very dirty nappy – or a sore tummy or are very constipated, but otherwise I think it is quite unnecessary to eternally be changing a baby's nappy.

I always felt that it is most important for a baby to be peaceful. I left my children alone to play or sleep and when it was time to feed them I would change their nappies and bath or dress them, or whatever was necessary, and then I would leave them to be peaceful again. Unless you feel insecure and need physical contact there is no need to disturb a baby constantly – or at least not under the pretext of a dirty nappy.

Having said that babies don't mind having a dirty nappy, I think they like having a clean nappy and may well feel comforted when a cold, dirty nappy is removed and a clean, warm nappy is put on. I always warmed nappies, especially in winter, by putting them on a fire-guard or radiator before putting them on a baby. You can't do that with disposable nappies but I don't suppose your baby will mind. In winter you can always warm his clean vest and clothes on the radiator before putting them on.

Normally I only change a baby's nappy either immediately before or after he is fed. After when the baby is very small (up to six months old) and before once they get a bit older. I always change a small baby's nappy after he has been fed, because I think if you change it first you disturb the baby, especially if you have just woken him up. It seems unfair to wake the baby up, then change him, and then disappear to wash your hands before you've given him his food. So when I pick up a baby to feed him I always feed him straight away and then when he is finished and replete, I change his nappy. Of course, if you go to feed the baby and he has a very smelly nappy then you would change it first.

Once a child starts on mixed feeding, at around six months, I normally change his nappy soon after he has defecated. Until then I would not hurry to change him, even if he had done a poo, if he was lying there perfectly happy. A small baby will not be crying because he has a dirty nappy; he is probably crying about something else.

18 · If my baby has nappy rash how often should I change his nappy?

Nappy rash makes the skin look as if the baby has been scalded and it will normally be on the buttocks or whichever bit the baby lies on, but it could also be on their tummy or the top of their legs (see question 11).

A baby can get nappy rash if he is left for too long wearing a wet nappy or if, when changed, his bottom is not cleaned properly. Both of these allow the urine to burn into the skin. If the skin then breaks, infection gets in and nappy rash is the result. A baby should never, ever get nappy rash, certainly not after one year old. But sadly they do get it when you are very, very busy and put off changing a nappy, which we all do, but shouldn't. Also some foods, such as fatty foods, can make a baby's urine quite acid so that it scalds the skin and creates a rash. You only have to get one tiny little blemish and in no time at all infection gets in and it spreads.

You can try and prevent nappy rash spreading by dealing with it is the moment you notice anything, from a tiny red spot on their tummies or around their genitals to a slightly red bottom. That's when I always apply a special proprietary healing cream to the area to get rid of the rash quickly. The cream is much thicker than ordinary zinc and castor oil cream and will prevent the urine further attacking the area. If I'm worried and there does appear to be a sore patch I also change the baby's nappy very often.

I do know that air and sunshine are meant to help heal a nappy rash, but I've never had a baby with such an extreme rash that I had to leave them naked. Where I was training, if a very small baby had nappy rash we would apply gentian violet to the rash and then leave the baby nappy-less in a warm room with the rash exposed to the air. But it is rather messy and the rash doesn't really heal much quicker, so I have never done it since. If it's a boy baby it's quite difficult to arrange as he will keep doing fountains up in the air; you have to make a pad of a folded muslin nappy and put that on top of his penis so the urine will get soaked up. You then have to change the pad each time the baby pees. It gets very complicated and rather a nuisance.

'I always warmed nappies, especially in winter, before putting them on a baby'

Nappy rash can normally be cured in under a week so it's not that long to have to be extra careful: changing the nappy every hour or two, washing the baby's bottom carefully with olive or baby oil and cotton wool and then applying a thick layer of healing cream on the bottom before putting a fresh nappy back on. I always keep plastic pants on top of my babies' towelling nappies as usual if they get nappy rash. I just change them and the nappy frequently.

19 · Do you think having nappy rash may make a baby unhappy?

It's difficult to know if having nappy rash upsets the baby. If they have a very sore bottom and they pass urine and it runs over the sore bottom they might well be very irritable. If the rash is on the stomach, I would always lie them on their backs and vice versa. I could imagine that soap does sting a little bit, so I wouldn't use it unless it was absolutely necessary and then I would only use a very little, even if it did sting, just making sure that I rinsed their bottoms very, very well. I would use a very mild soap and really only just enough to clean the bottom.

20 · What should I do if the nappy rash doesn't seem to go away?

I think if the rash was very ugly and it persisted, I would ask the doctor. The baby may have thrush, for instance, which will need special medication.

Urinating and defecating

21 · How often do babies and children urinate?

A new baby may not begin urinating until forty-eight hours after birth, but after that they will pass urine very, very frequently. As he gets older his bladder will grow and he will urinate less. What is dangerous is if a baby does not pass urine and I always keep an eye out for a dry nappy. In fact if I go to change a baby's nappy and it is dry I worry slightly and am very relieved when it is wet again. If the baby hasn't urinated for twelve hours (or six hours if he is under six months), I would seek medical advice. If a toddler has not urinated I would take it as a sign that he doesn't need to wear a nappy any more.

22 · Is there anything I should look out for in a child's urine?

If I saw blood in a baby's urine I would definitely seek medical advice. Quite often it is nothing at all to fuss about but it is best to be sure. Although it could be a sign of bladder or kidney infection it might just be that your baby has eaten beetroot or drunk the juice of some reddish berry as both of these have a tendency to turn urine red.

23 · How often should babies be passing motions?

You don't need to fuss, but just keep a casual eye on how often your baby is defecating. A new baby should pass the first stool within twenty-four hours of being born. The first stool and others over the next two days or so consist of a substance called meconium which is black and very, very sticky. Meconium must be passed before the digestive system can start working properly. When this has happened the baby's stools will turn brown, and then yellow.

24 · Is there a difference between the stools of breast-fed and bottle-fed babies?

Very small bottle-fed babies normally have frequent motions, often about three to four a day, whereas breast-fed babies can go for quite a few days before passing a motion. You'd think there would be some waste but the baby just takes what he needs. One of my babies used to pass a motion once a week – usually on my day off. He was entirely breast fed.

The motions of a breast-fed baby are possibly a little yellower and perhaps a little looser than those of a bottle-fed baby. I think they are normally also a little less smelly. When babies start mixed feeding their motions become firmer and a lot smellier, especially when the baby starts eating meat. They also often take on the colour of what the baby has been eating, such as beetroot and spinach.

25 · How often do older children need to pass motions?

As children get older their need to defecate decreases to a couple of times a day and then around the age of four it usually becomes just once a day. Some children don't go for several days. When I started my training we were told children should go every day, but it's now recognized that that is quite unnecessary.

Normally children defecate at the same time of day. One girl I looked after went early in the morning, straight after her fruit juice, but most go after breakfast. It automatically happens as soon as they are up and about exercising and then have something to eat. But one would never ever fuss about it. It really doesn't matter when they go.

26 · What should I do if my child is constipated?

Only if babies or children pass very, very hard stools is it time to worry. I was taught to give constipated children fig syrup or something to help them, but I never give children laxatives, not even when they are older. I find that with a proper diet it isn't necessary. I occasionally used to give one of my children who always had very hard motions an enema but I think nowadays I wouldn't, I would change their diet instead. I would give them lots and lots of fruit juice and raw fruit, vegetables (raw and cooked), wholemeal bread and plenty of water to drink. At night I might also put a little petroleum jelly just inside their rectum to help them pass the stools. Sometimes constipation or hard stools is a medical problem, but only in a very extreme situation.

27 · What do you do if a baby or child has diarrhoea?

If your baby has diarrhoea you will notice his stools will be very liquid and slimy, and he will be generally not very well. The first thing I do when a baby has diarrhoea is to stop giving him milk but make sure he drinks a lot of water. I also only feed him a little. I give him either grated or mashed raw apple, cooked apple, plain boiled potatoes mashed up on their own or plain rusks. Unless it's a serious infection (see below), when you must seek medical advice, it will pass. Give your baby plenty of water or water with glucose to drink, or buy some packets of Dioralyte from the chemist and follow the instructions. It is some kind of sugar and salt solution with added minerals.

If he is a very young baby you should call the doctor if the diarrhoea has persisted more than twelve hours, in case he has gastroenteritis. This is an inflammation of the stomach and small intestine that may be caused by a virus and a baby suffering from it will usually have both diarrhoea and vomiting at the same time. Until antibiotics were discovered, gastroenteritis was almost always fatal. Babies often used to get it through feeding bottles that were not properly washed. It was called 'summer diarrhoea' as that was the time that the milk was most likely to get infected and it would usually end with the baby becoming dehydrated and dying.

28 · Nanny, what should I look out for when changing my baby's nappy?

If when you change your child's nappy you notice something a little unusual but your child is perfectly happy, it would be no cause for alarm. It's only when a child is obviously not well, accompanied by strange motions or urine that you would have to take note.

29 · My baby has slimy green stools. Should I be worried?

It would attract my attention if the baby's stools were green and slimy. He might have a chill or have eaten something that disagreed with him, in other words, it might pass. But if it persisted for longer than two days I would seek advice.

30 · What should I do if my child has blood in his stools?

If I saw blood in a baby's stools I would take him to the doctor immediately. It could be that the baby had been constipated and now a mucous membrane has torn slightly.

31 · *What should I do if my baby has food particles in his stools?*

If there were little identifiable food particles in the baby's stools, I would avoid those foods until he was more capable of digesting them. Currants and sweetcorn are not digested at all, they go through as they go in, but I don't think that matters. You may well find bits of silver paper in a child's stool, as he goes through the phase of putting everything he finds on the floor in his mouth. I do know of a nanny who found a small closed safety pin in one of her children's stools. It just shows how carefully you must clean your floors.

32 · *What equipment do I need for toilet training my child?*

Really the only thing you need is a pot. This can be simple or decorated, so long as it has straight, rather than curved, sides, or at least a solid flat bottom, so that it sits very firmly on the ground. It should be a 'good' size, large rather than small so that the child sits comfortably. Having said that, most pots are the same size. I do sometimes see very tiny ones on sale and I would never use them; a large one can be used for a longer time. Boy's pots need to have a shield at the front.

Originally our baby pots were miniature chamber pots made of plastic with straight sides. Sometimes they were enamel which was cold to sit on and chipped easily. We also used to have splendid chair pots, made of wood with a strap to hold the child on, but I don't think they are necessary. I now see pots that look like cars or turtles. If you want to buy one for your child that's fine, but I don't think they are necessary. They are also often more inclined to tip up when the child stands up which can be rather messy. If it's a comfortable pot that's enough.

33 · *Is there any other equipment I will need?*

A child's toilet seat, although not essential, is useful. I first sit my children on one when they are three although sometimes earlier if their pot is becoming too small. Before that they are always on the pot. One of the chief reasons for using a little toilet seat at all is that they are very light to carry and can be taken anywhere. Some children do not like using strange loos and the seats, being familiar, do help. At home I always have a little stool or box for the child to rest his feet on, I don't leave them dangling in mid-air. I never use boxes so children can step up to the loo, I always lift them on to the loo myself. Children can fall off those boxes. But don't try and hurry things, there's plenty of time to use the big loo.

Toilet Training

Equipment

At around three your child will also be old enough to sleep without his nappy and you will need a waterproof mattress for him (see SLEEPING, question 15).

34 · Nanny, what are 'training pants' and do you use them?

Training pants are like ordinary knickers only they are made of towelling on the inside and plastic on the outside. I'm not sure why they are called 'training' pants, but anyway I do not use them. As far as I'm concerned they must feel the same to a child as wearing a towelling nappy; I suppose the thought behind them is that they soak up the drips in case you cannot get the child to the pot on time. I would think that wearing training pants might just give a child the feeling that the nappy is still on, so I would always rather put him in knickers. That way he can feel the nappy isn't on and it might make him start thinking that maybe he should be peeing in the pot.

Toilet training

35 · At what age do you start potty training?

I always start pot-training at what these days they would call early (nine months) because at that age they are still young enough not to notice. If they hated it I'd wait for a month, but I normally found they did not mind. Very often if you start later when the child is crawling or walking he resents the idea and it becomes a much longer and harder process. I also think it very anti-social to have a big child defecating in a nappy because by then his stools are extremely smelly.

36 · Do you have any rules about potty training children?

I don't really have hard and fast rules, apart from staying relaxed. Of course, a nine-month-old baby won't know what he is meant to be doing on the pot, so don't expect him to. It is just to get him used to the idea of having to sit somewhere for a while every day so he doesn't resent it later on. After all, it's so much easier for him to do a poo in his nappy whilst he is playing, so you have to get him used to the idea of sitting on the pot and later the toilet.

If you wait for the child to understand what a potty is before you put him on it you may have to wait a very long time. Most babies really only get bladder control by between eighteen months and two years. Before they do you can't 'train' them to use a pot anyway because they can only be 'trained' to do it in the right place once they have control over their bladder. By nine months however a child is often more or less regular so putting him on a pot after breakfast has results. Of course there is nothing wrong with three-year-old children who are still in nappies during the day, but it is rather unfair on others.

'I don't really have hard and fast rules'

37 · How do you go about it?

Every day after breakfast, I put the pot with its back to the playpen. Then I take off the baby's nappy, sit him on the pot with his back to the playpen and tie him firmly, but not too tightly, to the playpen using a square muslin nappy around his waist. If I hadn't a playpen I would find something else convenient to tie him to, or use a chair pot (see question 32). I only tie babies on the pot for a few months, until they are able to sit up straight on the pot by themselves, which may be by the time they are a year old or possibly a little older. Then I put the pot in the corner of the room to make sure the child cannot fall off backwards.

If I think it will make him happier I sit the child on the pot with a small toy – one that he specially likes at that time – and I leave him there for ten minutes. I never leave him on the pot too long. Ten minutes is quite long enough, but as usual, I am flexible. If he hasn't defecated and is perfectly happy to stay, I leave him a few more minutes. Whilst he is on the pot I either stay with him or leave him on his own depending on what I have to do. I always stay in the vicinity though, certainly within earshot.

I never say anything to the child once he gets off the pot. There's no point congratulating him if there is something in the pot, or scolding him if there's not, because he won't understand at nine months. It is just to get him used to sitting still. If you want to say 'Well done' when there is something in the pot, then do. But never fuss if the pot is empty. If nothing's happened on the pot I just take him off without wiping his bottom, but if he has done something I clean his bottom with a wet flannel and dry it very, very well and put new botty cream on. Then I put his old nappy (or a new one if the old one is wet) back on. One of the good things about towelling nappies is how much easier they are to pull down than disposable ones. For the rest of the day we carry on with nappy changes as usual.

Once the child has been sitting on the pot after breakfast for a month I start putting him on the pot after tea as well as after breakfast, also for ten minutes or so. Then, after a few weeks, I might just put him on the pot before going out to the park or to visit a friend, if he were perfectly happy about going on it. He might use it, he might not. It really doesn't matter and he will not know what he is doing anyway. It's just introducing the child to a new situation while he is young enough not to mind, and once he is used to it, gradually extending it.

By the time a child is eleven months he is still wearing a nappy full time but could be sitting on the pot three or four times a day. By now I should have very few, if any, dirty nappies. All the child's stools should be going in the pot.

38 · When will my child know what he is sitting on the pot for?

Children don't normally mention when they've wet themselves, but about the

'Never fuss if
the pot is
empty'

age of one and a half there is a stage when your child begins to know what a 'Poo' is, though he can't yet control it. (This is when he tells you when he's just done it.) But I think it will be around another six months before he is able to connect the feeling he gets when he is about to do a 'Poo' with the purpose of the pot (see question 39).

From now on toilet training is really a case of playing it by ear. If when you change your child's nappy it is dry I would sit him on the pot and if it had been dry for quite some time it's quite possible he would then use the pot. Again, if you went to the park for instance and he came back dry you'd suggest he might like to sit on it. I just say 'Why not do it on the pot?' very casually.

You will probably find that within six months you can dispense with nappies in the day – although you would have to be prepared for wet knickers now and again – and just use a nappy at bedtime. The thing is to be fairly light-hearted about it. When you feel like scolding your child for being 'Wet again', just stop for a moment and think how awful it would be if he couldn't urinate at all because he was ill. Another time not to get angry is when they proudly arrive saying 'Poo' five minutes after you've taken them off the pot. I don't believe children decide if they want to control their bowel movements or not. I think if they are capable of control, control happens automatically. And I don't think that by eighteen months it has.

39 · When do I start leaving my child's nappy off during the day?

Around a child's second birthday I no longer put him in nappies during the day; instead he just wears knickers except when he goes for his daily nap or out for a few hours (see question 47). By this age he may well be finding it restricting having to lie down whilst his nappy is being pinned (or stuck) on. I have also found that there does come a moment when a child doesn't want a nappy on and taking the nappy off and using underpants instead very often means that he does become trained quicker. I think a child feels that the nappy is there to be peed into, so if the nappy isn't on he will go and pee in the pot.

I keep the pot in the same place so I can quickly pop the child on it when I think it's necessary. You can see by a child's look of concentration that he is going to have a bowel movement, or even wet his knickers, because he sort of pauses in what he is doing. Or you may notice him crossing his legs, clenching his buttocks, pulling a face, tugging at his knickers, clutching himself, or wriggling about when he wants to pass water.

When I see this happening I just quickly pull his knickers down and hold the pot under him, holding my finger under a boy's penis so that the urine goes in the pot or sitting a little girl quickly down on it. That way a child begins to associate the feeling that he is getting with the pot and it is when he first begins to understand about a pot and what it is for. Again, you have to be sensible. If I see a baby showing certain signs of bowel movement I put him on the pot, but if he is sitting in his highchair having lunch I would leave him unless I could quickly lift him out and calmly put him on it. The great thing is not to make a fuss; it is better to let him dirty his knickers than disturb his lunch.

40 · By what age will my child have control of his bladder and bowel movements?

By two years *all* my children were completely aware that they were about to spend a penny, although that did not mean they would let me know. They would also know when they needed to move their bowels, although again, they would normally only tell me afterwards. I could tell they wanted to go by watching them or very, very rarely when they would bring me their pot. There would always be some sort of an indication that they would want to do it. I would also look out for these signs. If they had not used the pot fairly recently, I would keep my eyes open for signs of them needing to use it. Often they would get so absorbed in their play that they would happily wet their knickers, but usually there was a slight pause before doing so when I would spring into action. You will find you quickly get used to noticing the signs and will get used to keeping the pot within reach. I always make sure that it is put back in the same place so the child knows where it is. Usually I keep it in the nursery bathroom or in a corner of the nursery behind a chair if there isn't a bathroom close by.

Children do get very excited when they first realize what the pot is for. I remember when one of my children was two-ish and just beginning to understand not only that the pot was to pee in but also that I would always bring it to him. For a few nights, just after I'd put him to bed, he would call out 'Pee pee' every fifteen minutes so I could put the pot under him. It became a game. Needless to say, after a few days the novelty wore off.

41 · Do you let children help you empty the pot?

I would never say to a child 'Would you like to empty the pot?' but very often, when my children are between two and two and a half and I am about to empty the pot, they ask to do it and so together we tip the contents of the pot into the toilet and then I flush the loo. Sometimes they just do it of their own accord without even asking me, they just copy me. They certainly very often empty their own urine, obviously with a motion you would want to lend them a hand to avoid spillage. Again, it's important to be relaxed. If they tip a motion in the loo and spill a little I would never show displeasure, what does it matter? They are learning.

'What does it matter if he dirties the odd pair of knickers?'

42 · When will they be able to go to the loo by themselves?

By the age of three your child will be removing his knickers and sitting on the pot unaided. It's then that I first introduce the child's loo seat together with a box for the child to rest his feet on (see question 33). I don't leave the child alone, though, at this age except during the night. I am always there to help him and, until he is at least five, I will always wipe a child's bottom. Simply because he can't yet do it very well and if it isn't cleaned then he can get a sore bottom. I ask him to bend over and then I wipe it properly myself. Sometimes children will say they want to do it themselves, then I let them and just casually say 'I'll just have a look and see if it's clean'. I would not discourage them. If it's well done then I'll praise them, but if it isn't then I'll ask them if they want another go or I'll do it myself. How can a small child do it well? If children do wipe their bottoms themselves, then fill the basin and tell them to wash their hands afterwards – that's part of toilet training.

By three, boys will also be urinating standing by the loo, depending on its height. I wouldn't encourage a little boy to stand on a step or box by the loo in case it toppled over, so I sometimes hold them over a loo to help them. Once boys are standing up to urinate in the loo I always teach them to shake their winkie after they've been to the toilet. I remember saying 'Shake the drip' to one of my little boys and he'd shake his head. I give a boy trousers with fly-fastenings only when they're about five. Before that they just pull the trousers down. It's so easy.

43 · When do you think my child won't need a nappy at night any more?

Until a child is three I always put a nappy on him both at night and for his daytime nap. Even then I would normally leave a nappy on during the night unless I noticed that for seven days or so in a row the nappy is dry in the morning. Then I'd take it off and wouldn't put it on any more. But there does come a moment with toilet training, both day and night, when it can help a child become trained quicker if one just takes his nappy off – provided he is ready. Just wait for children to give you the lead if you think they want to, otherwise just take it yourself – providing you don't push them.

One night one of my girls, having been dry at night for a week, stood waiting for her night-time nappy to be put on. I told her she wasn't going to wear a nappy tonight. She didn't seem to mind but the next morning her bed was sopping wet. Of course I didn't remark on it and from the next night on she was dry in bed every night. I suppose she must have felt quite naked, suddenly not having a nappy on at night any more.

Once a child was sleeping without a nappy I would leave the pot in his bedroom so that if he needed to go to the loo in the middle of the night he would use the pot (see SLEEPING, question 32). I wouldn't fuss about toilet paper, he wouldn't have used it anyway. He would very rarely use the pot in the night, but if he woke early in the morning he would go. All children urinate different amounts and it is difficult to know why, but I never stop a child drinking before bedtime if he wants to. The amount of fluid taken makes little difference to the amount a child will urinate unless it is an excessive intake. Most of my children have never wanted much to drink after tea (except an occasional drink of bath water). If they do take a drink it doesn't necessarily mean they will pass more urine, in fact quite the reverse; a child who doesn't have enough to drink may have an irritated bladder and therefore pass urine more often.

'Tell them to wash their hands afterwards — that's part of toilet training'

44 · Should I put my child on the pot before I go to bed?

I have heard of people removing a child from his bed and sitting him on the pot at 10 p.m. or whatever time they go to bed. Often the child won't wake but he almost always automatically passes urine. I don't do this because I think it's training the child to pee at 10 p.m. It's much better if a child can learn to sleep right through the night and be dry in the morning, or even if he does have a few accidents or has to wear nappies for a little longer. None of these really matter but I think it is important not to get into the habit of sitting a child on the pot at 10 p.m. when a child most probably won't need to be potted.

45 · What if my child suddenly starts wetting his bed?

Often a child who has been dry in the night may start wetting his bed. One of my children became a bed-wetter on starting nursery school where he was very unhappy. In all cases bed-wetting stops eventually and is best ignored. I would never put a nappy back on a child who had not been wearing one for a while even if he was wetting his bed — it doesn't take that much time to wash a wet sheet. Instead I would try and remove the problem he is having during the daytime (see SLEEPING, question 53).

46 · Do you think it is easier to toilet train a boy or a girl?

I have never noticed any time difference between boys and girls first getting control over their bladder and bowels although I do think first children often take longer than subsequent children to potty train. I think really everything is easier for second and following children because if the older child is already using the pot, say, they will want to copy it.

As one of my little girls once said of her brother: 'He's lucky. All he's got to do is hang it over the edge'. Of course it is not such a performance for boys to pee as it is for girls and it is much easier for them to go anywhere. It is also easier to get a squirming boy with a full bladder to the pot, providing you don't dress him in dungarees, because you can just hook his little tail out from his trousers and hold the pot out under it. With little girls, by the time you've heaved their knickers down, they've done it.

Going out

47 · What should I do if my child wants to use the loo when we are out?

Of course it depends on the child, but if we were going out for a few hours I would probably put a nappy on a child until he was about two and a half – just in case. I would put the nappy on under the child's knickers. And, for children up to the age of three, I always took spare pants, toilet paper and any other creams and lotions I was using at the time, whenever we went out. We also always took the pot with us because children do like their own pot. Some children refuse to squat down in the park and even when you take them for tea they'll only go in their own pot, so I always take it in a plastic bag.

I have known easily shockable nannies not let their children urinate in the park – sometimes the poor children wet their knickers on the way home. Of course I always take my children behind a hedge or tree. Certainly in the park I find that little boys like doing it behind a tree – it becomes a game for them – but taking little girls to have a leisurely picnic in the park can be more difficult. If they need to go to the loo you can't expect them to wait and you wouldn't want them to be uncomfortable in wet knickers. I always take them behind a tree to go, like boys.

First I completely remove the girls' knickers otherwise they invariably wet them if they are left round their ankles. Then I would encourage them to crouch but at the same time I would stand behind them, or at their side, and firmly hold them under their arms, at the top of their armpits, so they didn't collapse on the ground. If they found this uncomfortable I would hold them suspended. To do this I would stand behind them and hold their calves so that their thighs are almost resting on my forearms. This might make them feel more secure. Again, the important thing is to keep relaxed. If you make it fun they'll think it's fun.

48 · Nanny, my child is one and a half and has never been on a pot. How should I start?

I would start the same way as with a nine-month-old (see questions 36–41) once a day after breakfast, only you will not be tying him on to the pot, and just try not to be at all aggressive about it. I would give him a book to look at and if he does use the pot I would say 'Well done! Aren't you clever!' because by then he will understand what you are saying. I wouldn't praise him if he was just sitting patiently, but I would not be negative either. I would then just put his nappy back on. If there is any resistance, don't make a fuss or a cross face. Just say 'No? Would you rather not? Let's wait until another day then.' It isn't so much what you say as how you say it. Just put the pot away for a month and don't mind.

49 · What should I do if my child doesn't want to sit on his pot?

I've never had a child take against his pot because I introduce it before the child has got too set in his own ways and because I have never been an over-potter. If a child doesn't want to sit on his pot, then I don't force him. Obviously children mind being taken away from their toys and interesting situations and being stuck on a pot; so refusing to sit on it or refusing to go in it is their way of rebelling, especially if they can sense that it is something you really care about. Often you will find that a child who takes against his pot is doing so because he has been put on the pot too often and he is rebelling.

  If a child, having been perfectly happy to sit on his pot, took against it and refused to go on it, I would simply put the pot away in the cupboard for at least a week. If he still minded after a week I would put it away for two more weeks, but after that I would put the child firmly on the pot and try and make it as cosy as possible for him to be there. I would sit beside him and talk to him.

  Ironically, you may find that the more intelligent the child is the longer and more difficult it is to make him understand that you want him to go in the pot. It is as if at first when the child is put on the pot and does big jobs he just does it, but then he thinks 'Well, that was fine, but I don't need to do it on the pot. I can use my nappy.' Pooing in the pot is convenient for the adults looking after the child but the intelligent child, of course, doesn't think like that. He just thinks how much simpler it is to poo in his nappy. He may well sit on the pot happily from nine months to two years and then when you take his nappy off it is also fine for a short time. But then somehow most children start doing it again in their knickers or their nappy when you put it on for their rest.

  With many children this phase does not last very long because it clicks in their brain that really it is more comfortable for them to defecate in the pot. But some children take much longer, they can regress for almost a year sometimes. It is nothing to worry about. Make as little fuss as possible, and talk about it as little as possible, but if you feel you can encourage him to do what you want that is a good idea because it is easier for everyone all round.

50 · Once a child is trained will he keep having accidents?

Very, very often, though not always, when you think a child is completely reliable, if that's the right word, he will almost always regress for a short time and go back to urinating – and occasionally defecating – in his knickers. Frequently this happens when a new baby comes along, but it sometimes happens for no apparent reason. That phase doesn't last very long and he soon once more will use the pot successfully so I would never put him back in nappies.

Mostly children only have accidents passing water when their bladder is full and there isn't an opportunity for them to go. Or they are frightened or excited. It need not be intense fear, and it does not mean they will regress permanently. I always just clean up the great pool on the floor and don't mention it. It's not important after all. If you are worried about your carpet smelling, just add a little disinfectant to the cleaning water. Children never seem to mind having wet or dirty knickers unless they have been scolded or made to feel dirty, otherwise they really truly don't mind. They will do it and just go on playing. If a child continued to have wet or soiled knickers in the daytime I would never scold him. I wouldn't even talk about it. I would remove the knickers, wash his bottom and then put a pair of dry knickers on.

Of course there is also the odd 'accident' with bowel movements, although this is unusual by the time a child is three. However, I have known of an eight-year-old who did occasionally defecate in his trousers. I didn't know why and I think it was only solved by the passing of time. He must have been unable to control his bowel movements or he wouldn't have done it, or he may have had a severe case of diarrhoea. Or it might have started when he went to school and was nervous. By then I would seek medical advice in case there was something physically wrong. I would always discuss a sensitive problem like this first alone with the doctor before I brought the child along on another day. But up to the age of four I wouldn't think it necessary to seek medical advice if a child occasionally defecated in his knickers or constantly dripped urine. I would simply replace the knickers and not make the child feel guilty.

'Accidents' do sometimes occur when a child has been put on the pot and left on his own for a minute. Once when I was looking after a little boy I came back into the room to find he had slipped off the pot, tipping it up, and was playing with his faeces, smearing it on his face and trying to eat it. I just gave him a bath.

I have also heard of children undressing and defecating in their cots in the morning, although I have never known a child do this. I think it would only happen if you'd left a child alone for a long time and he was bored. A child who is seen at 7 a.m., given a drink, put on the pot and given a book or toy would have no reason to do that.

Golden rules

Keep babies peaceful

1 Never disturb a baby to change his nappy. A nappy change every three hours should be quite enough, unless he has a sore bottom, a sore tummy or is very constipated.

2 A baby does not mind being wet or dirty (unless he is very wet or dirty) until he is at least six months old.

Indulge your baby

1 Warm his nappies in winter before putting them on. If your baby wears disposable nappies, warm his clothes instead.

2 Change your baby's nappy on your lap – it means you can do it anywhere – and he gets another cuddle.

Keep calm

1 A child will eventually toilet train himself even if no one helps him. You are just there to speed the process along.

2 Does it really matter if your child dirties the odd pair of knickers or a sheet? All you have to do is wash them.

3 Always be relaxed about your own body and bodily functions as well as your child's. Let children learn by imitating you.

4 Never over-pot a child. Always take it gradually. If he rejects the pot, take the lead from him.

5 Don't talk about a child's toilet habits in front of him.

5

Dressing

Dressing a baby up is really just to amuse the adult in charge, because babies are adorable without being adorned. I always find simple clothes so much more attractive – children used only to wear white or cream until they were two years old. I've seen people putting brand-new baby girls in little dresses for their own pleasure, but I think it looks absurd because for the first few months a baby's legs are so thin and long and bent. Of course, I don't mind looking at a baby's legs, but somehow I always felt that a long dress or nightie is much more appropriate.

We took such pride in what our babies wore – we were sometimes up until midnight ironing little sleeves. Years ago there were night-gowns and daygowns for small babies, both of which covered their legs. I think they stopped being used around the 1940s when the war changed so many things. Daygowns were made of nice fine lawn which meant they creased easily and had to be ironed and starched. You would put them on just before the visitor arrived, or in time to have a photograph taken, rather than keeping them on all day. They were usually embroidered, perhaps with tucks and with a bit of lace around the neck and the edge of the sleeves. They were like nightgowns, only prettier. They were a great extravagance and quite a performance to look after. A few of us nannies had daygowns which had been in the family for years. I remember putting them on one of my little girls, once she was three months old, to please myself or if we had visitors.

Often we made clothes for our children. For babies we would knit

OPPOSITE *At four months a dress is as good a toy as anything else* baby coats and bootees. At the sea we all used to be knitting for the winter – a semi-circle of nannies knitting jerseys, gaiters and things. Sometimes you would lend patterns and sometimes you would guard your pattern so your child would be the only one to have it. One nanny I know had a pattern for a bonnet that she would never let anyone borrow. Another nanny had a pattern for a pair of little bootees that were sweet, a little slipper without the straps, like a little pod; you put the child's foot in it and the slipper just stayed on. There must have been a lot of increasing and decreasing, but nanny would never lend that to anyone.

1 · What clothes will I need for my new baby?

The clothes you buy for your newborn child should last for six months, possibly more. Some people are superstitious and say 'I won't get a lot, just in case', but I think you must have some things ready before the baby is born. The layette I recommend is the minimum, because once the baby is born people usually shower you with clothes – not all of which you'll like. I base this list on a wash a day:

Essential clothing

4 nighties (see question 2)
4 vests (see question 3)
4 matinée coats or cardigans
    (see question 4)
2 bonnets (for winter babies)
    (see question 5)
4 pairs of bootees (see question 6)
2 pairs of mittens (for winter babies)
    (see questions 7 and 8)
6 towelling bibs (see question 9)
2 wool shawls (one in use and one
    in the wash) (see question 10)

Additional clothing from three months

2 woollen pram coats (for winter
    babies) (see question 14)
2 pair leggings (for winter
    babies) (see question 14)
3 little dresses (wool in winter and
    cotton in summer) (see question
    15)

Nappies

24 terry towelling nappies
18 muslin squares
6 pairs plastic pants
or
A large supply of disposable
    nappies
(*see also* CHANGING AND
    TOILET TRAINING)

Bedding

2 fitted sheets for each mattress
3 flannelette sheets for each
    mattress
3 woollen cellular blankets
    (includes 1 for pram)
(*see also* SLEEPING, question 15)
12 muslin squares (if using
    disposable nappies – otherwise
    you already have bought enough.
    Useful for face towels and to put
    in place of a pillow)

Bathing

2 soft white towels
(*see also* BATHING)

2 · Do I need to buy nighties? Wouldn't babygrows do instead?

I prefer nighties to babygrows for both boys and girls, although I don't suppose the baby really minds what he wears. I always had nighties made of a knitted woollen fabric or a wool and cotton mix fabric. If it was a really hot summer I would put them in a cellular cotton although in England a baby is rarely too hot in a woollen nightie. The nighties were either raglan style, falling from the shoulder, or on a tiny yoke and always very loose fitting and down to the baby's toes. They opened to halfway down the back and had two ties, one at the neck and one a little lower down. I always just unpicked and removed the sash ties they came with. They are restricting around the middle and I also felt it must be uncomfortable for the baby to lie on a knot. I also made sure that the elastic around the wrists wasn't too tight – if it was, I just cut it.

I never put any clothes over a new baby's head, and even when they get older children mind dreadfully about things being pulled over the head. Once they are a few months old you can pop things over their heads if the neck opening is large enough. If any forcing at all is needed just discard the garment – you cannot pull things over a very small baby's head. Nighties are very easy to put on a baby. You just lie him on his back, preferably on your lap, slide the nightie up him, put his arms through the armholes, then turn him round and put him tummy-down over your knee and fasten the two ties. To change his nappy all you have to do is lie him on his back, clutch his ankles to lift up his legs and pull the nightie up – it couldn't be simpler. With a babygrow there are poppers to do up and undo, all in all, a lengthy procedure.

I remember when babygrows were first imported from America around the early 1960s. Nannies never had them although I do remember one nanny friend being quite upset because the family she was with wanted their baby to wear tie-and-dye babygrows! I have never liked babygrows. For one thing, the baby does *not* grow with them, or rather they do not grow with the baby. Of course you can buy them a little too large so the child can wear them for a while, but babies grow fast and it is important that a baby's toes and leg movements are not restricted.

Most importantly I do not like babies to have their legs completely covered; air can circulate through a nightie, but not through a babygrow. With a nightie their legs can touch each other and the whole body can breathe much better, rather than just the face and hands. I discovered in one family that the baby had a babygrow on all day and all night; except in the bath his entire body was covered. Rather like a Victorian baby who had layers and layers on, but houses were much colder then.

People do say that the baby gets uncovered in the night if he is wearing a nightie – well, I suppose some do, but I never worried about it. Some nannies who had wriggly babies used to run a string through the bottom of their babies'

OPPOSITE *Putting a vest on a very young baby. I pull it up from the bottom and I put it on before the nappy to keep the baby warm*

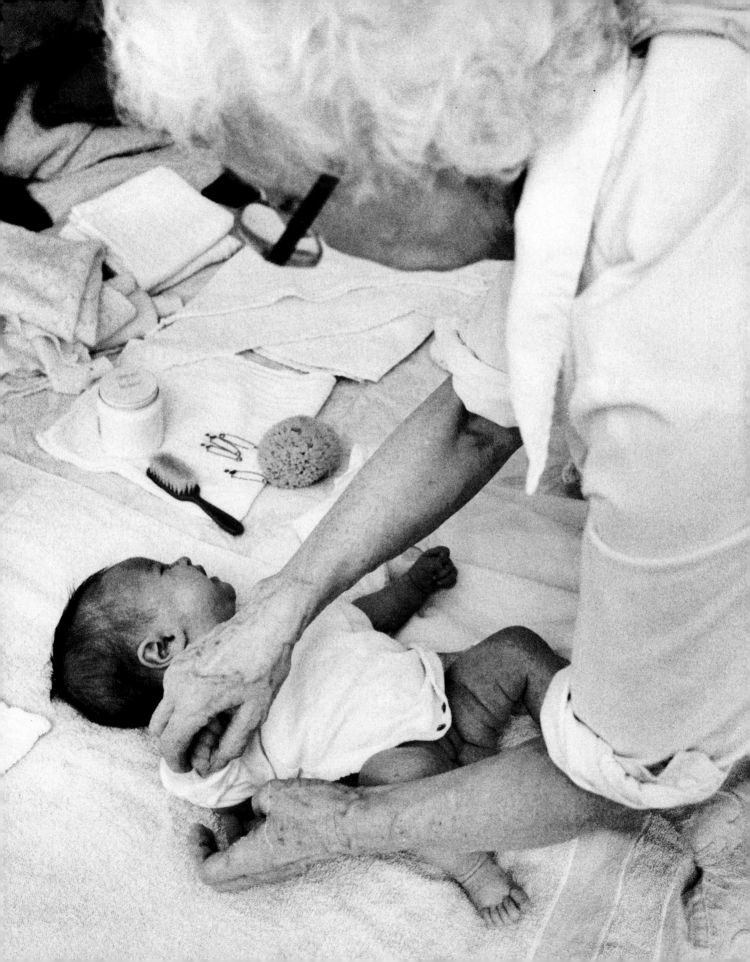

nighties to keep their feet under cover. Nighties in those days were lovely and long and voluminous. From six months there were also sleeping bags for wriggly babies; quite a few of my children had them (see SLEEPING question 34 and GROWING AND LEARNING question 4). They were very useful in a pram as they kept in all the body warmth.

3 · Is a vest necessary even for a summer baby?

I always put very tiny babies in woolly vests no matter what time of year it was because babies cannot move around to warm themselves up. I had short-sleeved vests for winter and sleeveless ones for summer. I don't think long sleeved vests are necessary for winter babies. My children all wore those cross-over waist-length vests which tied at the front, but there was always a gap around the baby's tummy which would get cold. Some people pinned the vest to the nappy but it was never very satisfactory. Today you can buy vests which fasten between the baby's legs; I think they are an enormous improvement. The vests I like are usually made of a mixture of cotton and synthetic fibres, but I am sure they would be warm enough. You just put them on legs first and pull them up the baby's body until you can put his arms in the holes. Then do up the poppers.

4 · What are matinée coats and will I need them for a summer baby?

Matinée (afternoon) coats or jackets are like a knitted cardigan. Sadly I think their day may soon be over because my chums don't seem to be able to find knitting patterns for them any more.

Matinée coats used to come in many different pretty designs and the one you bought just depended on which you thought looked the prettiest. I always bought woollen ones, but these days the man-made fibres are probably just as good (see question 18). Most matinée coats fasten at the neck with a button or ribbon, but some have four buttons at the bottom and a 'V' neck. I have heard people say 'I never put buttons on a baby in case he swallows them', but I have never heard of a new baby pulling a well-sewn button off.

They also used to worry in case the baby pulled the ribbon around his neck and strangled himself, but if you fasten it in my special way, if he does pull the ribbon, the neck just opens more and more. To do this with a matinée coat that has a ribbon threaded around the neck, don't tie a bow at the neck, as you would with an adult's bed-jacket, as the ribbon could tighten and choke the baby. Instead, first thread the right-hand ribbon through the first hole on the opposite (left) side and the left-hand ribbon through the first hole on the opposite (right) side before tying the bow. Even then, do not tie too tight a bow or knot. It may restrict the baby's breathing and you may find a knot rather awkward to undo.

It can also be complicated putting the sleeves of a matinée coat or cardigan on a baby. Some older children can hold their dress or shirt-sleeves in their hands, but others cannot and, of course, babies can't either. I always roll up the sleeve of the coat or matinée coat or cardigan first, then reach my hand up through it and clutch the child's arm and shirt-sleeve and then pull the outer sleeve up along the child's arm.

On a cool summer evening I would always dress a new baby in a matinée coat, or even during the day if there was a slight breeze and he was in the shade. Otherwise they are usually for winter babies, although they may not be necessary either unless it is very cold as a long-sleeved nightie will protect the baby's arms from cold (see question 16).

(see question 16)

'I often embroider the ends of bootee ribbons – solely for my own pleasure'

5 · When does the baby wear a bonnet?

In winter it is essential to put a little bonnet on a baby when he goes outside during the day as the air is often very cold and he loses a lot of heat through his head. I would always buy a woollen bonnet; it is nice and stretchy and if it does come down over his face he can still breathe easily through it. I never put any kind of bonnet or nightcap on a baby indoors.

I don't put sun-hats on very new babies even if it is a very sunny day. I simply put them in the shade or, if they are out in their pram, I use a canopy to protect them.

6 · Do you put all new babies in bootees?

Yes. I would put little knitted woollen bootees on a new baby all year round, until he started crawling, to keep his feet warm. Usually the ones put on for the night are kicked off by the morning, and the ones put on for the day are pulled off sooner or later. I do find that little babies' feet get cold, but if the room is warm and they pull them off I don't worry. Bootees that are too big come off anyway so don't tie them up too tightly to try and prevent this. Make sure that they are not too small, either; bootees that are too tight and restrict the child's feet could damage the soft bones in his toes (see the photograph on page 118).

Most bootees are tied with wool string or a ribbon. I find ribbons look so smart, you can iron them and they don't get into a knot as easily as a wool tie, but I never use double-satin ribbon as it is too slippery. I often embroider the ends of bootee ribbons – solely for my own pleasure. I always stitch the wool string or the ribbon to the back of the bootee, just above the heel, so the baby can't pull it out, as that is maddening. Or when I thread the ribbon or wool I put it through a hole twice at the heel instead of stitching which secures the thread equally well.

'If the child was a thumb-sucker I would knit mittens with a little hole to poke the thumb through'

Sometimes I knot the loops of the bow once the knot is tied, depending on how long the ribbon is, to deter the baby from pulling it undone. I suppose you could substitute a gentle elastic garter for the ribbon or string (see question 7).

7 · How do you get mittens to stay on a new baby?

I always had woollen mittens that looked like little bags with no thumbs – or, if the child was a thumb sucker, I would knit the mittens with a little hole to poke the thumb through – and I would only put them on the baby if it was very, very cold; otherwise being wrapped up in a shawl should be enough. The mittens tied around the baby's wrist with ribbon and I would put them on the baby first and then put the matinée coat or pram coat on top to hold them in place.

Rather grand nannies would sometimes make a little pair of garters from elastic, cover them with a tube of ribbon and put them round the baby's wrist over the mitten to hold it on instead. That was rather a sensible thing to do as you didn't have to fiddle around tying anything. Of course, the elastic would have to be tight enough to do its job, but not too tight or the pressure would stop the blood from circulating. I find that as soon as they can, babies do take off their mittens and their hands become purple, but they rarely seem to mind. So we didn't lose the mittens I always sewed them, and later gloves, on to a length of tape or ribbon – one mitten at either end – and threaded them through the sleeves of the coat. This prevented them being thrown out of the pram, even if they were taken off (see question 17).

8 · Do you put special mittens on babies who scratch their faces?

New babies often do scratch their faces and some people do put cotton mittens on so they can't. Some unkind people even put them on to stop the baby sucking his thumb. I have never used them, but I have seen babies scratch and claw their faces. I don't think it hurts if a baby scratches his face a little and I would just tuck him up securely so hopefully he couldn't, but I don't approve of him having his hands covered – I am sure a baby is comforted by having his hands available.

9 · Does a new baby need a bib, even if he is breast fed?

It doesn't matter whether a baby is breast fed or not, because sooner or later he will probably bring some of his milk back up, and wearing a bib means that you won't have to change all his clothes afterwards. I like towelling bibs with a waterproof backing best. I find them very useful, although the waterproof side of the bibs you buy today tears easily once they have been washed a few times.

10 · Do I really need a shawl? Wouldn't a blanket or baby nest do instead?

I like wool shawls for my children. They are so cosy and stretchy. Any size is convenient, so long as it is thin enough so that a baby can be well wrapped up in it without it being too bulky. People go on about children's fingers being caught in lace or in the stitches, but I can't imagine they would ever get broken or seriously caught. It's just a bit of a bore for you, if you are wrapping him in his lace shawl or dressing him in his matinée coat and he stretches his fingers and traps them in the holes and you have to free them, but I don't think the baby minds. Of course you can wrap a child in a blanket or anything really, but a blanket cannot be wrapped as cosily as a shawl (see SLEEPING, questions 13 and 17). I also think it is far easier to roll a baby in a shawl than stuff him into a baby nest and just as convenient for carrying him to the car or to wherever else you want to take him.

11 · How often do I need to change a new baby's clothes?

For the first three months of their life babies are not doing very much. They do not move about, and they do not get dirty either, so as long as they are cosy that is all that matters. I always let a new baby wear the same outfit for twenty-four hours. I just put a clean vest, nightie and jacket on when I bathe them in the morning and then leave it on until after their bath the next morning. I only change a baby twice a day if his nappy overflows or if he is sick and gets his clothes wet. Once he is about three months I start changing him twice a day (see question 15), after his bath in the morning and at night, because by this time he is kicking and moving.

12 · What size should I buy the new baby's clothes?

We bought 35 cm (14 in) – measured around the chest – or, if we were being economical, 40 cm (16 in) so they would last for longer. You can't buy a much bigger size because it would not be comfortable for the baby and also he does look so very sweet if his clothes are not too big. Sizes seem to vary so much these days according to the generosity of the manufacturer and from country to country – for example, French sizes are always smaller than British. It also makes a difference if you want your child to wear terry nappies as they take up so much more width than disposable nappies.

13 · Do you wash new clothes before you put the baby in them?

We always washed most of the baby's clothes, blankets, sheets and nappies before

Buying the layette

I put woollen bootees on a young baby all year round to keep her feet warm, but most get kicked off sooner rather than later

we put them on the baby, certainly their layette and nappies and anything we had knitted, just to make quite sure they were clean. One used one's discretion – a pretty dress arriving in tissue paper would not be washed. Nappies we would boil up in clear water, other clothes we would just wash normally. I never use biological detergent because some people are allergic to it, but I suppose if you want to, you must just make sure it is completely rinsed out.

Additional clothing from three months

14 · Isn't a snow suit more useful than a pram coat and leggings?

These days even tiny babies have snow suits. I have nothing against them, but they are so difficult to put on. You have to put their feet and legs in first, then getting one arm in isn't so bad, but getting the second arm in they hate. I would first put a snow suit on a sitting-up baby, not a lying-down one. I suppose in a pushchair you either have to have a snow suit or one of those envelope-shaped, fleecy lined bags made of man-made fibres, but in a nice, cosy pram neither is necessary – unless they like throwing their blankets out of the pram.

In my day we would knit or buy a pram outfit for the three-month-old baby to wear in winter. He would wear it until he was sitting up when he would get a cloth coat and matching bonnet. The pram outfit would consist of a coat, which was a jacket with a collar, a bonnet and leggings. It was either cream or white, usually white, all wool and matching. Underneath the baby would wear his indoor outfit. Wrapped round him, up to his armpits, was his shawl and he would be tucked up with a pram rug or blankets. In the summer we would have the canopy up and the child would just wear a little cotton outfit (see question 15) or possibly a cotton coat or woolly cardigan if it was a chilly day.

15 · When did you take a baby out of nighties?

Once babies – boys or girls – were three months old, during the day I put them in little dresses which they wore over their vest and plastic pants and nappies until they were about six months old. It is so easy to change the nappy of a baby in a dress. You would find some nannies putting boy babies into rompers at a very small age, just because they were boys, but I never did.

The dresses we used to have were always plain white or cream, with tiny yokes and sometimes they had lace insets or little appliqués of chickens or whatever cut out of the same fabric. They came down to just over the knee and had little puffed sleeves. As it was warm in the nursery the dresses were made of nun's veiling (a fine wool which looks crinkly and rough but is smooth to the touch) in winter, and lawn (a fine cotton) in summer. In the evening I would put them back into their nighties.

16 · How will I know how many clothes to dress my baby in?

In winter, to keep small babies cosy, I always work on the three-layer principle – basically a woolly vest, nightie and little coat or jacket. From three months, if the baby was wearing a long-sleeved little woolly dress, I would put him in a woolly vest and plain petticoat under the dress. I wouldn't put a cardigan on top; it looks so cluttered. If we were going to have tea in a cold house I would sometimes put a cardigan on underneath the dress, which looks so much nicer.

I do put bootees or socks on a small baby, in winter; they often kick the bootees off, but they rarely seem to mind. Sometimes they cry, but not normally. They

Keeping the baby at the correct temperature

119

are more likely to cry if they are too hot. But use your common sense. If your room is very cold (I always aim for my room to be 16°C (60°F) both day and night so it isn't too cold), both you and your baby will need to be more warmly dressed – a little baby who is not yet moving about should be wrapped up well in a shawl. Once a baby starts being a little agile, as long as the room is warm, he will be all right. I always let toddlers have bare feet indoors until they have been walking for a while. It means they don't slip and it strengthens their feet.

In the summer you have to go by our very variable weather. I always used to put very small babies in a woolly vest all year round, only changing it to a cotton vest in summer once they were moving about (see question 3). It makes no difference whatsoever whether your baby is fat or thin – they all need the same covering. It is only as they grow older that they need less covering; a new baby you keep nice and warm, though not hot, no matter what his size.

17 · Could my baby easily become too hot or too cold?

To have a cold baby is rare. But you could tell if a baby was too cold because his hands would get purple, his little face would be very pale and he would be crying. This would be a very neglected baby – an extreme case.

Babies can certainly be too hot from being over-wrapped and that is much more common and more dangerous than their being too cold. Their faces get red and their hands sweat; when you pick them up they feel like little furnaces. The worry is that if they sweat too much they risk becoming dehydrated. And a baby who is too hot might not cry, he would probably get lethargic and sleepy instead. But if they are sensibly dressed and kept out of direct sunlight they should never get too hot. It is worth remembering that when you take babies or older children into a shop, especially a large department store, it is often much hotter than the temperature outside. At the same time as you undo your coat and remove your scarf, take a layer or two off your baby until you go back outside into the cold air again.

18 · Why do you dress your new babies in wool?

Because I think you can get very hot in a man-made fibre such as acrylic. It doesn't breathe, it doesn't soak up any perspiration whereas wool (like cotton and other natural fabrics) is very absorbent and much pleasanter to wear. Sometimes a baby is allergic to wool (though I have never had one who is), in which case one should make sure he wears cotton next to the skin, with wool on top. All my jackets, bonnets, bootees and shawls were always knitted from wool, but I know that man-made fibres are greatly improved since I first came across them – and of course are easier to wash and quicker to dry.

'All babies – whether fat or thin – need the same covering'

Golden rules

Babies are adorable without being adorned

1 Clothes for a baby should not be restricting, uncomfortable or difficult to put on and take off.

2 Nighties are easier for nappy changing than babygrows and they let the baby's legs breathe.

3 Cotton and wool are more comfortable for the baby to wear than synthetic fabrics, although man-made fibres are improving all the time.

4 Remember that new babies cannot move around to warm themselves up.

5 Make sure your baby is neither too cold nor too hot. To see what he should wear look at the weather and what you are wearing, then use your common sense.

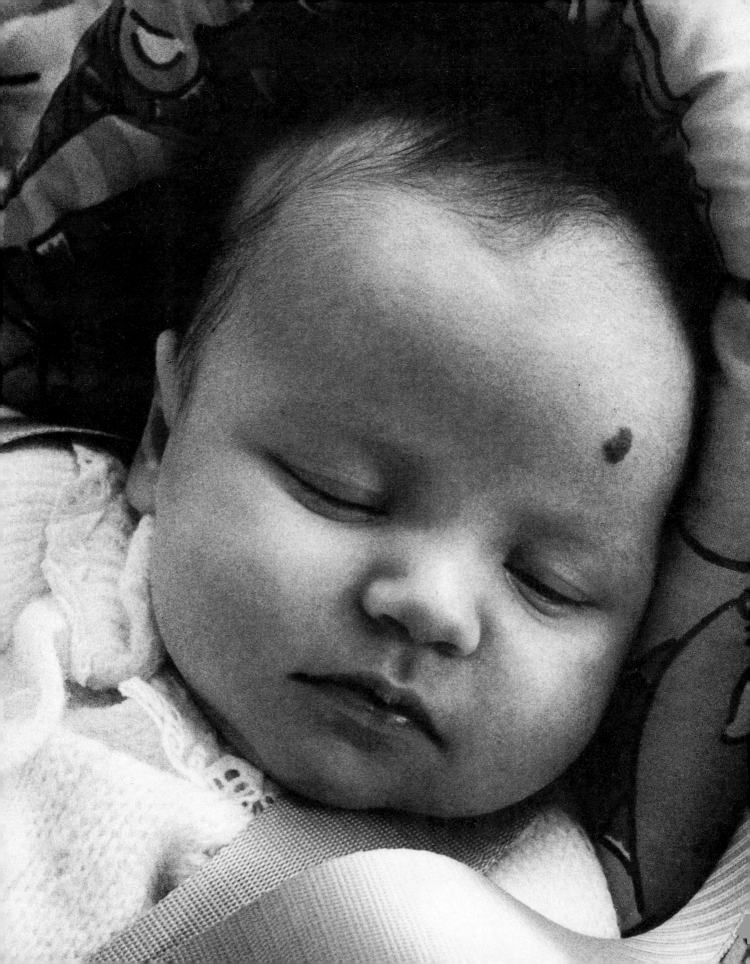

6

Sleeping

I find having children up and about in the evenings is very boring. How can adults relax and have a conversation with a small child around who is getting more and more fractious? I have seen children kept up until 9 p.m. and they have been crying and fussing and crying and fussing. All they have wanted is to be put to bed because they are too tired and over-excited to drop off to sleep where they are. I used to stay with a friend who kept her child up every night. It would drive me mad and the child was not happy either. One night my friend threatened the child with bed and you could see how delighted the child was. She wanted nothing better than to lie down and sleep.

It is very easy to tell if a child is tired. He will start putting his hand up to his face and rubbing his eyes, possibly sucking his thumb and playing with his hair, whimpering, getting bad-tempered and losing interest in things. You should put him to bed straight away. Although in a calm atmosphere a tired child can go to sleep anywhere (one of my children used to fall asleep on the nursery landing and another, at around six months, would just drop off to sleep on the floor of her playpen), an over-stimulated child cannot relax and sleep no matter how tired he is and will stay awake until he is gently calmed down and put to bed.

Going to bed is a luxury and should be treated as one. I find it extraordinary the way some people send their children to bed as a punishment; I suppose you are banishing a child to show your displeasure. But it is quite beyond my imagination to see bed as a punishment and it destroys the idea of bed being a treat. In fifty years of being a nanny I have only very occasionally sent a child to his room but never sent a child to bed.

1 · Should there be a bedtime routine?

Yes. Children need to be peaceful last thing at night. In winter after tea we played games quietly until bathtime. In summer we would come home from a picnic in the park and return just in time for bath and bed. Returning from a party the children were often quite excitable so I would try a little harder to keep a calm atmosphere until bed. Children need a bath, a bedtime story, a cuddle or whatever bedtime ritual you feel you will be able to stick to. Keep it simple and cosy; there is no point in setting up a ritual that involves reading your child a bedtime story if you cannot do it every night. Instead read them a story whenever they want one during the day.

My children always had the same bedtime. I kept to my routine no matter what happened and no matter who wanted to come and see the children, unintentionally disturbing their day. I felt it was important that their lives were consistent and that they knew where they were. Children love knowing what is happening next. It makes them feel secure and it makes your life easier too. A new baby will accept the pattern of the day sooner if he has a routine than if he doesn't. A small child, too, will be happier with whatever time you decide he should go to bed, so long as it is the same time every day so he knows when it is. Changing a routine can be done, but takes time (see question 4).

2 · How can I ensure a happy bedtime?

I keep bedtime as part of the day, not a cut-off point, a chopping-off finish. Bathtime to bedtime is always casual, never a hurried affair. When it gets to 6 p.m. I go and run the child's bath and I might take off his jersey. But I never say 'Bathtime now!' or 'Finish doing that, it's bedtime.' Since bathtime is as much fun as playtime my children always run in to have their bath. Then they have their hair brushed and their teeth brushed, all in a quite unhurried fashion. Then I snuggle them down into bed and read a story or occasionally sing to them, either a nursery rhyme or a song I make up about the events of the day.

Once they are about five I read them a chapter a night, rather than a short story, and then we say prayers. After that I tuck them up so they are all nice and cosy (see question 36). I also leave the curtains open; if you think the room is too cold with them open, then close them, but I think the sun coming in in the morning is so nice for a child. Then I say 'Have a lovely sleep' and just come out of the room without long good-night kisses and hugs. I loved my children very, very dearly but I hardly ever kissed them good night unless they wanted it, and then I did so with pleasure. I just tucked them in and said 'Good night, sleep tight'. I never made a big thing of it.

I do not believe in elaborate night-time routines, such as saying 'Good night'

Keeping bed-time happy

'Going to bed is a luxury and should be treated as one'

'Children love knowing what is happening next'

to each and every teddy. I never introduce those things. I never suggest anything like leaving the light on or the door open either, I always wait until they ask me (see question 38). I just made sure there were lots of nice things about bedtime and told them about something fun we were going to do the next day.

3 · How do you determine when bedtime should be?

My children have always gone to bed at some time between 6.30 and 7 p.m. from the day they were born until they were about seven, when they went to bed half an hour later, having had their bath at 6.30 p.m. At eight years they had their bath at 7 p.m. and bed followed. It was always bathtime that was prompt and bedtime that was a little bit flexible. I put my children to bed early because an early bedtime was thought to be best for growing children.

Nowadays it seems quite usual for a mother to keep her child up so her husband can see him when he comes back late from the office. I would say 'Too bad'. The husband can peep at him whilst he is asleep and play with him at the weekend. I do not see any point in keeping children up. A young parent may feel it is charming, having the new baby around all evening to fuss over, but it does over-stimulate the child. It also means that when the parents one day want their evenings to themselves again the routine they have established is hard to break and their child may be very reluctant to be put to bed (see question 4).

4 · How do I change my baby's bedtime routine so he sleeps earlier?

If you have always put your baby to bed at 10 p.m. and now want the child's bedtime to be earlier it can be done, and the younger the child is, the easier. But I would do it gradually. I would stagger bedtime, knocking half an hour off every week until I had reached the new time. It would take a few weeks, but it would be worth it. You would have to talk a great deal to the child, keeping him calm, and telling him that he had to go to bed earlier.

Any change in a routine you have set up can be difficult. From nine months or so, babies become creatures of habit. One of my girls had problems with her first child who she brought into bed with her every morning until one day she had had enough. Of course the baby was still enjoying being with his mother and was most put out. It is difficult anticipating what routines you are going to tire of and trying not to start them in the first place, but you must if you possibly can. How can a child understand why suddenly their routine should change – and just because that's what a grown-up wants.

OPPOSITE *Reading a bedtime story: children should be peaceful last thing at night*

Daytime resting

5 · How many rests a day does my child need?

I always put children to rest in the morning until they were two. The afternoons tended to be rather elastic and I would have to be guided by the child. They sometimes, not always, became sleepy after lunch. If they did, I put them down again. I think it is very important that children have some kind of rest during the day and if they have had to miss their morning nap I would always put them to bed in the afternoon.

I put children up to two years for daytime rests in their pram in the garden or on the balcony, unless they were ill when they would stay indoors. I would fix the pram straps so the baby could lie down or kneel up and I would put three or four things in the pram for him to play with. Of course, he never played with them, he just hurled them out, so why I bothered I do not really know since I never picked up the toys once he threw them out. He was usually still awake when I put him out and would get up on his knees and look around and shout and play or whatever. When he got tired he just shuffled down and fell asleep, usually for about an hour and a half. Sometimes babies would wake up and play after the nap until I fetched them for lunch.

Once a child was two years old his rest period would change to after lunch. I would put him into his bed or cot and leave him for an hour and he would sleep. Once the child was older, three or four, I would give them a book to read and I didn't mind if they slept or read – it just got them into the routine of simply resting and gave them the experience of sitting quietly with a book or a puzzle and not always saying 'What shall I do next?' It also gave me a breathing space. It does not matter if a child sleeps or not, children should relax and so should their nurses or mothers. Of course, like all routines, the daytime rest had to be flexible. If we were going out walking after luncheon I would not necessarily put bigger children to bed. I would put the smaller ones in the pram where they could sleep as we walked if they needed a nap.

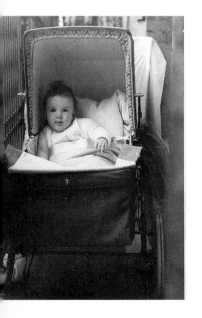

Nina in her pram on the balcony

6 · If my child has a long nap will he still be able to sleep at night?

Children will always sleep at night even if for some reason or other they have a very long nap or had to have a very late nap. I would make the bedtime just a little bit, maybe half an hour, later, but normally even if they do not want to sleep at bedtime they are happy just lying in bed and talking or singing. Until she was three one of my girls would have quite happily slept twice a day and I always had to wake her up or she would have slept the whole afternoon away, which would have wasted the lovely day. She certainly exemplified my motto 'The more they sleep, the more they sleep'.

Usually I avoid waking up a child from his nap. Sometimes you have to collect another child from school or something and then of course I do wake him up, but if it was just missing a meal time I would never mind, I would simply feed him when he woke up.

7 · My child is always a bit grumpy after his nap. Is this usual?

Very often children are a bit grumpy when they wake up from their naps. I must say that if I sleep during the afternoon when I wake up I feel cross too, I do not know why, but a cup of tea soon puts it right. Just cuddle them and let them stay quiet until they feel ready to move on to the next stage of the day.

8 · How many hours sleep does a child need?

Some children do seem to need remarkably little sleep and there is really nothing you can do to change whether a baby is very sleepy or very energetic. All my newborns except one girl have been very sleepy and for the first month or two they have usually slept, or just been very peaceful, more or less round the clock between their four-hourly feeds unless they were troubled by something. The girl was very, very tiny when she was born and I fed her approximately every three hours according to her needs. In between feeds she would look from side to side and wriggle about and thrash around and lift her little tail. She was very wakeful.

At three months most babies will be sleeping through the night (see question 9) which should continue forever, although of course it won't and there will probably be several wakeful periods as your child is growing up. By six months the daytime sleep will be lessening. At six months a baby will usually only sleep about four hours during the day and by a year this will be down to about two hours, although occasionally it will be more. Occasionally it will be less – some one-year-old babies may not need any sleep at all during the day.

The child's sleeping pattern changes all the time but by the time a child is four he will normally have stopped having any daytime sleep at all, although I still like him to read peacefully for an hour in bed after lunch. Until they started full-time school at the age of five, my children always rested in the afternoon. Sometimes they would fall asleep even when they were quite big children, which just showed they needed it. Once school started the rests had to stop, although I think if given the choice, even most adults would still like a siesta.

Up to the age of five most children can still sleep twelve hours at a stretch, but again some just can't. One of my boys could never go to sleep before 10 p.m. From the day he was four I used to let him have a book in bed and would leave it to him to switch his light out. If he had been able to sleep he would have, but

Newborns to nine months

'*Children should relax and so should their nurses or mothers*' he could not. In the mornings he was always very sprightly. Had he been tired I would have tried to help him sleep earlier by sitting quietly by his bedside and holding his hand until he dropped off, but he just did not need that much sleep.

9 · How can I get my child to sleep longer?

In an ideal world I suppose a baby would be born sleeping through the night. But they are not, and sadly you cannot immediately teach a brand-new baby to sleep through the night or even to know the difference between day and night. Even when they do sleep longer at night you can never encourage them to sleep more than they need to. All you can do is to make sure they have enough food in their tummies and that they are comfortable, neither too hot, nor too cold, and surrounded by a peaceful atmosphere.

Many young mothers seem to play with their babies the whole time. It uses up precious time and over-stimulates the baby who really and truly is far better relaxing in a quiet atmosphere, watching the clouds overhead and going to sleep. I would expect a new baby to be asleep, or at least quiet, most of the day except during his feeds. I always try and keep a child calm and quiet so he can sleep should he want to. Usually I find that after three months a baby, having had his last feed at 10 p.m., will sleep until 6 a.m., in other words, through the night.

10 · Where should I put my new baby to sleep in the daytime?

During the day I like all my children, even a new baby, to get as much fresh air as possible. After both the 10 a.m. and 2 p.m. feeds I put a new baby in his pram and let him sleep in the garden if it is a nice day. I see that he is well tucked up and in the shade with an insect net over his pram to keep out the wasps and deter cats. If the weather is bad I leave him indoors in his crib but I open the window a lot or a little, according to the season, so he gets some fresh air in his room.

11 · What temperature should you keep a new baby's room?

There used to be a terrific vogue for always keeping the window open at night, but I keep the window closed in the winter and on very cold spring or autumn nights. In the summer I would leave it open a little when the babies are all tucked up, both day and night. On a warm summer day, I put the baby in his pram outside during the day (see question 10).

These days, with central heating, having the baby's room warm enough is not so much of a worry. I always keep it at around 16°C (60°F) when the baby is in his bed, but have it much, much warmer while I give him his bath. I never really check the temperature, I just make sure it feels warm enough to me. And

I always keep a dish of water in the room to moisten the air and counteract the dryness of central heating.

If you have not got central heating I think an electric convector heater is the safest form of heating to use in a baby's bedroom. But once the child can get out of bed you do not want any sort of heater other than central heating or a night storage heater in the room as it could cause a fire. So put the heater on before the child goes to bed to warm up the room, and then remove it. I think smoke detectors are an excellent idea providing you keep making sure they work.

12 · Would you share a room with your new baby?

In the olden days, nannies always slept in the night nursery with the children. I always had my children in the same room with me until they were at least a year old and one of my girls stayed with me until she was seven. If the baby was being breast fed I simply carried him into his mother's room when he was thirsty and waited until the end of his feed to take him back to his bed.

I do not have any strong feelings for or against having your child sleep in the same room as you. I don't think it matters if you do not want your child to sleep in your room, but you must of course be able to hear them. I would always share a room with a new baby for the first three months of their life, although you may feel a baby alarm is good enough. A lot of people do find a baby makes too much noise, but I would rather hear them snuffling and snorting than be worried that if they did start gasping or choking, or whatever, that you could not hear what they were up to. If they were in the same room you would know if there was something wrong. I also think a child can sense the presence of another person in the room and it calms them down (see question 30).

Nina in her crib

13 · Would you sleep in the same bed as a new baby?

I would never sleep with a new baby, but I do not think it would matter if you wanted to and did, except I suppose you might roll over on him when you fell asleep yourself. If a new baby is crying I might wrap him tightly in a shawl, so it covers him from head to feet, and sit in my bed, or on an easy chair, with him and put him back in his crib once he is asleep – unless we've both fallen asleep together. There is such a lot of time to sleep with babies, for example when they are a little older and ill or unhappy, that I never feel it is something you need to do right away, although in the excitement of having a new baby you may feel like it. I always let children into my bed at night when they are older and have bad dreams (see question 40)

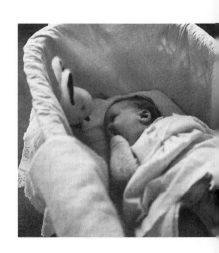

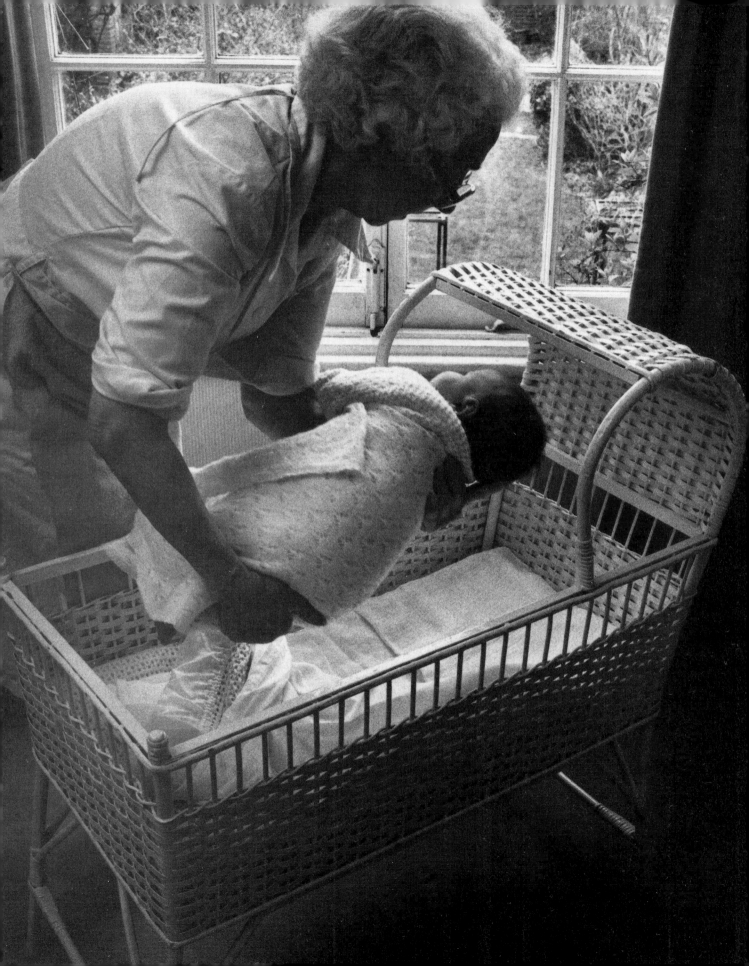

14 · What do you put a new baby to sleep in?

As long as the new baby's tummy is full and he is out of a draught and warm he will be quite happy anywhere. I have always put new babies in a crib or Moses basket on a stand. Both of these can only be used for the first six months, if that, when the baby grows out of them. So in a way either of these is an extravagance, although most cribs and Moses baskets are passed around from one baby to another, so lots of babies do use them. But I always feel the baby is very cosy in them, although he would be just as happy in a drawer from your chest of drawers. A crib is really just for the grown-ups' pleasure.

My cribs were always made of cane and were very light to move about. Some were painted white and some were natural, and covered with an organdie frill. A padded lining was tied on around the inside with string so it could be taken out and washed. You do not need a lining, some people simply tie a small pillow to the top end of the crib so the baby cannot hurt his head on the cane if he creeps up. I find it is a great joy when somebody has given birth to a baby and there is this tiny baby who looks so sweet in his beautiful crib.

I also always had a carry cot which I could use until the baby was about nine months. The carry cots I see now are shades of their former selves and babies grow out of them at around six months. The ones we used to have were like big, strong boxes that the baby could lie in as we were travelling and look all around him. They were fairly generous in size, very strong and usually navy blue – although I once had a yellow one – and you could fix a hood on to keep the draughts out. There was also an apron for it which we used if it was raining to carry the baby to and from the car or train. They were mostly carried by two people, one at each handle, because we didn't use them very often, only for going on a journey or out to tea at grandmother's when we had to take the newest baby.

Carry cots did not have a pram base; that is a newish invention. Instead they had a frame with four little wheels that folded flat and did not have a pusher. If you went somewhere overnight that did not have a cot you took the base. Day to day the carry cot stayed on the floor and the base was folded up. They could always have been used instead of a crib and even today I know of a young mother all of whose children slept in a carry cot until they grew too big for it. She found it very useful as they could be moved around and taken in and out of the car without ever having to be woken up.

Once the baby was six months, or before if they were long babies, I moved him into a cot where he stayed until he was almost five. We always had enormous cots which could have their sides removed so they could be turned into beds afterwards. I also found it useful to have a cot with a base that could be raised or lowered. The cot we got for one of my girls had one. As a tiny baby she had the base very high and I lowered it as she got older. I thought that was very good

OPPOSITE *Putting a very young baby to bed, cosily wrapped in a shawl*

because I did not have to bend over so far. I had twice hurt my ribs rather badly leaning over cots (see questions 16 and 32).

15 · How should I make up a bed for my new baby?

The mattress should fit the crib, Moses basket or whatever bed you are using perfectly. We always had a fitted rubber waterproof sheet (which we called a mackintosh) to tuck in around the entire mattress which in those days was stuffed with horsehair. These days most mattresses are already three-quarters covered with a waterproof material. I then put a fitted sheet on the mattress and then a flannelette sheet on top of that which made it very cosy. I always thought, now would I like to lie on top of that rubber with just one sheet between me and it? No, I would not. I then put a muslin nappy (folded double and tucked in on three sides; top, left and right) under the baby's head because it absorbs their dribble and you can change it easily when it is wet without changing the whole sheet. (For bedding requirements see DRESSING question 1.)

I always use cellular blankets, preferably woollen ones, and I have two in the crib and another in the pram, making three in all, and a pram rug. I think wool being a natural substance is warm without being sweaty. Acrylic may keep you warm, but wool breathes as well. A satin binding is very nice because if it comes into contact with the baby it is smooth and soft.

I change the flannelette sheets daily, or more often if the baby has a very dirty nappy and soils them. When I make a child's bed I never ever tuck the sheets or blankets in at the bottom, so if a child does go down the bed, as some do, he is not trapped. I once heard of a baby who got stuck and suffocated at the bottom of his bed. It is a rare case but very distressing.

I have never given a new baby or toddler a duvet, instead of sheets and blankets, or even an eiderdown on top. For one thing we didn't have duvets in England when most of my children were growing up, but I always thought little sheets and blankets were cosier and safer in any case. I was always worried that a child might pull an eiderdown or duvet up over his face and have difficulties breathing. I know current recommendations say that you should not give a baby a duvet or an eiderdown until he is one.

On her birth one of my children was given a beautiful eiderdown for her cot. I once heard her breathing so deeply and laboriously that I went in to see and she had pulled the eiderdown over her face. After that I used to move the eiderdown a bit further away from her hands. But best of all I really like the idea of a blanket and a sheet that you fold over and tuck in. Then the children are free to move but they are still cosy.

One of my mothers once remarked that she thought the reason the English were so secure as individuals was that they were always tucked into their beds.

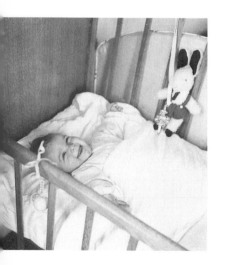

Nina in her cot

She was brought up with a duvet. I wonder if this new generation, brought up on duvets, will feel as secure?

I never ever give new babies pillows in case they suffocate in them. I also try and make sure they have a good firm mattress. I have never used an electric blanket for a child. Electric blankets can be dangerous and should never be used by anyone, whether child or elderly person, who might urinate in bed (see question 34). I have certainly used a hot water bottle in winter to make a bed cosy, but of course I always took it out before I put the baby to bed. Never leave a baby in bed with a hot water bottle.

'I roll them up, like a Swiss roll, from under the arms down'

16 · Do you ever give your baby a cot bumper?

The first time I saw a cot bumper I had no idea what it was for. I presumed it must be to keep draughts off the baby but you would not let a little baby lie in a draught anyway. I was told it protects the child from banging himself on the bars, but I have never known a child do himself any harm that way and I think a bumper blocks a child's view. It means he cannot look through the bars which is most unfair. I actually knew a little boy who got his head stuck under his bumper and did not know how to get back out again. I went in to get him up in the morning and could only see up to the nape of his neck. I do not see any point in them.

People always worry about children getting their heads stuck between the bars of a cot, but I have never heard of any child to whom this had happened – I only read about it. I would think that it might have happened because the child had been left too long to his own devices and got very bored. There are now rules about the widths of bars so you need not worry about that.

17 · How should I dress my new baby for bed?

I always dress my new babies in a vest, nightie and little jacket, and socks or bootees if it is cold (see DRESSING, questions 2 and 16). When I put them down to sleep I just wrap them loosely in a shawl on top of that, so that they are cosy. Or sometimes I roll them up in their shawls quite tightly, like a Swiss roll, from under the arms down, so they are warm but their arms are free. It doesn't matter which, it just depends what you are used to doing.

I see people swaddling their babies, wrapping them up very tightly with their arms bound to their sides, and they sometimes even look as if they are bound onto a board like in that Tudor painting, but I never do it. I only wrap them up when I need to keep their arms out of the way, when I wash their hair for instance, but I never do it for sleeping. Babies were swaddled thousands of years ago and I'm amazed the tradition is still being handed down. People who do this say they do it because babies have been so used to being in a tight position before they were born that they feel safer being wrapped up. But I do not think babies are very swaddled in the womb. After all they kick and thrash about and move their arms around, don't they? So I let them move their arms around now. I think a new baby enjoys stretching and exploring, and having his hands available near his face, so I never swaddle my new babies, except if I am cuddling them in my arms to keep them calm (see question 13).

18 · Do you lie a new baby on his tummy, back or side?

After rolling the baby cosily in his shawl (see question 17), what I always used to do was to put him in his crib, cot or pram on his tummy, with his hands up on either side of his face. Sometimes he would put his little nose straight down into the mattress, so I would move his head to the side, so that his ear was flat down on the mattress and sometimes he would jolly well put his head back again. Babies always do what they want. I would then pull his shawl and nightie down firmly so that they were covering his legs and not bunched up around his waist and put a blanket over him, folded over several times for extra warmth and placed right up over his ears up to the top of his head so he was warm and cosy. Then I tucked the blanket into both sides of the mattress so he was firmly wrapped.

I was trained to put babies to sleep on their sides, changing sides each time they are put down. First on the left side, next time on the right, then left again and so on. We tucked them in tightly so they could not roll but, of course, by the time they were three months they all fling their arms out and roll onto their back.

I remember in the early 1950s when the idea of putting a baby on his tummy to sleep first came over from America. At first we all scorned it but after a while it did seem to me that a baby seemed rather cosy on his tummy. It used to be thought better for various reasons, including that if a small baby swallowed some saliva or brought up some of his food it might make him choke if he was on his back, which would distress him, though it would hardly ever be dangerous.

The latest recommendation is that babies should not be put to sleep on their tummies but on their backs or sides until they are old enough to roll over and choose their own sleep position. This is because research shows that more cases of cot death occur with children lying on their tummies than on their backs or sides. Of course, that doesn't mean that sleeping on their tummies is the cause of cot death. Cot deaths can occur up to about the age of two, and the cause is sadly still a mystery. Children have been known to die suddenly while in their parents' arms or sitting in car seats. It is terribly sad for the parents and the keeper

Comforting a restless baby by wrapping her tightly in a shawl and sitting calmly until she is asleep

'Thumbs are
useful at tired
and sad
moments'

and they must be reassured that there was probably nothing they could have done to prevent it. But since the risk of a cot death is higher with babies on their tummies, obviously it is sensible to follow the current recommendations, so that the risk is reduced as much as possible. They are:

● **Place your baby on his back or side**
● **Don't let your baby get too hot**
● **Don't smoke near your baby**
● **If you think your baby is unwell, contact your doctor.**

19 · At what age do children start being interested in comforters?

Some children do not have any comfort things at all, but most children do, however, begin to form this habit during the first few months of their life. Thumbs are sucked from early on or it may be that they have a treasured piece of shawl or material. Often the comforters remain with them for life, becoming good luck mascots. One of my girls only stopped sleeping with her stuffed bunnies when she had her first child.

Thumbs are useful at tired and sad moments. I am always very pleased if a child decides to suck his thumb as it is something you will never forget to bring along for them. I recall a child who had obviously been intimidated about thumb-sucking saying to my small girl, 'Why are you sucking your thumb?' I answered for her saying: 'That is what thumbs are for!' I also valued the choice of a muslin nappy as a comforter as it could always be cleaned.

I would never automatically offer a child a comforter (see question 27), but one of my girls, for instance, as a tiny child in her crib would reach down for the hem of her nightie and hold it next to her cheek to go to sleep. It meant her tummy was naked and it was not very cosy, so the next time I tucked her down I put a muslin nappy next to her face for her to hold instead. One little boy I know had the corner of a shawl as his comforter so his nanny knitted six identical others so she could keep them clean. If children choose a large duvet or sheet to be their comforter you will notice that they always fondle the same corner. Instead of letting them drag it around and through the dirt I usually cut off that corner for them to have – not too small but not too enormous. One of my children liked the corner of his flannelette sheet, so when he went to school I stitched it inside teddy's pants – teddy was acceptable to take to school, a sheet was not. Sometimes you cannot replace things. If you notice a child liking something like a bunny, try and get another one as soon as possible so if it gets lost you still have one.

Even though I prefer a child to sleep in an uncluttered bed, most of my children have had some kind of a comforter and they have normally also had one or two favourite toys that they always take to bed. If a child wanted to sleep with more and more toys in his bed I would always let him (see question 21).

20 · *Do you ever take a comforter away from a child?*

A little boy I go to has a muslin nappy as a comforter but his Nanny will not let him have it except when he goes to bed. I abhor the idea that the baby should only be allowed his comforter at bedtime; what a curious idea, many times in the day such comfort is needed. I think comforters are like cigarettes. You sometimes just need something comforting during the day so if it is forbidden during the day it becomes guilt-ridden. It is much better to let a child have his comforter when he wants it. Never take a comforter away from a child of any age and never ever say to a child 'You are too old for it'. Who says? A child wanting a comforter is certainly not a problem and he should be allowed to have it whenever he wants it.

21 · *Do you mind how many toys a child takes to bed?*

By the age of two, most children will have a favourite toy, either a rag doll, a soft toy or a little tin or box or car, which they will carry everywhere and want to take to bed. They will usually single out one no matter how many they are given. I have never encouraged or discouraged a child to take anything with him to bed but I certainly never put all a child's cuddly toys in a neat pile or row on the bed. I never know why people do this. What happens is that the child adds other things to the pile and in the end there are so many toys which you have to move to make the bed. Of course it does not matter what you do, but I always think it must be an awful bore to have all that clutter on the bed. I just watch what the child takes to bed and put that out for him, or if he doesn't take anything to bed I wouldn't put anything there.

I would think it was more peaceful and relaxing to snuggle down with just a few select friends, but let your child decide. If he wants a lot of toys with him, let him have a lot. Some children will just throw things out of their cot if you put them in. I would rather children did not take anything sharp or hard or noisy to bed but if an older child did, I would always try and reason with him to let me place it in a corner of the cot or on the floor. However, if he insisted on taking a new or favourite small car or bus in to bed with him, I would let him and simply remove it when he was asleep and put it near the bed for first thing in the morning. Often when a child has something new he likes taking it to bed. When one of my boys was first a page he took his buckle shoes to bed for weeks; he thought they were wonderful (see question 52).

'Babies always do what they want'

22 · Do you go in and check a baby in the night?

When a baby is very new I have to admit I check him three or four times in an evening before I go to sleep, to see if he is all right, and then I would always sleep in the same room as a new baby (see question 12), so we are together during the night. When they are asleep new babies breathe in such a shallow fashion that you cannot hear them, nor can you see their chests rise and fall. I have sometimes touched a baby's hand to see if he moves it away, or even sometimes woken a baby up to see if he was still alive. You can see they are alive really, but I still worry. Normally I just put my fingers in front of a baby's mouth and nose to feel his warm breath. I have heard of people holding a mirror up to a baby's face to see if his breath clouds the mirror, but it is much easier to just feel if his body is warm. Sadly, cot death (Sudden Infant Death) and its causes is still a mystery and there may not be much that anyone can do to prevent it happening, but you should check a new baby regularly to reassure yourself (see questions 18 and 37).

23 · Should I worry if my baby is very active in bed?

All babies, even newborns, move about while sleeping. Newborns don't change position except for occasionally moving their heads from one side to the other. Sometimes it may just be that the baby is too hot and trying to kick his covers off. Often an older baby who has moved into the foetal position and remained there may be too cold and trying to preserve heat. I would feel his hands and adjust his blankets accordingly. If a baby is hitting his head at the top of the cot I take his ankles and pull them gently down, but he will probably wriggle back up again; so if you prefer, just leave him. If a baby is uncomfortable he will move himself or cry so you will always know if you need to.

24 · Why isn't my new baby settling?

For the first couple of weeks, if a new baby is crying, I pick him up because I feel that he needs to have human contact. I never, ever leave a new baby to cry. I always think babies must feel very lonely when they have been attached to somebody for so long.

I think the other most likely reason a new baby might be wakeful is if he is hungry, so I would feed him. If a baby who had recently had a feed could not settle, I would pick him up for a short time or I would touch him and stroke his head. Normally I find this settles a new baby and he will fall asleep, but if I saw him searching for food, I would feed him again. When one of my boys was a very new baby he would cry and cry after his 6 p.m. feed; I would pick him up and within minutes put him back down again and he would stop crying. He had just

OPPOSITE *If a new baby cries at night I go to her at once and pick her up in her shawl and give her a cuddle*

wanted some contact. Very often I wouldn't need to pick him up, I would just gently stroke his forehead and he would stop crying (see question 28).

25 · Is there anything I can do to help my new baby settle?

On the whole a well child who is neither ill nor in any pain will sleep. But babies are creatures like plants, you cannot do anything with them if they are hungry, except feed them. You always have to follow what your new baby decides he wants because he is only doing what his body tells him. You cannot yet teach him the difference between night and day, but you can organize it so both the baby and you know when his next meal will be.

I think that if you want your baby to keep to hours you like, and sooner rather than later to sleep through the night, there is an argument for routine rather than demand feeding, even though it all evens itself out in the end. I believe that routine is really essential to a small child because then they soon know instinctively what is going to happen next as it were. But no matter what kind of routine you decide on, you cannot really expect a little newborn baby not to need a feed for eight hours in the night when throughout the day their tummies are filled approximately every four hours. Once they are three months or over you can begin to expect them to sleep longer during the night, but not at first. Even then, you cannot ever encourage them to sleep longer, all you can do is make sure they have enough food in their tummies and that they are comfortable, neither too hot, nor too cold, and surrounded by a peaceful atmosphere.

26 · Should I cuddle or rock my baby to sleep?

Routine is a great thing. Once a baby has become used to his own routine, by the time he has been bathed and fed in a peaceful atmosphere he is normally ready to sleep the moment he is put down, possibly after a little cooing. I have rarely cuddled a baby to sleep (see question 13). Even if a baby has evening colic and I've been holding him upright for a while I would always try putting him down in his crib before he could actually drop right off to sleep in my arms. If he minded a lot, then I would rock him to sleep, possibly even singing a little lullaby, but I would try and avoid having to do it the next day as well. Otherwise the cuddling session will get longer and longer and before long I (or the parent) will resent it.

I don't understand why people start a routine of rocking their babies to sleep. They will undoubtedly get bored of doing it, and when that happens how can a baby understand that that is what has happened? All he knows is that he has always been rocked or cuddled to sleep, so why not now? I think when you want to stop something like that, you are just going to have to let your baby cry – and he will do – until it passes and do not blame him for crying. It is best never to start rocking or cuddling a child to sleep, unless he is unhappy. Never start taking him for a walk in his pram or a drive in your car just because he is having difficulties settling (see also question 4).

27 · Should I give my new baby a dummy to help him sleep?

I never, ever use dummies. For one thing I think if a baby wants to suck, he will suck his thumb (see question 19). Giving a baby a dummy is introducing a foreign object to him; also a dummy can be lost and the child, having got used to it, will be distraught. You can buy another one, but one dummy is not the same as another. I was once on the bus with a couple whose biggish baby was screaming. The dummy had been left behind and the baby was heartbroken. Sometimes when a small baby has an operation and mustn't scream, then you use a dummy or you could use a dummy if your child has colic (see question 29). Really only in those two instances is it a good idea.

28 · Why is my new baby crying?

Babies always have a reason for crying. Either they are in pain, lonely, hungry or uncomfortable (feeling cold or too hot), all things that can be remedied. If a new baby cries in the night I go to him at once and pick him up in his shawl and hold him firmly against my shoulder. Very often I have found that he stops crying more or less at once. I hear people say 'He only wanted to be picked up' and I think: Well, why not? Often a very, very short cuddle is enough and the baby just goes back to sleep and does not cry any more. If he carried on crying when I cuddled him and was not ill I would check that there was not a nappy pin sticking into him, which of course there wouldn't be, so I would presume he was hungry or would like a bottle for comfort, I would put him on my lap and feed him even if it was between feeds. If it was not long (only two hours or so) after the last feed the baby probably would not be hungry, but even so I would offer him a little milk. I think warm food is security to a baby. If he was still screaming a lot I would rub his tummy.

Once a baby had reached six months of age I would rarely rush the second he began crying unless the crying sounded urgent. Some babies do cry for ten minutes or so before they go to sleep. I don't know why they do it. You have to use your judgement – if they are clean, well fed, warm and so on, you might just have to leave them to cry for a bit. But I wouldn't leave a new baby crying at all and I would never leave a baby of any age crying for more than ten minutes.

'Often a very, very short cuddle is enough'

'I say "Have a lovely sleep" and just come out of the room'

29 · What do I do if my baby has evening colic?

Some children are known as 'Six-to-Tenners'. You have a wonderful day with them and then at 6 p.m. they begin to scream, and scream, and scream and they usually only stop around 10 p.m. It is a condition which can last quite a few months.

The nanny of one baby I knew who had evening colic used to fill the teat from a bottle with cotton wool and give it to her to suck so she could suck without breathing in any air. I don't know why it worked; I suppose giving a baby a dummy would be the same. The sucking stopped her crying, but it did not get to the root of the problem. Another way to stop a baby with evening colic from crying is to pick him up. I always find that the moment you pick him up he will stop crying and if you hold him so that he is straight and upright, almost stretching him against you with his head resting on your shoulder he will fall asleep, as though there was a kink and you were straightening it out. It seems to give a baby relief being upright against you though on occasions it may take quite a time for this to take effect. This is of course a great nuisance if you want to get on with your life and not have to carry your baby about hour after hour.

I cannot quite put my finger on it, but I think evening colic may be psychological. Adults get indigestion when they are nervous, so why shouldn't babies get it too, possibly also caused by some underlying tension? Certainly as soon as a baby with evening colic is picked up he stops crying. Maybe it is because when you pick him up he is reassured and the tension stops.

I think the remedy is to accept that you will need to cuddle the baby for several hours, trying to put him down every now and again, leaving him for ten minutes each time and see if he stops crying. If you can't keep picking him up and have simply got to do a job, then put the baby down, shut the door and do the job you have to do. If you are really desperate I suppose you could keep the baby strapped to you in one of those sling things, but I would find that very trying. Otherwise, just put him down and as soon as you are free then pick him up again and cuddle him.

If you are very busy and other people are relying on you, you just have to let a baby cry, otherwise you begin to resent him terribly. The evening colic will end sooner or later, you won't have to spend the next year holding your baby hour after hour every night. You don't have to walk about, you can read a book or watch television and one evening when you put him down, he will not cry and he will never cry again. There is an end to it.

If your baby is crying all day as well as all night it could be that he is allergic to milk (see FEEDING, question 18).

30 · Do you think a new baby can be disturbed by noise?

I don't think new babies or older children are worried by the noise of ordinary things like people talking or doors slamming once they are asleep. I have occasionally known babies to jump and burst into tears when a door has slammed or an electric blender or vacuum cleaner has been switched on, but this is when they have been awake. I don't think ordinary noise stops children going to sleep if they are tired. In fact it may seem a funny thing to say, but I think children like ordinary noises to go on when they have gone to bed. They would far rather have that than silence or people talking in whispers. For the first six months of her life one of my babies did wake and lift her head when I went in and out of our room. She woke very easily then, she was a light sleeper. After that it never disturbed her when I went in and out or turned on the light to read in bed.

Most babies are not disturbed by a sibling screaming in the cot beside them – at the age of three one of my girls used to sleep soundly through the yells of her year-old brother in the same room. I have heard of children waking when their sibling cried, however. I think it must depend on the child and the amount of screaming and whether or not it is near the time they would wake anyway.

31 · *My nine-month-old baby cries in the night. What should I do?*

If a baby of this age wakes crying, I never, ever put the light on when I go to him, there is enough light from the landing. I pick him up and cuddle him and ask him 'What's wrong?' and he might be sobbing and, of course, he cannot answer. If he was very hot or cold I would adjust his coverings and change his nappy if he was very wet and then put him back to bed. It is like making a fresh start. I would ask him whether he was thirsty and say 'I'll go and get a little drink for you', and get him some warm milk and keep talking quietly to him as he drank the milk. Then I would just say 'Well, we'll snuggle up nice and cosy now', and just tuck him in. Make it a new beginning and be very peaceful (see questions 28 and 43). If he still did not settle, I would leave him a short time and then pick him up again and cuddle him a little more. If he simply couldn't settle at all I would wrap him tightly in a shawl or blanket and take him on my knee and sit in a comfortable chair (see question 13). You cannot leave a screaming child to wake the household. When he slept in my arms I would put him back.

32 · *When should I move my toddler out of a cot, into a bed?*

Nowadays parents put a child into a bed by the time he is two but we always used to buy the biggest cots we could so that a child could stay in them until he was four or five. A cot spells security for a child. It is such a safe and cosy place to be in. In a cot you can lean books against the railings and hang music boxes on the sides. I think a child must feel very insecure in a bed, especially one without sides. I always put off the move from cot to bed for as long as possible,

Nine months to five years

even if it meant buying another cot when the second child came along. If an under-five must go into a bed I would have one with half-sides, but if the cot is big enough I never see why a child is moved so early. Two sisters I looked after both had a cot that turned itself into a small bed. Both sides dropped until they were only about 15 cm (6 in) high all round. From when they were three I left one side down completely so they could get out of bed in the morning and go to the pot. It depends on the child; some children were able to sit on the pot instead of shouting upon waking, and then get back into bed again and read the books I had left out for them the previous night. Some were not and wanted attention. Most of my children slept in their cots until they were nearly five. They were very cosy.

If you put your child into a cot without sides or even a bed you may find them wandering about the house instead of snuggling down and going to sleep. It may be that you have transferred them when they were too small and that they are missing the security of their cot railings. Try putting the sides back and they will probably just go straight to sleep (see questions 37, 48 and 49).

33 · What bedding will be needed?

I always put my children on as firm a mattress as possible. A child on a good diet will always have good posture unless he has a bone disease or other illness. Since a soft mattress may affect a child's posture badly, it is not worth taking a risk. I also worry about a child's posture if he sleeps on a pillow. I never ever, ever give a child a pillow. I like to feel that he is lying on his back or front without being bent up or down. I only give a child a pillow when he says he would like one, age five or six, and then I would just give him one. If he slips off his pillow when he is asleep I just slide it out from under him and do not put it back.

34 · How can I keep my child warm in bed?

Often people say: 'He kicks off his covers', but the baby sleeps quite peacefully; it doesn't seem to worry a baby being cold. I don't think they feel the cold nearly as much as they do the heat. You don't need to worry so much – when they are old enough to kick off their covers they must want to. Just leave the window closed, unless it is the middle of summer, or they may get a little chilled. Some babies do get right out from under their covers and cannot get back. This can happen until they are about two or three, when I find that if they do get out then they can usually always wriggle back under the covers.

When I visit a child before I go to sleep I just make sure he is tucked up and has not thrown off his bedclothes. If he has I tuck them back in. I think some people used to use blanket clips so the child could not kick his blankets off. I have

'A cot spells security for a child'

even known people use safety pins to pin the blankets to the mattress to stop them being kicked off.

Today I have seen parents put babies at six or nine months in sleep suits. We did not have sleep suits for wriggly babies, we had what we called sleeping bags, that zipped up the front and looked like sacks with sleeves. They were always very roomy, and the bottom buttoned together. As the child got bigger, you could unbutton the bottom and use it as a dressing-gown; a cord was supplied for this. I suppose now most houses are centrally heated fewer people use them. If a child was in a sleeping bag I would still tuck him in with a sheet and blanket on top to make sure he was nice and warm. You had to start putting a baby in a sleeping bag before he could stand or he would be frustrated when he woke up in the morning and wanted to stand up.

Bedrooms are often well heated these days but if an older child was cold I would use a hot water bottle. I normally give them to a child when he is a bit older, say from seven to ten. That is when children begin to like them. You must make sure they are not too hot of course. As I said earlier, never give a baby, a child, or anyone incontinent, an electric blanket. I have heard stories of babies being dehydrated and dying on electric blankets.

35 · What do older children wear in bed?

I always used nightdresses on both boys and girls from birth up to the age of three. I especially liked cotton nighties. In winter I would put children in woolly nighties. I never used vests or bed-socks unless we were in a very cold house.

Once they are three I do put little boys in pyjamas, not the button-up type that men have, but with a 'T' shirt type top and elastic-waist bottoms because they are so easy to take off if the child wants to go to the loo. My little girls stayed in nighties or used pyjamas too. From the age of two my children also have slippers and dressing gowns; they are so cosy to put on and small children look very sweet in them.

36 · What is your night-time routine with older children?

A golden rule for children of all ages is that bed and bath should be very, very peaceful. Water is such a good outlet for the emotions that I have never ever rushed bathtime.

I start reading children a bedtime story at the age of two. Before then, after the bath, I just tuck them straight up in bed. Once they are two we either sit cosily on the sofa together reading the bedtime story or the child goes to bed and I sit next to him on the bed. Between two and three I read simple stories: adventures of a family, nursery rhymes, old-fashioned fairy tales, Peter Rabbit and other

'A golden rule for all children is that bed and bath should be very, very peaceful'

147

OPPOSITE *Tucking up an older child*

early Beatrix Potter books. Between three and four I read them fairy tales. They are not teaching sessions, but a gentle and cosy time together with a book. Then I occasionally sing a song or, after the story or chapter is finished I just turn out the light, say 'Good night, sleep tight' (if he is a little older, he says his prayers first), and then I leave.

Some of my children have had a musical toy by their cot and I think that is quite fun. When they are little babies I put them into bed, tuck them down and pull the music box string. I have noticed they do listen to it and when they get a little older they pull the string themselves. I think it must be a fun thing to have stored in your memory, a music box at bedtime. I think it's all part of the cosy, night-time routine.

37 · Did you go and see them last thing at night?

I always checked on the children last thing at night to see if they were properly snuggled down and not too hot or cold. If their pot had been used I emptied it and if their drink was empty I filled it. If I felt they had the beginnings of a cold I would put a vaporizer in their room for the night. Once they were four, I would always leave a book or some toys in the cot for them to find in the morning. I never kept toys in a child's bedroom, only in his nursery, so he would not be going out and getting things from around the bedroom. If he wanted them they were in his bed. A bedroom is for sleeping and a nursery for living and playing in.

38 · Do you keep your child's bedroom door open or closed?

When a child is small I always close their bedroom door at night, but usually once children get to be three-ish they like the door left open. I can see why. Having been with people all day, how awful to be shut away alone. I never say to children 'You're a big boy now, you don't need the door open.' If they ask for it, just do it. Or leave the light on, whatever they have asked for.

I have been told that it is a bad thing to leave a child's door open but I really cannot see why. If you can sleep better with the door open, leave it open; if you can sleep better with it closed, then close it. I always closed the child's bedroom door anyway just before I went to bed, but it is the finality of being shut away at bedtime that some children do not like. In the morning it does not matter that the door is closed. The whole thing is to be casual. Do not make a big thing of it. It is obviously very important for them to have the door open or they would not mention it.

Incidentally, I never close bedroom curtains. In summer the sun shines in, in winter the street lamp (see questions 2 and 45).

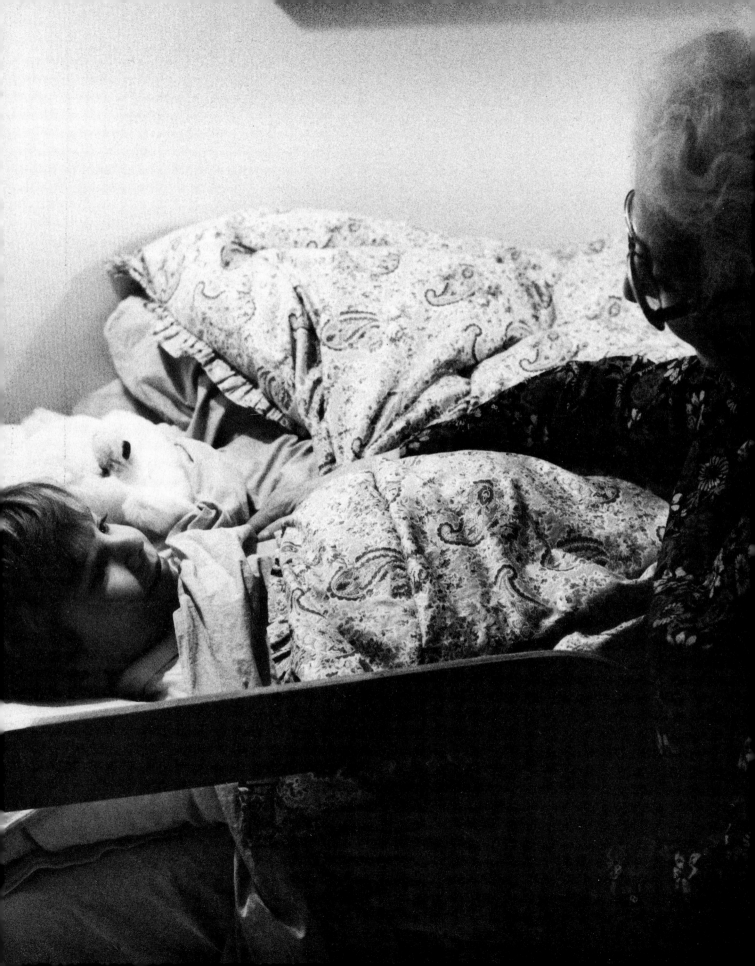

Bedtime problems

39 · My child does not want to go to bed. What should I do?

As always, the one essential thing is to keep to a child's routine. If you have a reason for changing their routine, like dogs, they will always know something is up, even if they do not know quite what. If you keep to their routine I usually find they will go to bed quite happily every night even if they do not sleep at once, but just lie in bed talking and singing to themselves.

Sometimes of course a baby who normally goes to bed without any fuss will actually shout and will not want to be put to bed. Then I sit down quietly with him on my lap and talk to him. Perhaps he has got a windy pain or some sort of worry I do not know about. Then, when he was quite calm and relaxed, I would gently tuck him in, stroke his head and back and sit with him for a few more minutes. Once I felt he was calm I would quietly leave him.

Older children, around the age of four or five, sometimes have problems that keep them from sleeping. They might be worried or feeling a little sad or lonely. If a child is not snuggling up and getting sleepy I just sit next to the bed and hold his hand. When he no longer feels unsure or unhappy he will fall asleep quite quickly and then you can slip out. At the time you may feel that now you will have to do that every night, but the problem is not going to last forever and it will probably never occur to him to say 'I can't go to sleep if you don't hold my hand'. Small children need a cuddle if they are feeling miserable and it never hurts to give them one.

40 · If a child is unhappy would you let him sleep in your bed?

If a child is having difficulties sleeping I never automatically tuck him up into my bed at night or even suggest that he might want to sleep in my bed. If he felt lonely or sad, however, and wanted to come into my bed in the middle of the night then I would never mind. I never discourage it because as I am always with them during the day I think that if they feel they want to be near me at night then why not? I never encourage it, though, either. Often a child will go back into his own bed after quite a short time. Sometimes he wakes early and comes for a snuggle in the morning. That is always cosy but again I do not encourage it (see question 54).

41 · What should I do if my child calls for me?

If a child calls for me I go immediately. I never say 'I'll come in a minute'. If they call, I go, as I know the chances are it will be something serious. They won't be calling for a drink of water because by the time a child is old enough to ask for this I will have left one near the cot for him to reach; nor will they be asking to go to the loo because there will be a pot left next to them. So I know a call means something else.

Occasionally a child will call out and want to ask lots of questions or just have a chat. It is normally when he is worried about something and I always go and talk to him. Sometimes, after I have put a child to bed and gone back to the nursery and am quietly knitting, a little person will just come and join me and say 'I've got a pain' or 'I don't feel very well' or something, and then I would deal with that. If a child were sad I would stay with him until he went to sleep. I have often watched children until they have fallen asleep.

You do have to work it out though. Sometimes it may be that the child has a feeling that you are going to go out that evening and wants you to himself. Then it might be best just to let him shout for a bit and be a bit stern. Wait for a while until you really think he needs you or if it is necessary. A child's second sense is incredible. You cannot peep through the door to see if he is all right, he knows you are there. But do not let him boss you around too much. He is not the only thing in your life.

'I never say "I'll come in a minute". If they call, I go'

42 · Why should my child have any problems at night?

'Problems' can stem from many different sources. It could be that the child is not exhausted enough during the day or, more likely, too exhausted and not calmed down enough at bedtime. If you notice your child developing what I have called a 'problem', make sure he gets lots of fresh air and exercise during the day so he goes straight to sleep after a cosy bedtime routine.

43 · What if my child wakes in the night?

Sleep disturbances

I always go in when a child screams in the middle of the night, or anytime. You feel now that it's something that will last forever, but it will stop – and then, of course, there will be another problem to take its place!

If your child cries and wants to see you in the middle of the night then by all means cuddle him; you might as well as you have got out of bed anyway. Then tuck him back into bed once he has calmed down (see question 31). I never feel there is any point in a child crying for his parents or nanny if they do not cuddle him. It is not fair. He cries because he wants to see you, to know you are still there. But I do not go in immediately unless he is a new baby (see questions 24 and 28) or his screams sound urgent. Sometimes when you have the intercom thing on you hear a child wake up and make a lot of noise, then there may be a space and he just starts talking or playing, it is so sweet. He may make some more noise and then talk again and then go back to sleep, he does not always cry.

So you need not always rush in. Judge each time on its own merits.

I would take a screaming child of eighteen months into my bed, as he would normally be in my room, and cuddle him, and then put him back into his cot, once he was calm. He might ask for a drink, so I would give him one, or I would offer him one anyway. I think to have a drink and to know somebody cares and then to be snuggled down is very cosy. For a few weeks one of my boys aged eighteen months, used to wake up in the middle of the night and shout and cry and I used to sit him on my knee, when he would look all round the room and smile. I would give him a little drink of milk and change his nappy and after about ten minutes I would put him back and tuck him up and he would go back to sleep. If he had not wanted to go back to bed and had made a terrible fuss then obviously I would have had to investigate.

Some children, like this little boy, stop crying the moment you lift them out of their cot and on to your knee. Then you can feel confident that they have not got a pain, or they would still be crying, and are not thirsty or hungry, though they might still like a drink; they just want some company. After a few days I would not lift that screaming child out of his cot any more, I would just kneel down next to him and stroke him and talk gently to him. If you treat it all very casually and are very calm the child will not wake again the next night. If you wake him up thoroughly and start playing with him, then you cannot blame him if he starts waking up every night expecting to have fun.

After the age of two, one of my girls never slept through the night. It began during my holiday, she just suddenly started screaming every night. A doctor's advice was asked and he suggested she should be left to scream. Of course, when I returned I ignored the advice and the result was that I was continually exhausted. Every night at bedtime I would put her in her cot and tuck her up and she would say 'Nanny's hand' and she would hold my hand for a minute and put it against her face. And then I would come out of her room and close the door behind me and she would sleep until she woke up in the middle of the night. She would cry and cry and so I would go in and talk to her and, when she was older and out of nappies, I would take her to spend a penny. Then I would wrap her in a shawl and cuddle her and sing to her and rock her in my arms and then put her down very, very gently after an hour or so. This happened every night. By the time she was four she still woke in the night but by then she didn't cry but used to come into my bed for five minutes. Then I would take her back and tuck her up and she would go straight back to sleep. At five she would take herself back to bed and tuck the blankets up back round me when she left.

44 · *Might my child be waking up because of pain?*

I have never had a child wake in the night from toothache, but I have had them wake up from an infection of the middle ear. One poor little girl screamed and screamed and there was nothing to be seen but she kept putting her hands on her ears. I called for the doctor immediately. Children do wake up from other pains, possible a tummy ache or a sore throat or if they have a very high temperature.

45 · What if my child is frightened of something at night?

Lots of children have night-time fears. I'm never sure where they spring from. When children play in doorways, for example, are they unconsciously behaving as their distant ancestors did in guarding the cave? One of my girls used to take a running leap on to her bed every night. 'You see, Nanny, there's a crocodile under my bed!' Was her beast under the bed a throw-back to primitive days when animals did lurk in caves? One never knows. Anyway, the crocodile was so real to this child that I just left it, I did not say 'I'll chase it away'. I suppose I could have said that but I did not. One day the crocodile just went away. The imaginary creature is so real to a child that in a way I think it is an insult to him to pretend that you understand. He might well say 'It's still there, Nanny' after you had supposedly chased it away and that would not do much for his confidence in you. Once this little girl was in bed she was safe anyway, she did not expect the crocodile to come out from under the bed. So I just accepted it and never talked about it to anyone in front of her in case she thought I was making fun of her.

My sister and I as children were always terrified of the large picture of Mr Gladstone that hung on my grandmother's bedroom wall. His eyes seemed to follow us around the room. We never told our grandmother we were frightened. Now if a child voiced his fear of a painting I would ask him if he would like me to put a scarf over it so he could not see it or I would even ask if he would like me to remove the painting. I was also frightened, up to the age of twelve or so, of going upstairs if I was alone in the house. I had a fear of what was round the corner and I had to go up the stairs accompanied. I have known children who have a different fear of stairs, of hands coming up from underneath and grabbing their ankles. If I knew a child was frightened I would always be by his side going up the stairs until they one day told me they would go alone.

One of my boys never liked the dark so I had a night-light for him in the country and would always walk with him through dark corridors. In town the street-lamps kept him company. I think a fear of the dark must stem from primeval times because why should children be afraid of the dark when nothing has ever happened to them? Another child always used to ask me to close the door 'so the black dog could not come in'. I just did as he asked (see question 38).

'In summer the sun shines in, in winter the street lamp'

46 · My toddler has been having bad dreams recently. Why might this be?

It is hard to say why some children dream more than others. I do not know if it is true that the more intelligent a child is the more nightmares he has, but certainly the more perceptive a child is the more bad dreams he seems to have. One of my boys for a long, long time from the age of three would run into my bed in the middle of the night and snuggle down and go to sleep. He had obviously had a nightmare. I never knew why this child had so many nightmares, he must have had a lot of fears I never knew about. He would often have a happy and peaceful day, with a peaceful bedtime and yet he still had bad dreams. He was a very, very sensitive child.

I think that having many nightmares in a row is a phase that passes but obviously a child will be very disturbed if he has nightmares night after night. If the opportunity arose to talk about them I think I might say: 'Well, what happened in your nasty old dream?' and I would sort of make light of it. If he said it was a horrid creature that tried to get him, I would say 'Did he hurt you?' and if he said 'No, but he was running after me' or whatever, I would say 'Oh, poor old thing, do you think it couldn't find its way home?' I would try and think and talk about his dream in a reassuring way. I would never dismiss it because as a child I too had very bad dreams.

I do not think that protecting your child from frightening things will stop them having nightmares, though it may help to do so if they are having a lot. My children never saw horrific things on television or in the cinema and none of them ever read frightening stories yet they still got the occasional nightmare.

47 · I am worried about my child sleep-walking. What should I do?

Children often talk in their sleep and I have heard small children laugh in their sleep, but I only ever looked after one sleep-walker. I found it very, very eerie. We were staying at the seaside when one night, fast asleep, the girl, aged five, sat up, then got out of bed, walked over to the bedside table, picked up her beaker, knelt on her bed and lifted her hands above her head with the beaker in them, like the vicar at Communion service. I very, very gently took the drink out of her hand and tucked her back up into bed. She was still fast asleep and didn't wake. It was so dramatic I have often wondered what it meant. I have heard that you should not touch people while they are sleep-walking but I would, and I did on this occasion.

As a child I was a great sleep-walker. I would wake to find myself at the foot of the stairs thinking I was trying to climb back into bed. I find it quite amazing that I should have been able to walk down stairs without falling whilst I was fast asleep (see question 48).

48 · How do you stop children wandering round the house at night?

There are so many potential accidents if children wander round the house that once a child is nine months, I put a gate on his bedroom door. I never suddenly introduce it once a child has begun climbing out of bed. I just always have it there, so he accepts it. He will throw things over it once he gets a little older but he cannot get out. Once a child is three if he does leave his bed I think it is very useful to have a gate on the door of his room so that he cannot leave the bedroom. The gate is really only to protect the child against any wandering round the house whether sleep-walking or not.

If you have not used a gate early enough and your child objects when you put one there, I would persist, even if he objected, especially if he was a wanderer. I do know people who have put a hook at the top of the door on the outside to stop the child opening the door but I think if he couldn't open the door at all that this would frighten him.

49 · What do I do if my child climbs out of his cot?

None of my children have ever climbed out of their cots. I knew one particular boy who was always climbing out of his cot; his parents had to put netting on top of his cot from when he was about eighteen months old. I think he must have felt awfully hemmed in. Later in life he was still always escaping and running away from home. I suppose there are all kinds of reasons for a child climbing out of his cot. It could be that they are simply not tired, or not exhausted enough or that they are bored. But it could be that they are over-tired and over-excited or want to see a parent who has been out at work all day.

If a child does climb out of his cot it is probably when he is fairly small and not old enough to reason with. If it happens at around two and a half I should think it was because he was very over-stimulated and over-tired. I suppose I would try very hard to give him a safe and cosy end to the day. I would tuck him down and say 'Now snuggle down' and I would stay with him for a few minutes, holding his hand. Then I would say to him 'I must go and have my supper/stitch a button on your jersey (or whatever), and then I will come back as soon as I have finished.' I would then leave him and go back after I had done whatever it was I had said I would do. I think lying there waiting for me would make him drop off to sleep.

Obviously, you have got somehow to keep the child in his room so you can have your sleep knowing he is not coming to any harm running around the house unsupervised. The problem is not new. There used to be special reins for a child to wear in bed; I always used to think it was an awful idea. The child could turn around with them and sit up, but not climb out. In this situation I would put a safety gate on the child's room without further delay (see question 48).

50 · My child always takes all his clothes off in bed. What should I do?

I have known children who on being put to bed have taken all their clothes off and all their sheets off and thrown them all out of the bed, including the mattress. You go in and they are lying there, exhausted and fast asleep. You could put young children who do this in a bag so they couldn't strip off and get cold. If they were a bit big for a bag I would make sure the window was closed, dress them in an outfit that fastened at the back and try and secure their sheets and mattress so that they could not be removed. I might buy a heavier mattress that they could not lift out and attach a string at each corner so it could be tied to the cot. If they cried I would go in and dress them but if they just fell asleep I would simply cover them up later, I wouldn't bother waking them. I would try and put their nappies on (if necessary) without disturbing them.

In future I would also try and give them a quiet peaceful bedtime and make sure that they went to bed unexcited. I would think it may be that the child had been put to bed too early after a rather uneventful day – a frustrated child, I would think. I would try to use up the child's energy more during the day so that he doesn't need to get so excited at night.

I even knew of a pair of four- or five-year-old children who dismantled their cots and threw the whole lot out of the nursery window. In this event when you put the cot together again you would be well advised to glue as well as screw it and in future keep the minimum furniture in the room. If possible perhaps the best solution would be to put the children to sleep in separate rooms.

51 · Why do children head-bang?

Lots of children head-bang when they are asleep and luckily they do not injure themselves doing it. Head-banging or crib/cot-rocking, like thumb or finger-sucking is a comfort habit and one that can take several different forms. Some children bang their foreheads on their mattresses, others on walls and some rock themselves as well. A four-year-old boy I knew used to bang his head nearly all night against the wall, but it never harmed him, and a little girl I know would shake her cot, bang her head and cry a lot in the night. One night I was sleeping in the room next to her and I went in to see what was happening. When I saw her I just sat down next to her and gently stroked her head and held her hand and repeated softly, over and over again, 'It's all right, stop crying' and she slowly stopped and went back to sleep. I do not know why children start head-banging but I think it must be a cry for help.

52 · What do I do about a child who plucks his blankets?

Some children have phases of plucking their blankets or their teddies until they are quite bald. Occasionally a child will put the pluckings in his mouth which is quite worrying because you do not really want him swallowing great balls of wool. I suppose the answer is not to have a fluffy blanket or a soft toy out of which the hair can be pulled (see question 21).

53 · Should I worry if my child is a bed-wetter?

None of my children were bed-wetters, but I did hear of a boy who was, from another nanny. He was somewhat highly strung and nervous and evidently a very deep sleeper. He probably only relaxed when he was asleep and it seemed to me his bed-wetting was like a safety valve, it was a form of release. When he went away for weekends for example, he never wet his bed and at boarding school, too, for the first few weeks he had a dry bed. After that it started again, I should think as he began relaxing, and continued until he was about fourteen. It must have been wonderful for him when he stopped.

There is nothing sinful about bed-wetting. It is a damned nuisance but something that should be accepted and ignored. Children will grow out of it. I don't think you can do anything about it. It may even be hereditary, as various members of that boy's particular family had been bed-wetters. So many children do wet their beds and for some extraordinary reason the people looking after them, be they nannies or parents, are ashamed and never ever talk about it until it is over. Of course, it can be embarrassing for a boy and his family when he goes away to school, or with friends on holiday, and I do think it is only polite for the child's parents to mention it to anyone who will have to cope with it. Before the boy I was told about went away to his school the family arranged with matron to send extra sheets.

Another child I knew was taken to a doctor who prescribed a drug which meant that he never wet his bed, but his nanny told me that his face looked haunted, dark under the eyes and miserable. His parents then decided they would rather have a wet bed and a happy child, so they took him off the drug and he started wetting his bed again, but at least he was happy. They also bought him a pad which made a bell ring when he wet his bed; the first night it woke up the whole household, but he slept through it. Luckily, he was not sent to a special hospital I heard of where bed-wetters were woken up every hour and made to urinate. I hope that hospital was prosecuted.

54 · At what age can you expect early wakers not to wake you up?

Some children wake very late, some very early. Most wake very early but I do

In the morning

157

not always go in just because they are awake. If a child wakes unhappy I would go in and see what was up, give him a drink and a toy, change his nappy, put him back to bed and come out again. Until a child is nine months he would be having a drink of milk at 6 a.m. anyway and then going back to sleep. After nine months his first meal is breakfast at 8 a.m., so I rarely go in until I want to get him up and dressed. Usually until then he will be happy playing with the toys I left in the cot for him and talking to himself or his sibling if he shares a room.

I have never known anyone to train a child not to wake them up before a certain time, although one of my children, now a mother, did show her four-year-old son where eight was on the clock so he could play by himself or quietly with his sister until then and hopefully leave her to sleep. If children wake you by talking to themselves and shouting or playing I would not take any notice of that, but if they are shouting a bit after a few minutes I would get up and see why they are upset. If they wake up crying I would go at once.

If you started a routine like bringing your baby into your bed every morning so that you could read the paper and are now regretting it, you can always change your child's routine. However, I think you should try to do so over a period of days rather than abruptly as he will not be able to understand why suddenly you do not want him to come in with you (see question 4).

Golden rules

Make bedtime a part of the day, not the end

1 · Going to bed is a treat – never use it as a threat.

2 · Don't let a child get over-stimulated at bedtime. Put him to bed before he gets too tired to sleep.

3 · Keep bedtime the same every day. Don't keep your child up to show him off to adults.

4 · Don't start any routine, such as rocking your baby to sleep, that you will soon regret.

'The more they sleep, the more they sleep'

1 · Humans do sleep at night, so your child will eventually, too.

2 · If a baby has a full stomach, is neither too hot or too cold, isn't in pain and is surrounded by a peaceful atmosphere, he should be able to sleep anywhere.

3 · Of course, some children need less sleep than others.

Listen to your child's fears

1 · Keep your child's bedroom door open if that's what he wants.

2 · If at bedtime your child is lonely or a bit sad, then why not sit by his bedside and hold his hand until he drops off to sleep – it won't hurt once in a while.

3 · A child crying in the middle of the night may just need to know you're there, so go to him immediately.

4 · But if you think they know you're going out and are just bossing you about – be gentle but firm.

7

Playing

Parents are often worried about whether their child has enough toys to keep him stimulated and learning. But there is no need to bombard a child with toys, especially if they are the wrong toys for his stage of development. Any object at all that your child plays with is a toy to him and all the best toys are based on things that are in your child's life already, such as boxes, cups and a pot and wooden spoon which he can use as a drum and sticks.

What is very important is to choose the right toy for your child's development, the toy with the correct play value for your child. A toy he will be able to use and learn from. Of course, a child learns as he goes along, as he enjoys himself and does what he can absorb. A child of four months will enjoy a simple rattle and needs little more. Three months later the chain with discs or beads on it that you give him to play with will fascinate him. It will be the correct toy for him. There is no point giving it to him when he is only four months old in the hope of teaching him something quicker as it will just slip from his fingers. Similarly a seven-month-old child may pat a drum and pick up a series of plastic pots but he will not learn or derive the same pleasure from them as will the ten-month-old who can bang the drum and put the plastic pots inside each other. Giving a child a toy too early will only mean that the child is used to (and possibly already bored by) it by the time he is really ready for it. Given at the right time the toy will be a new challenge.

'Any object that your child plays with is a toy to him'

I so often see people buying things for children that really and truly have no play value for them. I recently saw an eighteen-month-old child whose mother had bought her a very nice little set of tiny feeding bottles and dishes and so on, for playing with her doll. But the child was not old enough to appreciate it; to her they were just bits of plastic. A child of three playing with a doll and knowing about little dishes and spoons and bottles would get a lot of play value out of it and greatly enjoy playing tea-parties and feeding dolly, but for this child it was a waste of money.

Children need to develop in stages – simply and slowly. It is repressive and frustrating for them to be made to play with toys they cannot yet cope with. It is equally repressive and frustrating to be made to discard toys before they are ready to. I find the phrase 'too young', meaning the toy is meant for a smaller child, most extraordinary. Why shouldn't a five-year-old play with a rattle if he wants to? Never tell a child that he's too old to play with a toy or that it's 'too babyish' for him. What nonsense. If the rattle is intriguing to the child, it doesn't mean it will have a lasting interest. Being scorned will take away the child's confidence.

Each stage of development is learnt gradually as a child goes along, whether it is walking, talking, playing or sharing and children should be left to work each stage out for themselves. They are very wise. It is always better to leave children alone and not try and make them develop in ways they are not yet ready for. A child who wants to play with something that needs two people begins to learn about co-operative play. In the same way a child will learn about sharing and you will soon notice that a child forced to share is very often much less likely to share of his own accord than a child that is left to use his own initiative. Let children explore at their own pace. They will learn much more that way.

The right play value

1 · How will I know if a toy is too advanced for my child?

One can always tell if a toy is too advanced because the child either will not play with it or he will pick it up and throw it around. I always put a toy like that away in the cupboard for a short time and then reintroduce it in a few months' time. Every child develops at his own pace and has his own interests. One child will be more physical than another and ready for a climbing frame at quite an early stage. Another at the same age may be so fascinated with cars that he could be given a toy garage. The list of toys that I have suggested for children, starting at question 22, may be used as an approximate guideline, but in the end you should be governed by your child. Everything on the list is, of course, a basic toy – and just a suggestion. It goes without saying that if granny brings a present that is more sophisticated or unusual but has the right play value he will probably enjoy that too.

I always think it is much better to give a child something slightly below his capability than above it. He will do whatever he can with it and will then be ready to go on to the next thing and get a lot out of that. A toy below his capability may not give him a feeling of achievement, but he will have the enjoyment of playing with it, and it could stretch his potential. If it is too advanced it does not mean anything to him and he cannot do anything with it. By the time he is able to do it, it has always been lying around and is no longer a challenge, no longer fun.

2 · Do you take any notice of the age recommendations on packages?

Because I have been with children all my life I never take any notice of the ages recommended by the toy manufacturers. I have seen ages indicated on toy boxes that I did not think were particularly relevant and often I think manufacturers put ages on toys that are really too young; I do not think they always have the child's interest at heart. The trouble is that a godmother or grandmother will look at the recommended age and may feel embarrassed giving the child (or rather, the mother) something with too young an age on it, whereas in fact it is only just of the right play value. It is up to you to put the toy away for a few months if that happens.

I do, however, take notice of any safety guidelines on a toy. If the package says the toy is suitable for children of thirty-six months or over, do *not* give it to a smaller child (see question 15).

3 · Can a child have too many toys?

As well as finding a toy with the right play value, it is also important not to swamp your child with toys. I remember an eleven-month-old baby in a playpen surrounded by thirty-two toys, none of them with any play value. There were things to pull along, but she was not yet walking so she could not pull them along; there were lots of soft toys; there was a thing that looked like a tea-cosy but it was a little house with lots of pockets to put things in which she could not yet do; there was a pyramid thing with coloured rings which she was not old enough for and there was a picture tray which she stood on, she did not yet know what to do with that either. I would have put her in the playpen with a book made of cardboard pages with simple pictures on them, one on each page, and some hollow cups or cubes to put inside each other. Those things would have held more interest for her.

Whether in a playpen or not, it is always better for children to have fewer rather than a lot of toys to play with. If they have a lot, I find they will not play with anything, they will just heave them all about the room.

4 · How do you control the number of toys a child has?

The first thing I always do is to put any toys away that are no longer of interest to the child. You will notice they just lie there and the child never plays with them any more. I then bring them out when a younger child comes for tea and my child usually enjoys seeing them again.

Every night I always put all the day's toys away and get out two or three others for my children to play with the next morning. For example, for an eighteen-month-old to two-year-old child I might put out building blocks, a posting box and an animal to pull on a string. For a two-year-old I might leave hammer pegs, large beads to thread on a string and a picture tray. For a three-year-old, some Plasticine and an easel and blackboard with chalks and so on. During the day, of course, they can take more toys out of the cupboard if they want to, and I never tidy any toys away until the children have gone to bed – toys are there for them to play with as they please. But I try to provide the opportunity for them to do things I feel they would enjoy.

Of course, as children get older they know what toys they have got so they just ask for whatever they want, but I always just put a few different things out every day for a younger child so he does not get fed up with all his toys. But if he does have a favourite he plays with all the time, like small cars, that is his decision and his fun. It is only when I see him getting bored with his cars that I would put them away for a while. I always take the lead from the child. Sometimes you can observe that when a child gets a new toy of the right play value he himself will put all his old toys back on the shelves or wherever they are kept, to clear a space, both mental and physical, for his exciting new toy. Do not put them out anymore. You can learn a lot from your child.

'You can learn a lot from your child'

5 · What are the other advantages to having fewer toys?

Children who have a few toys get more out of them than children who have a lot. You have to remember with children that there are so many years ahead. Often parents adore their children so much, they cannot resist buying them things, but if you can restrain yourself from buying too many toys you will find your children get so much more fun out of having a few things that they really enjoy. Having fewer toys also makes a child use his imagination: he has to invent his own playthings. You will often notice children preferring home-made toys to shop-bought ones. An old shoe box with a string attached is as much fun as a shop-bought pull-along toy, if not more so as you can fill it with things, and wonderful garages and buses can be made from toothpaste boxes as well as big cardboard boxes (see also other home-made toy ideas throughout this chapter).

6 · What do you think children learn from playing with toys?

I think children learn a great deal – they learn dexterity, first by holding a simple rattle, later by banging with a spoon and squeezing a rubber toy, then by posting shapes and pulling an animal or small cart along. They handle sand and water, thread beads and put their dolls' or teddies' clothes on: each achievement more complex than the last. They learn to solve problems, from fitting shapes in holes to building with constructional toys and working on jigsaw puzzles. They are also learning to use their own initiative and to occupy themselves without being told what to do (see question 7).

7 · Do you ever show a child how to use a toy?

I often hear people say 'Not like that!' or 'Let me show you how to do it.' Quite often children will attempt things on their own and are frustrated by adults. I never show a child how to play with a toy of any kind, unless of course he asks for help, otherwise I would assume he is enjoying the toy. Sometimes he will say 'You do it!', perhaps when he is perplexed and undecided, then of course I show him what to do, but I later remove that toy for a few months. He is obviously not yet ready for it.

I feel very strongly that children should be allowed to play alone. I do not mean alone in a room, I mean a child should be able to play without adults continually making suggestions and interfering and interrupting. I very rarely actually play with a child or join in his games unless he suggests it, until he reaches the stage of games such as snap, dominoes, donkey, happy families, ludo and snakes and ladders, when it takes two to play.

8 · Some children don't seem to want to play with toys. Does it matter?

Some children never play with toys. One of my boys enjoyed small cars and a little garage and he had a beloved rag doll, a drum and a ball. He also had a large dog on wheels that he pushed and a tricycle we took to the park but he certainly didn't enjoy construction toys or fitting shapes or building bricks. He could never be bothered with them. I remember him lifting the lid of the posting box and dropping the shapes in. He was always quite ambitious and from the moment he was born he seemed to know what he wanted to do and what he didn't. It certainly doesn't matter at all.

9 · Do you think I should allow my child to watch television?

If I say 'I do not allow children to watch television,' that is a sweeping statement. I did have a television set in the nursery which was kept in the cupboard. If we were going to watch the *Woodentops*, or another favourite programme, we turned it on for the programme and then we turned it off. It was never on all the time and the children never fiddled with it. Most of my children were not particularly bothered about whether they watched television or not because they were always busy doing other things.

I only ever allow a very little carefully chosen television because I have always felt children should *do* things and not watch other people doing things. The late lamented *Andy Pandy* and *Watch with Mother*, both of which I am told you can now get on video, were delightful programmes; short and charming. Apart from that the only things my children watched were football (*Match of the Day* was one of my boy's favourite treats) and the Trooping of the Colour (for the horses and pageantry). *Blue Peter* used to be an excellent programme, it had animals on it and showed the children how to make all kinds of things – it was enormous fun. I used to listen to the radio with my children, *Listen with Mother* was after lunch and we'd sit on the sofa together.

One of the families I was with had a television set in the nursery, but it was never, ever switched on. As it was never on, it never occurred to my children to put it on. On Sunday evening they would watch *Songs of Praise* with their father on the upstairs television. They were thrilled, it was a sort of weekly treat. I am always appalled when small school friends of my children have said 'Can we watch television?' and when I have said 'Why? What is on?' they have had no idea, but they just wanted to sit and gaze at the screen. I find it rather sad that children are reduced to such behaviour. I do not ban television, but I do not encourage it either. Television is a marvellous thing if used properly, but I do think it is unnecessary for children. And if you don't want to, and they don't ask, I certainly don't think you need to watch children's television with your

'Children should do things and not watch other people doing things'

children. It doesn't stimulate much conversation. If you've got something else to do, do it.

10 · Do you think children need shop-bought toys at all?

Buying toys

I do think it would be rather strange if children did not have any toys bought for them. I only heard of that happening once, in my era. At school with one of my girls there was a brother and sister who were both nice, intelligent children. Their mother's proud boast was that she did not approve of toys, her two children only had books. As far as I could see they were perfectly happy and well-adjusted. The toy-less home worked for them but I have always felt that a few toys are important because there is a limit to how many things you have at home that a child could play with. I also find children like the bright colours of toys and might be rather unstimulated living almost solely in a rather drab adult world. Toys have evolved to aid children's development while giving them pleasure – and as such I believe they have a place in a child's world.

11 · Do you think boys and girls need different toys?

I was in a toy department one Christmas and next to me was a father with two small boys, perhaps five and seven years old, looking at the exciting toys on sale. The elder boy picked up various dolls and the father said, with heavy sarcasm, 'I'll buy *you* a doll for Christmas'. So much psychological damage is done by such remarks.

Don't ever say to a child that they are the wrong sex for the toy they want to play with. All toys are toys for all children and if it is good enough for them it is certainly good enough for you. I hear so many people saying 'This is a boy's toy' or 'Darling, it's for girls'. So what. Why make the child as rigid-minded as you are? Up to the age of five or six most children do play with the same toys and then they do start to go in different directions. Of course girls also enjoy sailing boats and boys enjoy dolls' houses, but by then boys will be playing more with trains and cars and girls will be enjoying skipping and making things with canvas, wool and beads (see question 50).

12 · Do you check toys to see if they are defective in any way before leaving the shop?

Yes. I once saw a young mother on the underground who wanted to give her sons their new toy to play with. She pulled out the box and found it was empty. I felt most sorry for her, it can be very disappointing and aggravating to find you have come home with an empty box or a broken toy or even a toy that needs batteries

'Given at the right time a toy will be a new challenge'

that you haven't bought. I always look in the box, if I can open it, and check the toy while I am still in the shop.

13 · Nanny, were there any toys that annoyed you?

The only thing I can remember that I really did not enjoy was a little car with a perpetual police siren. It drove me mad. But I didn't remove it, the children loved it. Trumpets and drums don't worry me at all. I find gimmicky toys (My Little Pony etc) are annoying and expensive but there is a stage when children collect such things, it does give them so much joy at the time and it all passes so I don't mind about that. If you are a busy person and the child has a musical toy that drives you mad I think at night you must hide it away. It's important that it doesn't drive you mad. The only toys I ever forbade were guns and soldiers (see BEHAVING, question 17).

14 · Do you ever make toys for your children?

Yes. Making toys is great fun – we all enjoy it. It's a rainy-day thing, a game really. The children always made gifts at Christmas, too, usually only for their mothers. We would buy their fathers a small present at Woolworths. I didn't influence them at all and I remember one of my girls buying her father a tube of toothpaste one year!

Playing safe

15 · What potential dangers are there when children are playing?

One hears horror stories about dangerous toys and reads of small children swallowing tiny parts of a toy. Sadly there are tragedies but I do wonder why children are given such toys. People do not seem to use their common sense; surely one would never give a child a toy with sharp edges or a toy that is easy to pull apart. I also wonder about the child's lack of supervision; I think these things must happen when a child is alone for a long period of time, in a cot perhaps or on the floor, and getting very bored and frustrated.

Between one and two years almost all children will begin walking. They will fall over often and usually without hurting themselves. They will just get up and carry on walking over and over again. You have to be careful not to let them carry anything sharp such as a stick or pencil or rod-like toys like recorders, especially not in their mouths, when they are walking until they are quite sure on their feet. I once heard from an eye specialist about the eye injuries caused to children by pencils. He told me never to give a child a pencil before the age of five. He said so many injuries happened by children fighting with pencils or just walking with them in their hands and tripping up, or accidentally putting the pencil in their own eyes. These chubby pencils they have nowadays are safer but even so, I think they should not be given to a child before he is three. Of course, with second children these 'rules' are more difficult to apply, but do supervise when pencils are being used. I always sat with my younger children whilst they were drawing. It is so important and it is only for a few minutes a day.

Babies (and toddlers) should never be given anything that could be dangerous. Of course if there are older brothers and sisters they may come into contact with some potentially dangerous toys anyway and should be guarded against them as much as possible. In a busy household there are lots of things around, small children do put everything in their mouths and it is difficult to keep the nursery floor clean and tidy all the time. Often they may be handed toys that are too small for them, by visiting children who give babies things they shouldn't have, so you must always watch out and keep tiny babies in playpens where they are protected (see GROWING AND LEARNING, question 8). Beads can get stuck up noses and Lego can be swallowed. These things can happen in the best regulated families and you have to keep a look out for them. There used to be tin toys that were sharp and toys painted with lead paint which, of course, were to be avoided. I always remove any fluffy toys from a child if he has a tendency to pull out the fluff and put it in his mouth (see SLEEPING, question 52).

The main danger in the nursery is for children to be harmed by swallowing things, so you must always keep a look out. Nannies would automatically take out teddy's eyes. I used to think 'Poor bear, he can't see' and I have yet to meet a very small child who would pull teddy's eye out. Normally the bear's face is made so that one eye is attached to the other so they cannot be pulled out. I remember they used to have sweets in lipstick packaging which were such fun – you could paint your lips and then eat the 'lipstick'. They banned them because a child choked to death on one. He was eight months old. What a silly thing to give to an eight-month-old child. Do be sensible about what you give small children; sharp scissors, for instance, should always be kept away from them. (If you are worried about your child wanting to take his toys to bed, see SLEEPING, question 21.)

The nursery itself needs socket shields which, I must say, are the very devil to get out, but should be used on all wall sockets when these are exposed. It should also have bars on the windows and no trailing wires around the room. Since retiring and doing part-time care, I have looked after several children in their family kitchens. If the kitchen doubles as the nursery I think you must try and find a little alcove in it somewhere where the children can play safely while meals are being prepared and washed up. The kitchen is a potentially dangerous room and must be made as safe a zone as possible.

16 · Do you think I have to wash my child's toys?

For the first six months of a child's life it is especially important to keep his toys clean. Dirty toys are unattractive as well as unhygienic, so once a week during this time I take all the baby's rattles (and other toys if there are any) and put them in a lather I make with soapflakes. I then rinse them well, dip them in a mild disinfectant solution and put them on a tray to dry. One of my children now loves the smell of that particular disinfectant. Anything that was washable I would wash, a ball or a soft toy, but I was never obsessive. I find it awful if people are constantly saying 'Oh he can't have that, it's been on the floor,' it is just not realistic. Before you wash, look first to see whether soft toys are washable and then follow the instructions, or you might ruin a very old friend.

Toy storage

17 · Where did you keep the child's toys?

We had several cupboards for toys, puzzles, games, cards and so on; we also had a bookcase. On the cupboard shelves I stacked puzzles and things in boxes. If there was a collection of miniature animals or bricks, dominoes, beads or whatever, I always kept them in separate labelled bags, boxes or jars with lids. I remember coming back from one holiday to find that the temporary nurse had simply thrown everything together in one big box. I was so cross. Balls were always put in a net bag and hung on a hook behind the door.

All my nurseries had a toy box which contained masses of little odds and ends, like the things that came out of crackers. The toy box was great fun and was always pulled out of the cupboard and rummaged in when someone came for tea.

18 · Did your nursery ever have any toys out on display?

I always had teddy and golly and perhaps one or two other soft toys and a doll or two on the sofa at any one time and the other dolls and soft toys I kept on a shelf in the cupboard. I would swap things round a lot. The favourite ones would remain with a changing selection of three or four 'new' ones every now and again which I would get out of the cupboard. It was just so that they wouldn't become background, like wallpaper. I never had all the dolls and soft toys out on display because I have always felt it confusing for a child, like a market.

19 · Do you ask children to tidy their nursery up?

I never ask children to tidy up. I have noticed during the years that if children have to tidy up after them it sort of takes the fun out of their toys. If you expect a child to tidy up you are really just wanting the child to do what you want –

'Untidiness I do not mind'

and why should they? After all, putting things away in a certain place is entirely a matter of preference and what you are asking the child to do is really to do what you want. If you want a tidy nursery, then you should tidy it.

When children are small they like putting things away because they have seen you do this and so they like to copy you, they are not doing it because they are tidy. I think it is most unreasonable to expect a child who is ready for his bath and bed to have to tidy away his toys before he goes to bed. I have heard people say 'It teaches them to be tidy', but it does no such thing. Young adults are either tidy or they are not. It has nothing whatsoever to do with what they were told to do as a child. Of course, if you are very, very busy you might ask a child to put his bricks in a bag whilst you ran the bath, that sort of thing, but not everything, every day. If an older child wants to tidy his toys away or clean up his room he will do so and I would always help him.

My nurseries were always a little bit untidy during the day as I always let children get out whatever toys or books they want to and I never tidy up at all whilst they are still playing. I do always tidy everything away after the children have gone to bed, so the floor and all the work surfaces are clear. If children play with paint or Plasticine during the day I clear up after that, I would not want anything to get ruined, but untidiness I do not mind. Of course, if a child is playing in the same room in which you are cooking you will need a different routine. But even then I would try and find him his own special place in the kitchen or sitting room that can be left as a mess during the day without it interfering with your movements and just tidied up in the evening.

20 · *What do you do with broken toys?*

There is nothing more unattractive than a lot of dirty, broken toys so when I had spare time, which was usually in the evening, I would go through the toys, wash all the tea set things which would have bits of crumbs glued to them; clean all the painted and plastic toys; wash and press the doll's clothes and put everything neatly away into boxes. If a doll or toy was beyond repair I would throw it away unless it was a favourite, but I do not remember toys ever being broken by my children; they lost interest in them but they rarely broke them, the damage was always done by visiting children.

As children get older and their toys become more intricate they do worry about them getting broken; I have been known to hide a treasured or fragile toy before friends come so that it will come to no harm. Sadly, a small boy visiting us once stood on a beautiful drum belonging to one of my girls, who would never ever have dreamt of standing on it herself.

I remember the same little girl, when she was three or four, had a special doll that was broken in a way that was possible to have mended, but too complicated

for me to do. We took the doll to the doll's hospital in Sheffield, where we then lived. When we went to collect the mended doll several weeks later she was quite disappointed and cried: 'I so wanted to see them in their little beds.'

21 · Did your children play outside?

Most homes I worked in did not have very large gardens, and a few only had balconies, so we would always go to a nearby park at least once, usually twice, a day. I think a garden is wonderful for children, and whenever my children asked to play in ours I always let them, even if it was drizzling. They might not have stayed out long if it was raining but when it was fine they often stayed out for a few hours. I kept an eye on them but did not always join them. They would just take their truck, their teddy or their cars and play, sometimes in their sandpit or their climbing frame if they were lucky enough to have one. Of course, gardens contain hazards, such as gardening tools left out and poisonous plants and you must be aware of them. A swimming pool or ornamental pond can be lethal and both must be made childproof.

The flats I lived in were also made as much fun as possible. The brother and sister I was looking after had a sandpit on their tiny balcony, a swing in their corridor and a bar on which they could hang in one of their doorways. The little boy used to love just standing on the balcony and watching the cars go by. The communal gardens we had were always very useful; at first for a place to leave the pram where I could keep my eye on it and later where the children could go on their own and meet their friends.

22 · Does my new baby need any toys?

My sole aim is to make sure a new baby has a very peaceful time in his cot or pram. I always feel he enjoys stretching, looking and just generally being comfortable and calm. I certainly never play with a new baby and I neither show him toys or other objects nor poke or tickle him or talk into his face. His only stimulation would be the clouds and trees outside and a mobile indoors. When bathing or feeding him I am also very calm. I speak quietly, and had I a good voice, I might sing softly as I changed or tucked him up.

I never push a baby out in the pram until he is three months old, unless there is an elder sibling who is by then enjoying the park, or I have to buy something. Then I lay the new baby in the pram, under the hood, and sit the old baby at the other end of the pram or he walks. On reaching the park the toddler can then run or pick daisies or pull a toy on a string while the new baby rests quietly in

Nina in her pram

the pram. Otherwise I simply put the little baby in his pram in the garden or indoors in his crib beside an open window during the day.

23 · *What about a mobile or something else to look at?*

I find the idea of putting coloured cards around the inside of a new baby's pram to give him 'something to look at' quite extraordinary. Imagine lying in a confined space with rows of pictures a few inches from your nose. How very uncomfortable. I think those strings of small toys people hang across the baby's pram are also a form of torture. Think of lying on your back with a row of objects you cannot remove obscuring your view. But I do think a mobile hanging over a cot is a wonderful toy. I always hang one up over a baby's cot the moment he is born so when he does look up he can see this moving, brightly coloured thing which is of interest, just like trees and clouds will later be. When he reaches three months and goes into a playpen, I also clip one over the playpen, not too close, but near enough so he can see it. As soon as the baby can focus he will enjoy it.

People have asked me if a mobile will prevent a baby from sleeping. It does not, because if a baby needs sleep he will sleep, no matter what the situation. If he enjoys watching the mobile he will not give up sleep to do so. He will sleep and wake to see the wonderful toy hanging there. There are such excellent mobiles, but I find the ones made out of coloured card or perspex that are light and move easily are the best. I do not really like lots of small teddies or dogs or whatever, but I don't think it really matters what the mobile looks like so long as it is moving. I have nothing against musical mobiles, they are probably rather fun, but new babies really like looking at things and having peace and quiet. Once the baby is a little older I always have a musical box which is activated by a string attached to the cot. Children enjoy them from about three months until they are three or four.

Three to six months

24 · *By three months might my baby like any other toys?*

At this age babies begin to blow bubbles, look at their hands and hold things. I always give my three-month-babies two things: a small, flat plastic ring and a simple rattle, both of which they will enjoy holding. I always knot a ribbon round the ring and pin it to the baby's cardigan so it is always to hand and does not get lost.

Rattles used to be made out of celluloid and shaped like a stick about 12 cm (5 in) long with a ball on the end which had seeds in it. They were very light and the stick was narrow enough that the baby's little hand could easily get round it. They would hold the stick and shake it and it would make a gentle noise. Now

I see rattles and rings that are far too big for babies to get their little hands round with ease. Small rings are much better, so make sure that any you get are not too large in circumference for the child to hold. Occasionally you still see rings in jewellers with a small silver animal or bell hanging on them. They are quite good, but a simple small plastic ring, which sometimes has a bumpy surface, is better. A baby can hold it and turn it over and over and put it in his mouth and rub his gums against it when his teeth are coming.

It's not really necessary to give babies as young as this many toys, especially if they wear a nightie as they will just look at their hands, or pull up the hem of their nightie or dress, and look at that.

25 · What toys might my six-month-old baby enjoy?

Once he is sitting up (see GROWING AND LEARNING, question 7) he will be able to enjoy banging a little tin drum or the tray on the highchair or some wooden spoons on a saucepan. He will also like to push a big ball and will try to scramble after it and push it again or, if you push it back towards him, he will push it again and again and again. Remember that your six-month-old will still put everything in his mouth that he can find.

For the next few months a baby will also enjoy beads or discs on a chain or cord. Like worry beads, these make a nice noise when the brightly coloured plastic discs slip around the chain. Seven-month-old babies would also like a rubber doll or animal to squeeze and throw. Make sure it is made of nice thin rubber that they can really squash and, if it squeaks as well, that is even better.

26 · What about when he gets a little older?

The end of a baby's first year is great fun as he will be beginning to find life one big adventure. It is up to you to make sure the area he is exploring is quite safe. Until he is a very keen and competent walker, I still use the playpen (see GROWING AND LEARNING, question 8); he will hang on to the side and walk around it and play and throw toys out and sometimes reach out and take them back. If he throws a toy out and cannot reach to pull it back, I would always retrieve it for the child and give it back. Throwing is part of his development and should be encouraged, it should not be a cause for unhappiness. If the child is not in a playpen all the rooms he goes into must be completely safe, otherwise you will end up saying 'No' all the time (see BEHAVING, questions 7–8). Cupboards must be childproof, there should be nothing that can be pulled over and there must be a gate at the doorway to stop him wandering around the house (see SLEEPING, question 48).

Up to approximately fifteen months he will still find the drum and sticks are fun for a good old noise. He will also enjoy hollow cubes (or plastic cups) to fit

Six months to one year

'A mobile hanging over a cot is a wonderful toy'

inside each other, but don't expect him to build them up yet; he will do that later. At this age he will probably just enjoy putting them inside each other. You can give him any boxes and tins with lids to take off and put back on again. One used to be able to buy a lovely set of six little boxes with lids which all fitted inside each other; I have not seen them for a while. It is good for a child's finger manipulation to fit lids on. If I came across a nice little box or jar with a lid I always kept it to give my baby.

One to two years

OPPOSITE AND BELOW *Nina, almost two, with some of her favourite toys – a toy dog with a handle to push and rings which fit over a stick*

27 · What will my child like playing with after his first birthday?

After the baby is a year old he will enjoy a block to fit pegs into. Not different shapes, you just need all the same shape pegs and each with a knob on, if possible, so the child can grip them easily. Normally at that age a child cannot yet work out different shapes, he just enjoys putting the pegs into the holes. He will still like playing with a large ball especially if you roll it backwards and forwards to him.

Between one and two years most children will begin walking. Once children are walking they will love pulling a little cart or wooden animal behind them on a string. You will notice that at first they will not walk forwards because then they cannot see the cart so they walk sideways or backwards to see it coming along. You can tie a piece of string to a shoe box for the same effect and put teddy in it. Another treat is a large toy animal or trolley with a handlebar to push. It is important that this is well made and sturdy enough so it does not tip up on top of the child when he pulls himself up by the handle.

He may also enjoy simple board books with just one object shown on each page, not pictures with fussy detail. At this stage if a child sees a page with one object, such as a shoe or an apple, it makes more of an impact – just knowing it is an apple gives him great pleasure. If the picture is all little busy bits, it may not confuse him but he will not enjoy it as much. A little later he will enjoy more detailed pictures.

From about fifteen months some children begin to enjoy soft toys. Before then, although it amuses adults to see soft toys in cots and prams they mean little to small children. He will also begin to love his bath. A plastic duck or a yoghourt pot with holes in the bottom will soon be fun for him. Expect him to drink a lot of bathwater – that is fun, too.

28 · My child is now eighteen months, what else will he enjoy?

Children of eighteen months may also begin to enjoy a posting box to post different shapes through. Let them work out for themselves where the shapes go – don't prompt them or put half a brick in and let them do the final push. I often

think posting boxes are sold too early for children. Even at eighteen months many children are still too young to work out where the shapes go and only really begin to enjoy the toy by two years.

A more satisfying toy for this age is those coloured discs that fit on a stick, but don't scold your baby when he doesn't put the discs on the stick in strict sequence of size. The sticks always used to have straight sides and the discs were cup-shaped so they could go on in any order and could either be used to build a tower or would vanish inside each other. I notice they are now making the sticks with sloping sides so the discs have to go on in the order they are intended or they won't all fit. This is a terrible pity as it restricts the child's pleasure and imagination. It also reduces the length of time that the toy has play value.

29 · Nanny, what home-made toys do this age group like?

From about fifteen months and for many more years, children love getting into big cardboard boxes – monkeys love doing this too. I used to have to steer one of my boys away from empty boxes or he would stagger home with them to make things. I would also use shoe boxes to make cars and trains stringing two or more shoe boxes together for a train with carriages. You can let children pull each other around in a larger box too.

30 · What do children of this age enjoy playing with in the garden?

From about eighteen months many children enjoy playing with both sand and water – although I would not advise them being played with together. In the garden I give children a bucket of water and some cups or yoghourt pots or even a little watering can. I always fill the bucket with warm water because although it cools down quickly their little hands don't get so very cold. They also love playing washing up in the sink or with sieves in the bath. If children are lucky enough to have a sandpit, I give them a wooden spoon or a little spade, yoghourt pots and little buckets to make pies with. They can also make sand castles though that is easier on the beach. The sand has to be a little bit moist to make the pies so I add water if necessary.

An outdoor sandpit must have a lid so neither the rain nor cats and dogs can get in. These days some lids have a sort of race-track on top which gives the child something else to play with. I always keep my eyes on a small child in a sandpit, especially if they are in there with a friend, because some children are liable to throw sand – small children because they throw anything, and the older louts if they do not know any better. Even today when I see children throwing sand I immediately stop them. If I saw my children throwing sand after being in the sandpit only a short time, I would join them and we would make a few sand pies;

'Children love getting into big cardboard boxes'

OPPOSITE *I think a garden is wonderful for children, and whenever my children asked to play in one I always let them, even if it was drizzling or cold* if they had been there a long time I would assume they were getting bored, so I would simply take them out and put the lid back on the sandpit.

I am not all that keen about paddling pools, I think they are greatly overrated. They are fun to jump about and splash in, but only once the child is able to stand up and get in and out of the pool on his own. I am totally against small immobile children being put into a pool of water and left sitting there. Even if you start out with warm water in the pool, it gets cold very quickly and all the poor baby can do is just pat the water and get chilled. If you are going to use a paddling pool, you should always put warm water in it and keep it topped up with warm water the moment it starts getting cold, unless it is a very, very hot summer's day. I think for small children a plastic bowl or bucket or even their old plastic baby bath filled with warm water can be just as much fun.

A slide is a toy that can go in the nursery or out of doors. It is not an essential, but children do love sliding. It is a great idea to hire one for a party, even if you do not keep it permanently.

Two to three years

31 · What do you think my two-year-old would really enjoy playing with?

Once a child is two I find a sack of large wooden building blocks gives a lot of pleasure. We used to build the walls and then put a book on top to make a house and put soft toys inside. There are endless possibilities. A child may well enjoy blocks up to four years old, especially if his set comes with archways and so on. Psychiatrists, I once read, test children at eighteen months by giving them bricks to play with. I think one of my children would have fared badly; he never put a single brick on top of another one. He could not see any point in it at all. However all my other children loved them. I usually only gave them bricks once they were two, though occasionally at eighteen months. I think it is asking an awful lot of a child of a year to put bricks on top of each other. Maybe by fifteen months they might copy you if you did it, but they really begin to enjoy bricks only once they are two.

By this age your child will also be ready for a wooden picture tray. This is not quite a jigsaw, instead it has figures or objects which fit into holes in a board and can be easily pulled out and put back in. He may also enjoy large beads to thread onto a shoe lace and hammer pegs, which are wooden pegs with a split in them which your child can hammer through holes in a wooden bench. Unfortunately often they are not made properly and the pegs are too large to fit through the holes, or drop right through without needing to be banged so the child can get no satisfaction. If this happens I would return it to the shop.

At this age children often have a lot of energy, so a trampoline is a fun piece of equipment and an indoor version can be useful for exercising on wet days. It

is not essential. I have known children to slip and bang their teeth on the metal bar and also two children who tried to jump opposite each other and banged their heads. So use them with care.

32 · *I notice my child enjoys copying me. What toys would he like around this theme?*

From the age of two children do love to re-enact what they see around them and will copy what they see. They will enjoy following you about with a little duster and broom or playing tea-parties with a plastic tea set and some water and biscuits. A tea set and a small table and chairs are very important for playing, especially when they get a little older. 'Play tea-tarty, Nanny!' was a frequent request and, of course, my children would always invite their teddies to tea. I used to break up Marie biscuits to eat and put a little water in the teapot. Afterwards the table and chair can simply be used for doing puzzles on.

Both boys and girls will also like a doll with clothes as they will love taking the clothes off. People say 'Oh poor dolly, she'll get cold' or 'I'm not giving you a doll, all you do is take her clothes off', but that is part of the joy of having a doll, taking off its clothes. Of course a small child cannot put them back on again, it is far too involved for them to do, but they can drag them off and carry the doll about naked. If we are going to the park I may suggest we put a coat on dolly but otherwise I wait until the child went to bed when I would dress the doll again and put it back on the shelf for the morning. Often a child will also like to put their doll or teddy into a cot or a bed and tuck them in. They are imitating what happens to them. All my boys had toys that are traditionally thought of as 'girls' toys' and they all thoroughly enjoyed them. This is the age for rag or other soft dolls. It is usually only when children are a few years older that they begin to enjoy plastic dolls.

33 · *What toys could I make for my two-year-old?*

When one of my girls was two and a half I made her something very simple which was such a success. I stuffed an old nylon stocking with newspaper so it looked like a long sausage, then I stuffed another and tied them together and so on until it reached across the room. Then we got powder paints and painted it to look like a long snake. My little girl used to take it to the park and luckily I never cared what people thought. Eventually it fell apart but one could always make another.

34 · *What do you give two-year-olds to play with in the garden?*

I find that if ever children are worried about anything they play with water,

Nina with her teapot

OPPOSITE *A peaceful session on a rainy day – Nina's daughter with her teapot*

185

especially between the ages of two to three. Children love playing with water, it's very therapeutic. I often let children play with buckets of water in the garden or with their hands in a basin or even let the bath tap run – provided the plug is out and there's no flannel blocking the plughole. Quite often they will play with water themselves if they are feeling a bit tense. Water play I think is very, very important. Children always walk in puddles and will stamp in them. They don't avoid the puddles.

I also think sandpits are great fun (see question 30) and can always be put on a balcony if the child does not have a garden. Most children will play quietly in them and enjoy making sand pies with a bucket or using little moulds.

Children (and adults) do love swinging. I think a swing and a climbing frame are the two things one would hope to have for the child in a garden. When they are small (up to three) you can get those box swings with bars all round for them. Even though a child cannot work the swing by himself until he is four or five, he will still love swinging.

Three to four years

35 · What do I give my three-year-old to play with indoors?

As a child's dexterity and intelligence progresses he enjoys more involved and detailed playthings. A doll with hair that can be washed and brushed and eyes that open and close is much appreciated. When one of my girls was about six she wrote a little essay called 'Henrietta is Coming to Tea' which consisted of 'Henrietta is coming to tea and we're going to wash the doll's hair'. Our nursery was always messy by the end of the day and of course my child could wash her doll's hair whenever she wanted, but Henrietta could not and loved coming to visit us.

For quieter moments they will enjoy farmyard and zoo plastic animal sets which will help them learn all the different animal names. I would save shoe boxes into which I would cut barn doors as though they were stables or cages and put the animals in them. Town children today may have little experience of seeing animals outside, but I always found the children liked to set the animals out and pretend to make them walk and gallop and so on.

If there is room, I also think a rocking horse is a lovely idea and is always part of a cosy nursery. All children love going on a rocking horse. I think three years old is an age for 'hanging on' to the horse. Smaller children need to be carefully supervised as they forget to hold on and fall off.

36 · What kind of games would my three-year-old enjoy playing with me?

If you feel like playing with your child, they will now begin to enjoy picture lotto.

You each have a large card on the table with several pictures on it and cards of individual, matching pictures in your hand. You take turns covering the pictures on your card with the matching ones in your hand. Children of this age also enjoy picture dominoes. However starting games too soon is very frustrating for small children – they cannot see the point in them – whereas when a little older they concentrate and are enthusiastic.

37 · Should I give my three-year-old a personal stereo?

Most children do love listening to music. I find it has a similar calming effect to water. We had lots of tapes of nursery rhymes in the nursery which we would listen to, or sing together, sitting on the sofa. But I would never dream of burying my child away with a pair of headphones. You can't compare the feeling of a child sitting alone listening to a book on tape to the cosiness of snuggling next to a child and sharing a book. Tapes are very useful for when your child is ill. When you can't be there playing a simple game or reading or talking to him, he can listen to the tapes on his own and enjoy them. But I would buy a standard tape recorder that you can both listen to rather than a personal stereo.

If you do buy him a tape recorder, choose tapes that are suitable stories or songs or rhymes, maybe even with books that go with them. I find those tapes to help children learn their times tables or alphabet quite unnecessary. I would help a child learn them if he needed help.

38 · Do you let children paint and sculpt at home?

I never really offer my children either painting or Plasticine or other modelling before they are three, but once they get to this age they really enjoy being creative, so I let them. I did start drawing with one of my girls before she was three because I noticed what incredible pencil control she had; so every day I would give her a clean page in a small sketch book and a pencil and let her do a few minutes of drawing. I never suggested what she should draw, I just let her do what she wanted. Her drawings were very precise and very strange. She is now fourteen years old and draws beautifully – she enjoys it so much and does it constantly.

All children enjoy painting. I had a good-sized blackboard on an easel with a tray at the front. It was a double easel so that a child can stand on either side and they can either draw on the blackboard or you can clip paper on for them to paint. If my nursery floor was not linoleum, which it usually was, I would cover the carpet with a big, big piece of plastic and clip sugar paper (stiff coloured paper) on the easel, mix up a few jars of different coloured powder paints and find a couple of lovely thick brushes. Of course, I would dress the child in one

'I never suggest what children should draw, I just let them do what they want'

of those thick plastic overalls with sleeves. Sometimes they used wax crayons – those short, stubby ones – and sometimes chalks, but brightly coloured paint was enjoyed much more. It is fine if children want to use their fingers and feet to paint with, but I would never have suggested it and think it strange when adults often do. It calls for far more supervision than using a thick brush does, which I would have thought was just as much fun. Most children normally will not paint or model for long anyway, only for about ten minutes. I found that it was often a sudden urge that went as quickly as it had come. Afterwards I'd just fold up the plastic and drop it into the bath to tidy up later.

I find it so sad when a mother tells me that her child paints at playgroup and not at home. I think he may grow up thinking that being creative is something that has no place at home. I think children should feel able to do everything at home – after all, nothing takes that long to clean up. When people say that an activity is messy what do they mean? What is 'messy'? Does it mean things being out of order or maybe even sticky or untidy? But if you plan ahead everything can easily be cleaned up. I would never have my nursery look permanently like a zoo with things out of place and wet and sticky. That is a child's way of doing things and there is no need for an adult to let a nursery get so terribly out of order, but if it does for a while it really does not matter, as long as the child is having fun.

39 · Do you suggest to the child what they should draw or model?

Once I had provided the chalk or paint I would just leave my children to it. I never make suggestions as to what children should paint unless they ask for ideas. And I never, *ever* say 'What is it?' to the child's finished art. I think it's an insult. I say 'Splendid' or 'Jolly good' or 'What a lovely, lovely colour.' Normally it isn't anything, they are just expressing themselves with the paint and they think you are a fool for asking what it is. The same with clay. I just praise, I never question. What is important is that the child is enjoying himself and being allowed to explore and be adventurous.

I like children to do things themselves, not to be shown how to do things by people holding their hands to show them how to write and draw. At first when children start drawing they just scribble marks on paper. They normally only start making shapes when they are four. At four they can, after a fashion, usually copy simple numbers and alphabets and draw something round or long. Children vary. When she was three one of my girls drew her grandfather with a face and glasses. Obviously I have sometimes drawn things for the child, a little house or a funny face. It would not be for them to necessarily copy and I wouldn't say 'Let's draw Daddy' or 'Why not draw a picture of our house?' I would just join in their game if they wanted me to, but not otherwise.

OPPOSITE *I give my children chalk and, with a good-sized blackboard to work on, I just leave them to it*

40 · What do you use for modelling?

We always used modelling clay which these days you can buy in nice bright colours. I very much like modelling: I think it gives a child great scope. I always sat and worked with my children when we used modelling clay. I covered the table with newspaper first and we never did it in a carpeted room as tiny bits can drop and be trodden into the carpet.

You can make your own modelling clay, mixing a dough with flour and water and some salt to stop it smelling and a colouring agent (cochineal or any other colour of food dye); you can then paint it if you want to. Home-made modelling clay can also be baked in the oven to make it very, very hard so you can keep it – if you don't bake it it will grow mouldy. It gives you more flexibility; you can put a pattern on the wings of the butterfly and some spots on your cow's back and you can make pretend cakes or pendants. Older children can also use home-made marzipan and colour it all sorts of colours with food dye – a small basket of marzipan fruit makes a lovely Christmas present.

At first a three-year-old child will not do anything very sophisticated with the modelling clay, he will just like to roll it about and sometimes he will make a long, long worm. Later on we would make things, fruit one day, a few eggs in a nest or a Christmas tree with decorations the next. We had such fun, we made animals and I once made a most impressive hippo, I didn't know I had it in me!

41 · What toys can I make a three-year-old?

For one of my children I once made a lovely house using a wooden clothes horse that opened out into three, like a screen. I covered two sides entirely with linoleum which I painted with trailing roses, and the third side I covered only half-way up and put curtains on the top half. The fourth wall of the house was the nursery wall so the clothes horse stuck out like a bay window. My child got in by moving one of the walls, but my joy was that you could fold it flat at the end of the day. In those days you could get linoleum and everything you needed so cheaply. Another of my little girls and I once made a little house with the box that the washing machine had come in, cutting windows in the cardboard.

42 · What do three-year-olds enjoy playing with out of doors?

If you have a garden it is fun to have some things to play with in it. By now children are ready for a climbing frame. I like wooden climbing frames, I think the feel of wood is more pleasing than metal or plastic, but it is a personal choice. One of my families had a climbing frame which had two upright ends with a horizontal ladder across it, two swings, a slide and a few hanging ropes. The children liked to crawl across the top so I always stayed with them in case they fell. I found children never attempted things they could not do, so there were fewer injuries than you might imagine, but even so I always watched them. I never had a child fall off a climbing frame and I will not have any pushing – I soon stop that.

Another fun thing for the garden is a large wooden four-wheeled trolley or cart to pull; children put all sorts of things in it. Make sure it is light enough to be easily pulled even with a child in it. I found these lasted for ages as toys, we would collect wood in them for the fire and the children would take each other for rides. It was a great toy. We also always had a lovely solid metal three-wheeler tricycle, not a small two-wheeler with stabilizing wheels or a light plastic three-wheeler, because the solid metal ones are such fun. I think children enjoy them enormously. I would put a strap, like a dog's lead, at the front to pull the child uphill if it was a bit steep, even though he would pedal as well. I would change the strap and put it on the back so that he wouldn't go too fast downhill, too.

Three-year-olds will also enjoy a doll-size pram in which they can push anything, not just dolls. One of my girls had a lovely coach built one, an exact replica of the big one in which I pushed her baby brother.

43 · What do you find a four-year-old enjoys playing with?

The most favourite pastime of all is make-believe and a dressing-up box is the most favourite toy of all. I have never known a child not to like dressing up, especially wearing different hats. I used to keep a big drawer full of all the clothes I would otherwise have thrown out and they used them for dressing up.

Other make-believe activities are shopping, visiting the library and the Post Office. These were all very popular. Even if you haven't got a proper play shop you can save little jars and packets and just glue them back down so they look new and improvise a counter. A girl and her younger brother who I looked after had a proper shop and the small brother and I would have to go shopping as his sister would always be shopkeeper. She used to look at the two of us as we entered her shop and ask me 'Is that your little boy?' Then she'd peer over the counter and condescendingly look down at her brother and say 'Hallo, little boy'. All you need to play shops is a little table and chair and you just set everything out on the counter with pretend money which you can buy or make with a piece of paper and a crayon – just place the paper over the face of the coin and rub with the crayon until the image appears – and a collection of paper bags. The sister also had a library. She stamped all her books with a rubber stamp and lent them out to her brother and me.

Two sisters I took care of loved playing Post Office. They had a proper play set with lots of stamps and envelopes, but you can use cut-up sticky labels

'The most favourite pastime of all is make-believe'

Four to five years

as stamps and draw the Queen's head on them. The elder sister was always the postmistress and the younger sister and I would go as customers with money to buy stamps and stick them on envelopes. We played it such a lot.

Once children are about four they may also like to play hairdressers with their dolls. My children hadn't ever been to a hairdresser, they just did to their doll's hair what I did to theirs. Two of my children had a doll they used to take to the bath every night for a hair wash.

44 · What about making miniature worlds?

All my four-year-old children also loved building, I suppose it is innate in all of us. I always found small wooden bricks (enjoyed when the child is almost five) far easier to use than Lego for making lovely houses; I would say they were essential for a child, Lego an extra. One of my children had Lott's bricks which were a composition of some kind but looked and felt like stone. They were lovely. We also had construction toys to play with. These consisted of wooden pins, like dowelling, and blocks, squares and triangles of plain and polished wood with holes in with which the children made carts, houses, pushchairs, anything really. We also had coloured plastic Meccano.

I used to buy little houses, cars, trees and animals to add to the farmhouse set the children already had. We would set them all out with imagination: we would make a street and then we would put cars and animals and a mirror pond and make our own little village on the top of the nursery table.

45 · What other things would you do with four-year-olds?

From when the children were four I would grow mustard and cress on the nursery window-sill. We would buy a little kit, it was very cheap, and we would snip it off once it had grown and eat the cress in sandwiches at tea. We would also grow beansprouts between blotting paper. We would sometimes grow bulbs in water so we could watch the roots and we would even try and grow orange and apple pips. I once grew some grapefruit pips, but they are not so much fun as they don't grow as quickly, although they do have such beautiful dark green glossy leaves.

On a rainy day we would cook. Children simply love cooking but they need to be well supervised. If they are making something easy, like little cakes or biscuits, we always weighed the ingredients between us and then they mixed them all up in the little bowl. You have to help them but they can do a lot of the mixing and stirring. It was great fun to eat them for tea afterwards. We also played games together. Favourite rainy day games at this age were always snap and picture dominoes, or the traditional kind.

OPPOSITE *Children love playing shops, and if you haven't got a proper shop you can save little jars and packets and improvize a counter*

'Never turn
children
away from
the things
they like'

46 · Will he still enjoy painting?

Your four-year-old will still like painting and modelling but he will now also begin to enjoy making scrap books as well. Children like cutting pictures out of old magazines with a pair of blunt-ended scissors, then putting glue on the pictures and sticking them in a book (see question 47). I always used Gloy paste with a brush, these days wallpaper paste is just as good and you need such a little bit. It was rather messy, but the children wore pinafores and I organized everything carefully. The other thing four-year-olds often enjoy tremendously is making plaster of Paris models although you may find they are still a little young. It is quite an art to fill the rubber mould and peel it off afterwards. One of my girls had a set of Snow White and the Seven Dwarfs which she made over and over again and painted them all with great care. She still remembers it today.

47 · Nanny, what toys did you make for four-year-olds?

For each of my children I made numerous scrapbooks which they (or I) then filled with pictures of whatever they were interested in at the time. I made them on the kitchen table, using large sheets of white cartridge paper which I covered completely using Gloy (or wallpaper) paste and a large brush. Once I had covered the whole paper I took a large piece of cotton bandage gauze (just a little bit bigger than the cartridge paper), stretched it until the gauze covered the entire sheet of paper and then smoothed it out onto the paper – it was awfully sticky. I left it overnight and the next morning it was dry, very stiff and completely untearable. I trimmed the edges and folded it in half and in half again and then cut the bottom so it became a four-page book. I stitched the spine with a needle and cotton using large stitches or I punched two holes in it and threaded a ribbon through.

When one of my boys was four I made a puppet for him using one of those round card cheese boxes with the edges cut off so it became a plain card circle. On one side I made a face using some sticky red pieces of paper, but had I been more artistic I could have painted one. On the other side I stuck the box cover of a box of matches (not the tray). I then cut out a circle of material and cut a small hole in the middle of it and two small holes at each side. I put my hand under the material and pushed my thumb through one little hole, my little finger through the other and my remaining fingers through the middle hole and in through the matchbox. The fabric became the puppet's outfit, my little finger and thumb his arms and my middle fingers controlled his head through the matchbox. It was very simple but with a few of them and a large cardboard box you could put on quite a fun puppet show. I also used to make very simple dolls which were just a stuffed nylon stocking tied tightly around near one end to form the neck and make a head, and then covered with a shift-style outfit.

48 · What do four-year-olds like playing with outdoors?

For the garden my children had a scooter. It was great fun and it helped them learn how to balance. They also had a large tricycle which was ridden until they were five, when they got their first bicycle. When I was a child I had a metal hoop to play with. In the park we would try and roll the hoop with a stick whilst running along beside it. The stick had a hook at the end which we used to catch the hoop. I haven't seen them for a long time. Those metal hoops would be too heavy to hula-hoop with, plastic ones are better and children love to hula-hoop.

Once a child is four I also start swimming with them. I never, ever left a child alone in a swimming pool until they were twelve or thirteen and could swim. If there is a swimming pool in your garden children should *never* ever be allowed near it alone and you should make sure it is impossible for a child to reach the pool without your being there. If a child is with a group of people near the pool then he should always, always have inflated arm bands on, even when he is not near the water. Then even if he fell in, he would bob around like a duck and not drown.

49 · What do you do when children get interested in toys that are crazes?

Once a child is five or six he knows the sort of thing he likes to play with and will tell you. His personality will have begun to develop and he will make it quite clear whether or not he likes playing games, reading or working with his hands. When children get to this age they also begin to develop their own interests. They long to have toys such as Sindy, Barbie, My Little Pony, Carebears, or whatever is the 'in' toy of the moment which none of us like particularly, but it is an interest. Of course other children have these things and they see them at school and on television. Or they may love drawing and want lots of coloured pencils and drawing pads. By all means give your child a My Little Pony, or more coloured pencils, but I would watch my moment and suggest that they tried something new, like skating or roller skating or even skateboarding. Take them to a rink and book a teacher so they learn how to skate or roller skate properly and do not fall over too much. Of course you should help them develop their interests, but why not suggest other things they might not yet have thought of. I would never turn them away from the things they like, you will find the most trivial interests pass and give way to something more substantial.

50 · Do you find that boys and girls are now beginning to become interested in different things?

Yes. By now boys' and girls' interests will be beginning to go in different

Five to six years

'*Restrain yourself from buying too many toys*'

directions. Of course girls will like playing with little cars and clockwork trains and boys will enjoy threading small beads and making necklaces and bracelets. But on the whole girls do find the act of threading more fun than boys do. Girls will be using canvas and wool with a large-eyed needle and sewing things from patterns. They will also be playing a lot with dolls' houses and outside they will be skipping. Together both boys and girls can play with jigsaws as long as they are large and without too many bits; and you can all play old maid, donkey and happy families and your six-year-old will be starting to want to win.

51 · What toys do you make for five-year-olds?

I am not particularly good with my hands but I found even the simplest home-made toys brought a lot of pleasure. My pièce de résistance was the doll's house I made for one girl when she was five. It was a surprise and I kept it hidden in my bedroom so she wouldn't notice it until it was finished. I made it from an orange crate which already had one division and I slid a board in so it had four rooms. I wallpapered the walls with wrapping paper and stuck pictures and mirrors on them made from sticking photos and silver paper on the insides of those plastic lids that used to come on the jam containers you would get on the train. I made some padded sofas and chairs, covering bits of matchboxes with very thin felt and then I made teeny-weeny cushions with bits of brocade. A lid of a toothpaste tube made a lampshade and another a tiny waste-paper bin and I found myself constantly spotting things that had been thrown away. I made the table from an empty cotton reel with a card circle on the top and made table mats out of small pieces of tweed and fringed the edges. A large chest of drawers was constructed out of three matchboxes, using three paper fasteners, with the prongs behind, as knobs. When it was all finished I put it on the floor one night so when my child opened her eyes one morning she saw it. She was so thrilled.

52 · What do five-year-olds enjoy playing with outdoors?

At five children are really too young for their interest in a garden to be properly stimulated. But if you do have a garden, in a year or two you could give them a little bit of the garden which they could call their own and which with supervision they could grow things in. Otherwise they will still enjoy their scooter, and by now all my children were given a bicycle. They will also still be swinging, using their climbing frame and swimming.

Golden rules

Don't be impatient, your child will reach the next stage as soon as he is ready

1   A toy given to a child too early can be frustrating, boring and, sometimes even dangerous.

2   It is pointless to buy toys which you hope will speed up your child's development. No matter how hard you try your child won't be able to do something unless he is ready to.

3   Don't show children how to do things, rather let *them* experiment.

4   Only join in a children's game if they ask you to, not otherwise.

5   Never turn a child away from the toys he likes playing with, you will find all interests change.

6   Remember, each child develops at his own pace. Never tell a child he's 'too old' to play with something. Don't frustrate your child.

Children need fewer rather than more toys to play with

1   To a child, any object is a toy.

2   Make sure each toy has the correct play value for your child. Put away all other toys.

3   Store your child's toys away so he doesn't get bored with looking at them. Just bring out a few different ones every day.

4   Cardboard box trains and other home-made toys can be great fun. They allow the child to use his imagination.

5   Don't make your child wait until school to be able to paint. Let him make a 'mess' at home if he wants to.

8

Weaning to Eating

The great point about feeding children is not to make any fuss, to keep calm about it because otherwise you can start so many phobias. If a child doesn't want to eat something I don't make him. Long ago if a child didn't eat something for breakfast he was given it for lunch and then for tea until he ate it. That sort of thing is best forgotten.

I never remark on it if a child doesn't eat or want to eat; when he wants to he will. For instance, if he is tired or there has been a difficulty or a tantrum or something that has meant he hasn't eaten very much, I don't take any notice. I just give him a little more for his next meal. Children can go for quite a long time before they come to any harm from not eating. By the age of two a child's whole eating behaviour pattern is fairly established. Some children have big appetites and some smaller and I would just follow their lead. I never comment about food or eating while we are at table nor praise a child for eating his food up or suggest he tries 'just one mouthful'.

It is a mistake to be obsessive about anything to do with food, even sticky fingers because then children can become neurotic about it and will always be holding out their hands to be washed. Even in the middle of the meal I knew children who wouldn't finish tea if their hands got sticky, until their hands had been washed. I think that's a rather unhealthy approach. I never minded in the least how sticky their faces or hands were when my children were having meals – I just dealt with it when the meal was finished.

OPPOSITE *At six weeks, very slowly and patiently, I start giving a baby a drink from a cup, that way a child accepts it readily*

1 · When do you first give a baby anything other than milk to drink?

When a child is one month old I introduce greatly, greatly diluted fruit juice which I give him on a small teaspoon at tea-time for a week. After a few weeks I start giving it by cup or a proper little child's mug. This way a cup is introduced very early and a child accepts it readily (see question 27).

When you first introduce a spoon or a mug to a tiny baby you have to make sure he cannot move his arms about. Given the chance he will grab the mug and want to pull it and look at it, so to prevent this I fold a muslin nappy into a triangle and wrap it around the baby so that the long side of the triangle is under his chin. I then make sure the two ends are firmly behind his back so his arms cannot move, not to be unkind, but to keep his hands out of the way. So, there you are with a baby with a mouth and you can introduce him to a spoon and soon a little mug. I hold the baby on my lap with my left arm right around him. In my left hand I have a saucer which I hold under his chin – so everything he doesn't drink drips into the saucer – and in my right hand I have the spoon or cup (I am right-handed) which I rest on his lower lip and from which I gently tip one sip at a time of fruit juice into his mouth making sure he doesn't choke. After a day or two he will be quite used to it.

Of course I make sure that the cup and spoon have had boiling water poured over them and I make the fruit juice with boiled water, leaving it to become body temperature (see FEEDING, question 31) before giving it to the baby.

2 · At what age should I start giving my baby vitamins and fluoride?

I gave all my bottle-fed babies vitamins once they were six weeks old and my breast-fed babies vitamins once they stopped being breast-fed. We never gave a breast-fed baby supplementary vitamins, because breast milk was reckoned to be perfect food. I believe that now vitamins are recommended for both bottle-fed and breast-fed babies from six months to two years unless they are not good feeders in which case they might be introduced earlier and continued till five years.

In the first year of a child's life he would have his vitamins every day. After that I gave children vitamins from September to April or May until they were five. I always felt that stopping and then starting the vitamins again in winter would give the children an extra boost. I would give them the vitamin drops, following the instructions on the packet as to how much they needed, in the bath in case it spilt as it would stain clothes. I also gave my children fluoride drops and later tablets if our dentist said it was necessary.

3 · At what age shall I start giving my baby milk in a cup?

Whether the baby is breast or bottle fed, at five months I begin to introduce milk

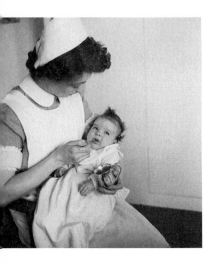

Feeding Nina with a spoon

in a cup at the 10 a.m. feed. By then the baby may well weigh, for example 5.4 kg (12lb) – some much more, some a little less – and is getting 850 ml (30 fl oz) milk a day to drink, 170 ml (6 fl oz) ounces in each bottle. I still make up the five bottles of formula as usual but just pour the milk in the 10 a.m. bottle into a cup, a little at a time, before feeding the baby and offer it that way. If you normally breast feed you would make up just one 170 ml (6 fl oz) bottle of formula (or however much your baby needed, see FEEDING, question 27) which you would give your baby at 10 a.m.

Compared to the bit of fruit juice they are used to this is a lot for a baby to drink from a cup and you have to be patient and keep pouring the milk back into the cup from the saucer (see question 1). It does exhaust them. So start, see how much they will take from the cup, and if they begin to lose heart give them the rest of the milk in the bottle or from the breast.

4 · When do you start giving other feeds from a cup?

At six months I give the baby his 2 p.m. feed from a cup as well. By now he has had a few weeks of taking one feed (see question 3) from the cup so I try and encourage him to hold the cup with me. He is still sitting on my lap, but now wears a large bib to protect his clothes, leaving his arms free. I hold the base of the cup so the handle is free for him to hold. A month later I start giving the 6 p.m. feed in a cup as well (see questions 7–9).

Starting solids

5 · At what age do you start giving solid food?

I was taught only to give children solid food once they were nine months old, but I always start at six months. I believe the current recommendations are that you should start introducing solids at four months. Of course, babies are individuals and you should always keep an eye out for whether or not your baby still appears satisfied with his feeds or if he is starting to demand food between feeds more often. If he seems to be getting hungry then I would start him on solids. Nowadays people do wean their children much earlier than I was taught, though like most fashions it swings back and forwards. At one stage children were given solid food almost the moment they were born. I begin at the midday (2 p.m.) or lunchtime feed, literally with one teaspoonful as an introduction. Before their cup of milk (see question 4) I give them one teaspoonful of cooked, sieved apple purée and I have never yet met a baby who did not like it. I put a little sugar in if the apple is very sour, but not otherwise. I then give them their cup of milk. Very soon the baby enjoys the newly introduced food and in a day or two you can increase the amount to two or three teaspoonfuls once a day.

You can judge for yourself how hungry your baby is. I would give them that first teaspoonful, making it up to three teaspoonfuls once a day, at 2 p.m., for a week. Then, after a week I would start introducing cooked, sieved carrot, or spinach purée to ring the changes. I monitor all new foods carefully to make sure the baby is not allergic to them. We had a baby where I was trained who always vomited potato; her mother could not eat potato either. Sometimes a baby might be sick when they have eaten a food they cannot digest.

Once the baby has eaten solids at his 2 p.m. feed for two weeks I would introduce a little cereal at the 10 a.m. breakfast meal where the baby is already on a cup. I would start with three to four teaspoons and let the child decide if they want more or less. I always gave my children baby rice cereal, made without sugar, just with milk taken from their feed. It means they will eat some of their feed rather than drinking it. Then I give them the rest of their feed in the cup.

After a week of cereal at 10 a.m., I give them a little baby rice cereal in the evening at the 6 p.m. feed, again mixed with their milk. I start with three to four teaspoons, as above, and work up slowly. Then I give them their bottle.

Introducing a cup to a young baby, very gently, one sip at a time

6 · My baby screams and screams after his feed and most of the day. What's wrong, Nanny?

Once some babies have tasted their first teaspoon of food, they want more. If your baby cries all the time when he first discovers solids he may well be hungry. Give him more food. Be guided by your baby. When a brother and sister I knew were weaned from the breast, one at four months, the other at five, they both cried solidly all day, neither of them having cried much before. For the first few days their mother thought the food must have disagreed with them, but then she tried giving them more food and they both ate a small plateful three times a day. They must have been starving.

7 · My baby is sleeping later in the morning, do I wake him for his 6 a.m. feed or leave him to sleep?

Very often by seven months the baby is sleeping longer so you can substitute both the 6 a.m. and 10 a.m. feeds for an 8 a.m. breakfast with cereal and milk (see FEEDING, question 26) in a cup. If the baby still wakes up at 6 a.m. and cries and seems hungry I would continue to give him the 6 a.m. bottle or his usual breast feed, and then put him back to bed. If he then sleeps on and misses his 8 a.m. breakfast he can have it at 10 a.m. or whenever he wakes and has been washed and dressed.

Lunch could then be at around 1 or 2 p.m. offering a savoury first course (see question 8) and then a little pudding, such as semolina; I would make this with homogenized and pasteurized cow's milk and serve it with either raw or cooked fruit puréed. At 5.30 or 6 p.m. I would then give him more baby rice cereal and a drink of milk from a cup; this is when I start giving the 6 p.m. feed in a cup. If he can't manage to drink all the milk in the cup, I put the rest in the bottle for him to drink. And at 10 p.m. the baby would have his 230 ml (8 fl oz) bottle of formula milk (see question 9) or his breast feed.

8 · What sort of food will my baby like at lunch time?

Once the baby has been having solids for a month you can start giving him a more adventurous midday meal. I don't think babies mind what they eat at this stage – they will happily suck soap – unless they are allergic to it. I think they may first notice bitter tastes; I have observed a baby screwing up his face in distaste when needing medication. But up to two years babies eat and drink most things – after that they sometimes protest and people say 'I can't understand it – he used to eat it.' I think the taste buds develop then.

What is important is that they are fed a balanced diet. Suitable foods at this age for the small baby are eggs (although some children are allergic to them – one of my boys came out in a kind of eczema rash on his face if ever he ate egg so I kept him off eggs until he was a year old and then tried again), white fish, chicken, liver, potatoes, rice, root vegetables, prunes, apricots, peaches etc. (see questions 13 and 14). Food was cooked simply and thoroughly, often steamed; fish, liver and chicken were all poached rather than roasted.

You can either use bought jars and tins of baby food which are expensive or you can make your own food. I have always thought that jars and tins are much better for the baby because they are made under hygienic conditions and the food is very concentrated. When I cook, half the goodness goes up in steam and the other half goes down the drain, although this is avoidable if you steam baby's food or use a pressure cooker. Possibly the simplest solution, when a meal for the family is being prepared, is to take a little of this and that before any seasoning is added and purée the baby's lunch from this. I have heard of some mothers cooking food for their babies and putting it into an ice cube tray and then into the deep freeze. When they need a little they can just push out the food from one of the cubes and have a portion of the right size which they then heat up. It sounds like a very good idea (see question 11).

9 · *What do I feed my baby now he is eight months old?*

Once a baby is eight months old I stop the 6 a.m. and 10 a.m. feeds altogether and move on to breakfast at 8 a.m. with cereal, usually baby rice cereal, mixed with milk and then a cup of milk (see FEEDING, question 26). So, if the baby is by now 6.8 kg (15 lb), he is getting four feeds of 230 ml (8 fl oz) of milk a day (8 a.m., 1 p.m., 5.30 p.m. and 10 p.m.), although at breakfast and lunch some of the milk will either be given on cereal or in puddings. He would get approximately the same if he was around 1 kg (2 lb) lighter or heavier; at this stage you go more by age than by weight, although obviously a hungry baby will be given more milk than a not so hungry baby. You must judge for yourself. Never leave a baby hungry and never force one to eat. You can tell if a child is hungry. You have finished giving him the pudding and he turns to you in disbelief and starts crying. You will know when to give him more.

10 · *Once my baby is nine months old does he need as much milk as before?*

By the time a baby is nine months, the importance of milk in his diet has diminished. People used to say children should have 600 ml (1 pint) of milk a day and if they didn't like it you should make milk puddings, but I never followed that. By the time a child is nine months if he is eating a good balanced diet you need no longer worry about the precise amount of milk he is getting.

> *'Never leave a baby hungry and never force one to eat'*

At nine months, as a baby is now more or less having breakfast, lunch and tea, I stop all his bottle or breast feeds. I never give a baby a bottle after nine months; instead when he wakes in the morning I give him a drink of fruit juice in a cup. Then breakfast is some time between 8.00 and 8.30 a.m. and consists of baby rice cereal made with milk (see FEEDING, question 26), a bit of toast or a crust to chew with a little butter or margarine, honey, yeast spread or golden syrup and 110–140 ml (4–5 fl oz) of milk in a mug. Lunch is now any time between 12 and 1.00 p.m. and the baby has a savoury course of fish, liver, egg or chicken mixed with two vegetables (see question 8) and a sweet course of a milk pudding, with cool

Enjoying every last crumb

boiled or bottled water to drink. At this stage I still sieve their food if I cook it myself, I don't like too large lumps in it.

Tea is around 4 to 5 p.m. when I would introduce rusks and crusts and little sandwiches with a yeast spread or honey or jam filling for the baby to eat with his fingers. You can go by the child as to how many little postage stamp sized sandwiches they can eat and how much milk they want to drink. I also give them a little fresh or stewed fruit or a bowl of baby rice cereal depending on their appetite. I don't then give them anything more until the next morning.

'Never suggest he tries "just one more mouthful"'

11 · Should I serve foods separately so my baby will be able to see all the different things he is eating?

When we cooked for babies we used a Mouli or sieve to put all the child's food through until he was eighteen months or so – possibly a little over, because children don't chew, they just swallow things. Tummies are tough and can cope with pieces of food, but we were taught to sieve and mash. I know mothers now are more likely to use an electric blender to purée their babies' food.

Children develop at different stages and when you are little food is just food. I never thought it mattered if different foods were mixed together. When you are older there will be a few little piles on a child's plate, but why rush it? We certainly mixed up the foods of their savoury course until they were about two and the sweet course also. Sometimes, to encourage a baby to try something new or eat something he did not especially like, we would even mix the courses as we were feeding him so he would eat a teaspoon of milk pudding, followed quickly by a teaspoon of chicken and carrot, and then quickly back again to the milk pudding.

12 · At what age will my child stop needing especially prepared food?

Once the child was three our cooking became slightly more sophisticated. We weren't so worried about steaming or poaching food, we would give them roast meats and casseroles, wholesome food. They would begin eating the same food as a grown-up, within reason. When he was three I would begin giving a child a cooked breakfast with bacon or scrambled or boiled egg served with fried bread which people scorn now but which is delicious. I might give him herring or kippers or smoked haddock, sometimes with a poached egg. And bread and butter or toast with honey. Sometimes children would have porridge (with milk and salt, never sugar) or muesli but I have always felt cereals did not have enough nutritional value. I always found that on the whole children enjoyed a good breakfast. They had had tea at 4.30 p.m., so it was a long wait to breakfast and I suppose they were hungry.

Healthy eating

13 · What foods do you consider essential?

I think a child should be given as large a selection of foods as possible. He should have plenty of fruit, milk, meat, fish, vegetables (especially green ones), pulses (peas, beans and lentils), eggs (three a week maximum) and bread (always stoneground wholemeal). In fact a good mixture of foods, well-balanced, not too much of one or the other. Yeast extract is very good for children (and most like it) as are oranges and spinach and liver. A lot of children don't like liver so I always cooked it in the pressure cooker, minced it and served it with mashed potatoes and gravy. You can always disguise the taste with a little yeast extract (see question 17). Until a child was two we used to give him a lot of offal (especially brains and tripe) and herring – fish is always good. My children always had very simple food which I suppose is not a bad thing.

Watch out for any cravings your child seems to have, they might point out a deficiency in his diet which he is attempting to balance himself. When one of my girls was little she used to eat the blackboard chalk and the shell of her boiled eggs. It was as though her body was telling her that extra calcium was what she needed – to this day she has trouble with her teeth – no doubt she did need extra calcium (see question 16).

14 · Are there any foods that you don't give children?

When I was trained there were many foods that were considered to be bad for children: pastry and cheese were reckoned to be indigestible, and only to be introduced to a child's diet at the age of five. Now they give babies cheese almost the moment they are delivered. We were taught never to give fried or highly seasoned food although children quite often like it.

Cucumber was also considered indigestible. In order to eat it we would peel it and place it in a basin with a heavy plate over it so that the liquid could be drained away. It was then served to children. Bananas were never to be given to small babies for the same reason although by the time a child was two, mashed bananas were considered acceptable. Ham and bacon we first gave children at five, pork we were taught never to give little children. Sweetcorn and currants were frowned upon as they stay whole. Baked beans which are now considered very nutritious and used a great deal we also never gave children. We gave them butter beans and kidney beans.

I would also avoid letting children fill up to the top with starchy foods, such as puddings and other sweet things. I do find that children on the whole take what they need but especially if they were a little on the heavy side (see question 22) I would watch that they did not eat too much sugar and starch. All in all I give children very, very little added sugar – if they never have it, they don't miss it.

15 · Should I forbid certain foods?

I never actually forbid a child any food although on principle I am against sweets. I would not forbid them, but I do not introduce them and my children do not demand them. I think if you don't treat sweets as anything special children are not particularly interested. If you forbid sweets (or anything else) they become like stolen fruit, children want them all the time and may eat secretly. If aunts or visitors produced sweets I would allow the gift but if asked I always said 'No chocolate before the baby is two years old'. I must say I was always able to keep the rule for the first child but when the next one saw chocolate, chocolate buttons or whatever, the older baby invariably gave a chocolate button to the sibling, and one could not forbid them. If a child is given some chocolates I would always keep them in a safe place and only hand them out at the end of tea, otherwise they do ruin the child's appetite.

Ice-cream is another treat and I think to give one to a child when they know it is a treat is fun, but I wouldn't give a child an ice-cream or ice lolly before they were at least two and a half and then only when we were at the seaside. I preferred those little tubs with spoons to cornets as they were much less messy. But I don't really like all this licking in the street and licking in the park. People give children ice lollies far too young and you see them standing there with the lolly dribbling down their arms. Often it is too overwhelming for the child. If they are standing there not licking the ice-cream, I would simply say 'Shall I hold it?' and then try and dispose of it quietly.

16 · Does it matter if my child refuses to eat?

I always offer children food and then if they don't want it, they just don't eat anything. I never offer them anything else that isn't planned in their diet for the day. If an indulgent grandparent wants to do that, let them. Once in a while won't hurt. But I do think the less fuss the better. I just serve them their first course and if they don't eat that I give them their pudding when we all have ours and then that is that. I find it extraordinary that some people won't let a child have his pudding just because he has not eaten his first course. Why not? It's all part of the food. Nature tells children what they need to eat.

Quite often, one day they will eat a lot of one thing and reject another and another day they might eat a lot of what they previously refused. You can leave it a lot to children what they want to eat. They will know what they need, provided it is offered to them. And I always offer them some more once they have finished eating or even if they have just finished all their meat and still have some vegetables left. I would then ask them if they wanted any more meat. I would certainly not mention the fact that they hadn't finished their vegetables.

> '*I don't really like all this licking in the street*'

209

17 · Nanny, my toddler will only eat bread and peanut butter, does it matter?

I once knew a nanny who looked after three children, the eldest of which ate only ice-cream. That couldn't be entirely true, but she probably ate very, very little else. Of course, she grew up and survived. We make a great deal of fuss about having a well-balanced diet and giving children a good selection of food, but children do survive even though they go through periods of disliking certain foods.

It takes a lot of cunning as a cook to get children to eat what they don't want to and mostly it's impossible (see question 11). A baby who doesn't like fish can taste it through most disguises. Yeast spread is a great disguiser of tastes and very useful. I know many mothers offer tomato ketchup as a sort of bribe, although I have never introduced it.

I have heard of people occasionally offering the child the pudding first if they want it and then giving them the first course later. I don't think I'd make a habit of that but every now and again it doesn't do any harm. No one makes an adult eat food he does not want to eat, so why make a child?

18 · Do you make a child finish everything on his plate?

No, I do not. One thing that drives me mad is children being forced to eat food they don't want. If he says he does not want any more I just say 'Well, put your spoon down then'. I never ever make a child finish what is on his plate. I think it's very important to have respect for the child's point of view. What's the point of saying to a child 'Why don't you just *try* a tiny bit of carrot or one sprout?' Let him make up his own mind. If he does not want to eat his carrot then why make him. I think some adults enjoy the feeling of power over a child and I do not approve of that at all. I think it is very cruel.

It's amazing how little food children can exist on, and they won't starve. One of my boys once said to me 'When I have children I won't make them eat vegetables'. I never made him but he had to when he ate with other people. He always had his vitamin drops and I would never have forced him or any of my children to eat things they didn't want to eat (see question 16).

19 · How do you stop children drinking between meals and ruining their appetite?

If children are left to do as they please they will drink a lot. I give the child a drink of fruit juice first thing in the morning and then when I have a cup of tea at elevenses I would hand him a cup of fruit juice. Apart from that I never give children fruit juice to drink between meals unless he is ill and needs to drink.

If it is a hot day then I offer the child a glass of water but nothing else. Of course if he is very thirsty and asks for a drink then I give him one. I don't give children a drink during a meal unless they ask for one. I only produce a drink of water at the end of the meal or they get so full of water they have no room for food. I have seen children being given bottles or trainer cups full of fruit juice to carry around with them so they can be continually drinking. If a child gets in the habit of drinking out of a proper cup (see question 1), then he sits down at the table to drink, he doesn't carry his drink around with him. Not only does drinking a lot of fruit juice from a straw or a bottle ruin the child's appetite, it also is not good for his teeth. If the child is used to drinking fruit juice twice a day from a cup, that is all he will want.

20 · *Do you ever give children anything to eat between meals?*

No. I have never had a child asking for a biscuit or anything else. Of course if a visiting child asks for a biscuit I will give one, but only one. I would never make a habit of it.

21 · *Do you ever ask a child what he wants to eat?*

On birthdays I always allow children to choose what they want for lunch, but not on other days. I would never get into the situation where a child constantly says he wants something else to eat other than what he has been offered. If he scrapes his plate clean or finishes all his vegetables I would offer him some more, especially if he was an ill child and I noticed he felt he needed vitamins or whatever. But I would never say 'Would you like this?' or 'Would you like that?' or 'What flavour yoghourt would you like?' I would never offer things before or during the meal. Keep things simple (see BEHAVING, question 2).

22 · *What do I do if my child is becoming overweight?*

Even if a weaning baby is a little overweight I would still give him a little cereal if he liked it and one or two rusks a day to chew as well as fruit, meat and vegetables. If the parents are not fat I am sure the child would begin to thin down after a year. I did know somebody who used to give her child only half a bottle because he was a fat baby, but you cannot do this to a child, you really cannot.

Obviously you would feed your overweight child sensibly, no biscuits and no cake. I never give a child extra sugar on cereal or fruit or anything like that, there is sugar already in many foods but I never add it and if they don't know it they don't expect it. Once when I was away a temporary nanny put sugar on my children's food and of course they enjoyed it but I stopped it on my return and

'No one makes an adult eat food he does not want . . . so why make a child?'

they continued without sugar. I never myself provide sweets or chocolates at all (see question 15).

If a child is only moderately overweight it is most likely simply his nature. Of course if he is absolutely gross you would seek medical advice. There may be a problem of some kind which needs attention.

Sitting up to eat

OPPOSITE Over four, I like putting children in long-legged chairs so they eat at the correct level. An older child may enjoy sitting on them when they come to tea

Nina in her old-fashioned wooden highchair

23 · *When do I start using a highchair?*

Up to eight months a baby will have been eating and drinking sitting on my knee which means that I really have to feed him either before or after myself and the other children because you cannot serve people and have a baby on your knee. So, it is only once the baby first sits in the highchair at eight months and begins to join us for meals that we can all eat together. I have seen people put younger babies in a highchair, but they keep sliding down so I would not do that myself.

I start using a harness, the same kind of straps as I use in a pram, and I keep a child strapped into the highchair – fastened at the back – until he is two and a half years old. I once heard of a child who stood up and fell out of his chair and broke his arm; these things can so easily happen in a matter of seconds.

The old-fashioned wooden highchairs we always had were so wide at the bottom and took up so much room that parents were anxious to get rid of them. They were very useful though because they hinged in the middle and would bend in half until the base turned into a table and it became a little joined-together table and chair. The highchairs you buy today are of course more convenient though more difficult to keep clean. Some can be folded completely away which is handy if you haven't got much space. Others can also be turned into a table and separate chair by dividing in half. This is useful because children like ringing the changes.

Once the child is three I remove the tray from the highchair and push the chair against the table. You can buy plastic boxes nowadays that allow children to sit on an adult chair, but why buy an extra piece of equipment when their old highchair will do unless, of course, you have a new baby to put in the highchair (see question 24).

24 · *Does my toddler really still need to be in a highchair?*

There is such a fuss made about children 'graduating' from highchairs. A highchair is fun. You'll quite often find that eight-year-old children coming to lunch will want to sit on the child's highchair and you should let them do so. It's an exploration for them and they find it very interesting. It's not at all 'babyish'

I don't mind if a young child makes a little mess when she eats — what does it matter? Good table manners come later

(see introduction to PLAYING). I've seen so many children put in ordinary chairs far too early and they wiggle about and fall off and it is so difficult for them to eat when they can only just see above the table. I keep my children in a highchair for a very long time, until they are about four, depending on their size, because I think it much easier for a child to eat from a higher vantage point rather than having his little chin resting on the table.

Once the child is four I take him out of his highchair and put him in a chair which looks like an adult chair except it has much longer legs. They look like long-legged miniature Windsor chairs. It means he can feed himself at a correct level and also feel part of the party. I believe that around the beginning of the century all hand-made dining room sets of chairs would include several matching long-legged chairs for the children of the family. I think they are an excellent idea.

25 · What did you take for the child to sit on when you went out for tea?

Once the child was old enough to sit in a highchair we also bought little folding chairs which we used until the child was two. They were very useful – we all took them with us. They had a little tray in front when they were opened and they could either be used on the ground in the park for a picnic – I don't approve of children sitting on the grass and getting wet bottoms – or they could be hung from the backs of large chairs when we went out to tea with friends, or from the car seat. They had long, rubber-covered hooks which meant they would not scratch the wood or upholstery. I've seen little collapsible chairs that hook onto tables that you can buy today but very often the table won't accommodate them and they certainly can't be used on their own in the park. Today it seems you need many different chairs: a plastic box seat for visiting friends' tea-tables, a car seat for the car and, I suppose, a park bench for the picnic.

Nina in her folding chair in the park

26 · At what age will my child start feeding himself?

Feeding himself

At nine months I give a child food he can easily hold to eat with his fingers (see question 10). I wouldn't give him anything like banana, although I know they do nowadays, because it can easily slip out of his fingers and might be frustrating for him. At this age I also begin helping him to use a spoon. We eat with two spoons, I have one and he has one. You will notice him turning the spoon over just as it is about to go in his mouth. I do not correct him immediately but let him carry on for a while unless he gets exasperated; only then do I guide the spoon into his mouth. I think adult aggression directed at children at the table is really the cause of a lot of neuroses.

I let him play with the food and try and feed himself as best he can. One of my children had a dish with a suction thing at the bottom to keep it in place but he found it very frustrating as it meant he couldn't pull the plate closer. I just hold the dish firmly on the tray so he can't hurl it, but otherwise I always had a big sheet of plastic on the floor under the highchair so the child could make as much mess as he liked.

Some children cotton on to feeding themselves very quickly and some take ages. I remember one of my girls used to 'wash' her hands in her food, she would rub them together in her plate until they were coated with food. I just wiped them clean at the end of the meal. A nine-month-old baby needs a teaspoon sized spoon with as short a handle as possible so he is not forever poking himself in the eye.

'What does a little mess matter?'

They now make baby's spoons with curved handles. I think they are quite unnecessary, but if someone has given you one, you might as well use it.

I wouldn't trust a child under eighteen months not to throw his plate away, but after that he should be able to eat quite happily. I would then begin to cut food up into small pieces rather than purée it as an eighteen-month-old child should be able to feed himself alone using a combination of teaspoon and fingers. I usually keep an eye on children of this age, just to see they are eating enough food. If the food does spill I help them feed themselves until they get better at it. By the time a child is two years old I begin to give him little helpings of food so he can see all the foods separately and knows what he is eating.

27 · At what age will my child be able to drink from a cup on his own?

When helping a baby learn to drink from a cup I never use those plastic mugs with a spout (see question 1). I have always had a proper cup and I have actually always had a *silver* cup which does sound rather grand, but it was simply because most of my children were given one at their christening. Silver cups are wonderful – they do not break when they are thrown and they keep warm liquids warm and cold ones cold for a very long time. Of course plastic does not break either but it does not taste as nice. If you give a child a trainer mug then he has to learn to use that as well, so I think, 'Well, why not go straight to a proper cup and cut out one extra bit of unnecessary learning?' By one year a child will normally try and hold his cup by himself and invariably he will wobble and spill a little. By the time he is eighteen months he will usually be able to drink from a proper cup holding it himself.

28 · When do I give my child adult utensils instead of a teaspoon?

I have come across children who have been given adult utensils, such as dessert spoons and forks, as young as two. A child of this age cannot manage unwieldy cutlery designed for adults, then they are told off and it is all so sad. If they can enjoy their food and eat it easily with a spoon, then why not? My children always ate with a spoon until they were at least three, and by the time they were heading for four I gave them a fork to eat with as well. It is only when a child gets to be five that I first give him a knife and show him how to use his knife and fork properly, and if he cannot cope with it then I take it away. There are no firm rules, I just give children what they can cope with. I would always cut up meat and sausages for children, if they ask to do it themselves then of course I give them a small knife so they can try. If they find they cannot manage then I simply offer to help. At the age of five I also give children a napkin and start trying to help them with their table manners (see questions 32–40).

Pushers seem a good idea but I have rarely seen them used. I think the idea was that the child used them to push the food onto the spoon but I think it might be difficult for a child to use. Scooping up the food with a spoon comes naturally, but using the scooper is a more complicated motion and one I would not worry about. You don't need to buy those special children's plastic teaspoons either, your baby will be able to manage perfectly well with an ordinary small metal teaspoon.

29 · Do you wash a child's hands before or after eating? *Cleanliness*

I always wash a baby's hands and face after a meal, and those of older children beforehand. Once children can wash their hands themselves I always ask them if they have remembered to do so and if they haven't I ask them to do it. Most children, even ten-year-olds, need reminding. But I never mind who washes their hands. If they want to do it themselves, why not? As long as their hands are clean it is all that matters. I always kept it casual, and automatic.

30 · Do you mind if children make a mess when eating?

When some people first start feeding babies with a spoon, they will automatically wipe off the excess on the baby's chin after each bite. I would never, ever do that. I think perhaps it gives the children a feeling that they shouldn't have food stuck on their faces, but I think eating should be enjoyed without having to be thinking about one's face. Some children mind so terribly when their faces are wiped. I think it must be children who get mopped up all the time or whose tender faces are treated roughly, because none of my children ever minded. It is a great thing to be relaxed – what does a little mess matter? (see question 26).

31 · How do you stop a child getting food all over his clothes?

What's wrong with bibs? Why are people so against their children wearing bibs? I dislike hearing people say 'You're too big for a bib'. Well, who is too big for a bib? Why has it become a crime or a sin for a child past the age of two to wear one? Adults have napkins with quite a few foods that are difficult to eat and a bib is really just like a napkin except that it is tied on. One of my children had a big bib or pinafore or overall until he was five because he was always spilling food. I only gave a child a napkin once he was five and if it kept falling onto the floor I would pin it on so it was available to him without being a nuisance. Until then I always put nice big towelling bibs, or what I call 'feeders', on children and I certainly never scolded a child for spilling food on his bib – what else is it for?

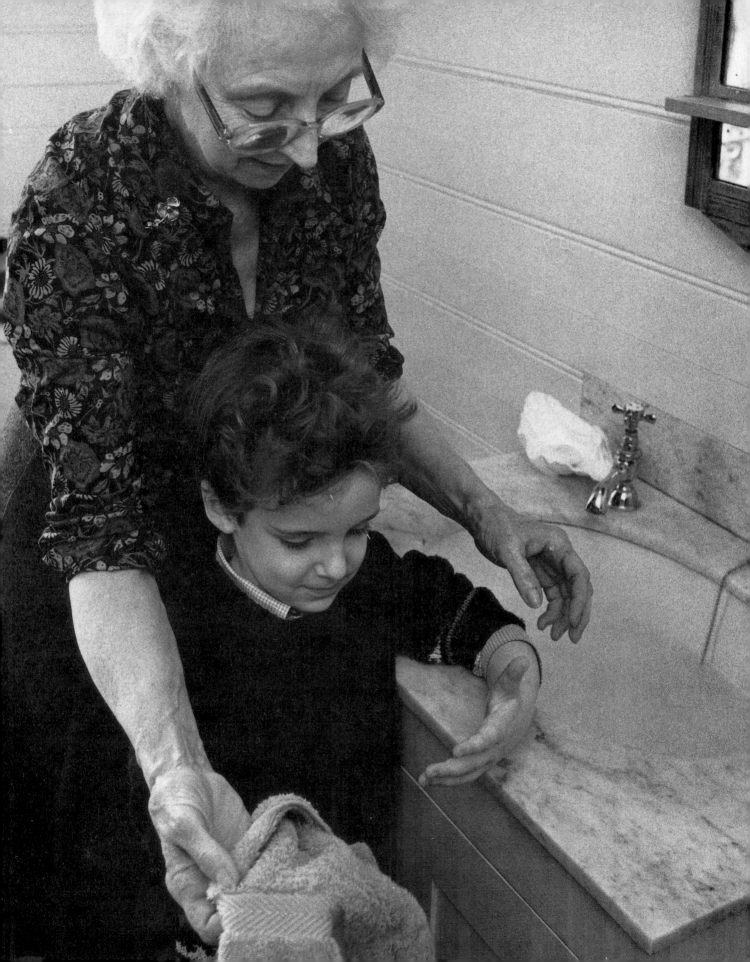

32 · Why do you think table manners are so important?

I think most table manners have evolved from a worry as to what would happen if . . . ? For instance hot soup tipped towards a lap could scald it, elbows on the table might knock things over and too much food stuffed into a child's mouth could make him choke. Fortunately children normally just spit the food out as they cannot chew it, but that is not very elegant, so I would tell them not to put too much in their mouths in the first place. I would never get angry and say 'That's very rude', I might say 'I wouldn't push so much in or you might choke'. I think the most basic table manners are about safety.

33 · Do you worry whether a child will ever have 'good' table manners?

Having good table manners shows consideration for others and of course one wants a child to acquire them. However, I have always believed you needn't be repressive about teaching manners; children brought up in a civilized atmosphere will become civilized too. I work on the idea that manners are learnt by example – that children copy. I learnt my manners at home from my parents who had the most excellent table manners and my children learnt their manners from copying me. Once children were two I always ate my meals with them (that is why all nannies eat so quickly, you have to finish your food first so you can cope with the children afterwards) and I always found that after the age of three children very quickly had civilized behaviour at table.

There are some manners you cannot teach children, they will learn them as they grow up, but they can pick up a lot from watching you (see BEHAVING, questions 22–24). That's why it is so important that the adults sharing the table with the child should have good manners themselves. If you put your elbow on the table then why shouldn't he?

34 · From what age can I expect my child to have good table manners?

I certainly never do very much about table manners before the age of three. Before then all you can try and do is very simple things like making sure your child does not try and drink when he has got a mouth full of food or that he does not choke from taking in too much food at a time.

It is only when children become five that I start making them use their utensils properly and pay a little more notice to the way they are eating. But as with everything in child raising, the best thing is not to fuss too much. I would never say to a child of any age 'Close your mouth when you are eating!' or 'Don't drink with a full mouth!' Instead I would just gently say 'Can you swallow your food before you tell me because I can't hear when your mouth is full of food' and 'Why

OPPOSITE *I always remind older children to wash their hands before a meal and I help them if they want me to*

2 1 9

not wait until your mouth is empty and then let's have a drink'. I would never pounce on a child or fuss too much or I might put the child off eating – although probably only temporarily.

35 · *Do you do anything to help your child learn good manners, or do you think they are all learnt by example?*

Even though children will learn from the way you eat, you do have to gently remind them even when they are quite old. Some manners can only be learnt as a child gets older anyway – eating soup, for example. A three-year-old will scoop soup up as if it were pudding, so I would only begin to teach him to eat soup at six or seven. It is only when he is a little older and you can say 'Try and do it the way I do it, that's the correct way', that it is worth beginning. Even then, at first, I would hold the bowl for them and they would scoop the soup up. I would also help things along by always serving a thin soup in a mug and a thick soup in a bowl.

It is good manners for children to sit with their hands in their laps when they have finished eating, but I would only start encouraging a child to do so when he was three or four. I might simply say 'Just take your elbow off' or otherwise explain 'Be careful with your elbow as you might knock something off'. If I was sitting next to the child, I might not even say anything but just gently take his elbows off the table and put his hands on his knee.

I always taught children to take a biscuit or sandwich or little cake from any tray offered to them and put it on their plates first, not straight into their mouths. They were taught to do this with their right hand, then eat it with their left, reserving the right hand for holding the cup.

I also made sure they put food, like sandwiches, back down on their plate between bites rather than holding it. This is especially important if a child is eating a chocolate biscuit or cake which is melting in his hands. I would just remind him by saying 'Why not put it on your plate so that it does not get too sticky in your fingers'. If he does not want to put it down I would just gently take it from his hand myself and say 'Come on, let's put it down or it will get rather squashy'. I never keep going on about it.

36 · *Nanny, do you allow children to take toys to the table?*

No, I don't allow toys to be brought to the table. The question never arose. If a child was loath to leave a favourite or new toy when it was time to eat I would put it where the child could see it and explain 'When you have finished breakfast, you shall play with it'. I have sometimes given teddy a chair near the table, but never allowed a car or train on the table.

37 · How do you stop a child putting too much food on his plate?

I see children at parties filling their plates with food, but they can never eat it all. I always used to stand behind my children at a party and simply pass them one sandwich at a time. If I was gossiping to my chums, then the child would help himself to a single sandwich – he would never pile his plate full of food. I wonder why children do it? Is it the way they are served at home? Or are they just not used to having anyone offer them a plate of food? If I am passing the platter of sandwiches and a child takes too many I just say 'You can have another one, you don't need to take two now' but if children stack their plates with potato crisps and twiglets I do get a bit fierce. I remove most of them and say 'You don't need to have so many now'. I find it terrible when children stack their plates full of food and only eat about one-third of it.

38 · At a tea-party do you mind if they eat the biscuits before the sandwiches?

When biscuits appear there are always a few rather fierce nannies who say 'No. You can't have a biscuit before you have finished your sandwich', but I would never do that. I might finish my child's sandwich myself so that he could have something else; after all, the sandwich might not have been what he wanted. Or, if I don't want the sandwich, I just let him leave the sandwich on the side of his plate and have the biscuit (see questions 16–18).

39 · What do you do if children start throwing their food?

To me, food-throwing is an obscenity, I really mind it so much. I am not sure why children do it, although I do think that often for children dumped at tea-parties without anyone in charge of them the tea-table sadly seems to have become a playground. If I see children throwing food I immediately tell them to stop it and if they do not I very firmly remove the ringleader from the table and from the room and tell him off in private. I would have no nonsense about it at all. I would simply make him sit down on a chair in another room and forbid him to get up. I do not threaten him with going home because you should never threaten a child with something you cannot carry out (see BEHAVING, question 9). But there is always a ringleader and it is him you should take aside.

40 · When do you let a child get down from the table?

I rarely let children get down from the table until everyone has finished eating, and so they never asked to because they were used to staying there. It's so

'Children brought up in a civilized atmosphere will become civilized too'

disruptive to have some children running around when others are still eating. If I had to feed an eight- or nine-month-old baby first and was therefore a little behind with finishing my own food, I would give the baby a little rusk to nibble at, because otherwise it is very boring for him to sit and wait whilst I eat my meal.

One exception that I would make was that I might let a toddler get up once he had eaten his meal as it does make him fed up always having to wait at table for a younger sibling. I think, as with everything, one must be flexible. A baby of not yet three years waiting ages for a nine-month sibling would be a case in point.

I would also make an exception if there was a child who was a very, very slow eater and you really could not expect other children to wait for him as he could take up to one hour over his meal. Quite often these slow eaters are great talkers; I found that if I got down as well as the other children they would have to eat their meal because there was no one left to talk to.

Golden rules

When a child wants to eat, he will

1 Don't talk about what your child is eating even to praise or to encourage – the less fuss the better.

2 It's a mistake to be obsessive about anything to do with food. Aggression at the table is the cause of a lot of neuroses.

3 Never leave a baby hungry and never force one to eat.

4 If a child misses a meal just give him a little more at his next meal.

A child expects what he is used to

1 Introduce a cup early and your child will readily accept it.

2 If children never have sugar they never miss it.

3 A highchair is fun – why call it 'babyish'? With an ordinary chair a child's nose is on the table.

4 Always see that a child's hands are washed before a meal. Keep it casual – and automatic.

Eating should be enjoyed

1 Be patient and relaxed. What does a little mess matter?

2 Don't scold a child for getting food on his clothes – or on his bib. What are bibs for?

3 At first the only manners that matter are those that concern a child's safety.

4 Never make a child finish what is on his plate.

9

Behaving

There is always the child who will have behaviour problems, no matter what his home is like; often they are part of his make-up and he will have been born with them. But in this situation the home background can contribute to making things better – or worse. Although it is far better for him to have a safe home with a well-balanced background of one male and one female parent, if a child cannot have this I do not think it matters terribly, it is not vital. In the war families went without fathers for many years. But as children learn by copying it is, of course, better to have two parents to copy than one – there are always some things one parent can do and the other cannot.

Childhood should be a happy, cheerful time and it seems so sad if it is unpleasant. In later years children will rarely remember unkind nannies, or unhappy circumstances, although these may well leave their mark, but I think a happy home makes a much more attractive, confident child, one who is civilized and responsive rather than aggressive or withdrawn. It is nice to meet a well-adjusted child who is friendly, who does not hide his face, who is uninhibited, who can take anybody on. One of my children used to hold out her hand when she was introduced to strangers, she was such an attractive little girl and it made people's day to meet her. Of course, there are shy children who are not so relaxed when meeting strangers, but I think as long as you can fill a child full of confidence he will be able to cope all right in the end.

OPPOSITE *That's what thumbs are for*

225

Because a home atmosphere is never perfect, children sometimes seem rather unhappy, although young children often feel frustrated rather than truly unhappy. I think that true unhappiness in little children only concerns relationships – either at home or at school with a bully. I have known little children who cry every morning when their mother leaves for work. I think it is insecurity that makes them like that. I think they often do not mind their mother leaving that actual day but in their subconscious they feel their mother is going for good. I think this insecurity is worse in families where there have been a lot of different keepers, but it could also be that a new sibling has arrived in the family or some other cause of unhappiness. If a young child is unhappy, there must be a reason and it is up to you to find the reason and remedy it.

1 · How do I build up my child's confidence?

Making your child feel secure

You should let your child develop without having to worry whether anybody is pleased with him or not. You should also avoid saying 'No' whenever possible. Children should always be treated like fellow human beings – you would never say 'No' flatly to a contemporary, you would think of a nicer way of putting it. So why should you say it to a child (see question 7)? Saying 'No' to a child either kills his initiative or makes him over-determined to succeed in what you want to repress. Once you, the 'No' person, has gone he will rebel. A friend of mine never allows her children to suck their thumbs and I was once with them when I saw her little girl, about four, doing this. This poor child was immediately told not to and so she obediently took her thumb out but it soon popped back in. The moment her nanny was out of the room of course she sucked away as hard as she could. If a child is continually frustrated from his earliest years, by all the time being told not to do things, all the time having a wall built up, when an opportunity comes to do something he is not allowed to do he jolly well does it. I think that fosters aggression. Some little boys I knew had a very good, but very strict nurse. These little boys were always most beautifully behaved. One day they were taken to a party and left there on their own as their nanny could not stay. They were like wild animals, they were rushing about and pushing and shoving, you couldn't believe they were these well-behaved little boys. Without their nanny they just went berserk. If their nanny had been there they would not have been allowed to.

As far as possible children should be able to please themselves in a home environment and should not be bullied and reprimanded; that way they are not repressed. We used to have children home to tea and they would be amazed at how much freedom my children always had: they were never restricted. Once when one of my boys was six, and he had a little friend home for tea, the two of them vanished into the bathroom for quite a while and when they appeared their faces were covered with some face paint. His nurse nearly went mad, she took him to the bathroom and scrubbed it all off. I was quite angry; after all, those face paints are washable and they had had such fun doing it and she just spoilt all the fun. If children can do as they please in their own environment, if they are not restricted and if there is somebody there who cares, then they have no need to be aggressive. They feel secure.

If a child can have his way within the safe environment that you have created for him it allows him to develop his own self-confident personality. At the playground if he wants to go on the rocking horse for thirty seconds and then on the swing for thirty seconds and then on the roundabout and then back on the swing and so on, then let him. It might be hard work for you but it is his fun time and opposing it will sow a little seed, he will have met with a bit of repression and a bit of aggression. Make it a happy hour. If you do not want him to have his own way in the playground, then do not take him there.

2 · Should I always let my child decide what he does?

No. When a child is very small he needs guidance and he needs to feel safe. He should not be asked to make a decision because being continually offered a choice of what he wants to eat or do makes him feel insecure and insecurity may make him a little aggressive. I have seen little children being constantly asked to make decisions that do not mean very much to them and often then being reprimanded ('Mummy did ask you, darling') if they do not want to eat the food they supposedly asked for. A little boy I know was continually asked and was an extremely aggressive child. It was because his mother looked to him for guidance and had done so ever since he was small. A pattern had been set in which this little boy always decided what he wanted to do and what had to be done. He was not mature enough to make proper decisions, he had not had any experience of life. He should never have been given any choice because he could not see the consequences. He was also so used to being asked that if his mother suddenly said 'We are going to do something' he would say 'No'.

Most children are potentially aggressive, although some more than others. It's very difficult to say exactly how or why aggression starts, but I think one of the most common forms of aggression is unknowingly caused by parents giving their children too much freedom of choice. Of course, you wouldn't want to repress your child so that he never makes a decision, but somehow giving a small child too much freedom of choice can lead to aggression. Although parents offer a choice from the best possible motives, I do not think it is conducive to a safe feeling in a child, and I do believe that it can lead to behaviour problems.

3 · What can harm a child's feeling of security?

I think a child is likely to become confused unless treated consistently. If the child has a series of keepers, who all have a different way of doing things, some doing their job well, some not so well, he doesn't know where he is. Something he was once allowed to do he can no longer do. Some children become quite withdrawn and some become very aggressive. The quieter child can become more and more withdrawn, and the bright child can become aggressive. With the withdrawn child it is as if they have had so many different people looking after them that they have somehow learnt not to mind what happens to them anymore; and nothing seems to make an impression on them.

When two children I knew were five and three their very caring nanny went away on holiday for two weeks and they were left with a very aggressive nanny

'My children were never restricted'

who hit them. In just two weeks those two children had been reduced to hollow souls. The sparkly younger child was sitting quite still on the sofa and the elder was twitching and blinking his eyes. They clung to their old nanny like leeches. They must have been so bewildered by suddenly being treated so repressively. They soon settled down once their old nanny was back, but I think many nervous habits are brought about by tension and repression.

4 · How do you think a child develops nervous habits from being repressed?

I think that if a child comes from a very relaxed home, nervous habits such as nail-biting, stammering and blinking can be brought about by an aggressive teacher at school or by an aggressive keeper at home. I think stammering, for example, is very often to do with the approach the keeper has to the child. An over-potting, over-correcting, over-aggressive person in charge of a child can lead to stammering because the child is afraid. Most children mispronounce words when they first start to talk. But if adults confuse a small child by over and over again aggressively pronouncing the word correctly in front of them: 'Animal, animal, animal, not "amnial"' a child might start stammering.

If a child has a true speech defect I would just pretend it is not there and stick up for him if I ever heard anyone making fun of him and the way he talked (see question 15). A speech defect should not be worried about and can be helped by speech therapy.

5 · Doesn't it annoy you if a child does something you don't want him to?

No. I let my children do everything. If a child has an idea and wants to carry it through, then let him. I am all for children experimenting. I remember so well taking one of my girls out one morning when she was about three. She wanted a little roll of sticky tape and so I bought it and gave it to her in her pushchair. All the way home she emptied the roll and she was really enjoying it, but when we got home she looked at it and started to cry as she could not get it back on the roll. I didn't stop her unrolling the tape – I would never have said 'Don't do that!' or 'No!' I just let her find out for herself what happens. After all, the sticky tape belonged to her. When she started to cry I did not say 'Serves you right' or scold her. I just said that we would buy a new roll tomorrow. But she had learnt about sticky tape and would never do that again. Within reason I like children to do what they want to do.

Unless danger is involved (see question 8), I never force a child to do anything he does not want to do. Never. I do not use any discipline, I simply encourage self-discipline. My sister always used to think all my children were absolutely

'Too much freedom of choice can lead to aggression'

The 'disobedient child'

ghastly. They said what they wanted and they occasionally broke things and behaved like you would expect children to. She does now think they have all turned out very well – and so they have.

6 · *Don't you tell a child off when he is being 'naughty'?*

No, I don't. During the first year of a child's life, nothing he does, however trying for adults, is his fault. From the age of one to two babies begin to get curious and 'into everything', but there is no need to reprimand them, simply alter your home a little to accommodate them while the phase lasts. One of my children always tipped up the waste-paper bin in the nursery, so I turned it into the toy container and we did not have a bin. If your child opens certain drawers in the kitchen then simply remove anything sharp or harmful, replacing them with wooden spoons and saucepan lids. I have known one-year-old children who have been slapped when they have done something 'naughty'. Often you will see them do that thing again and then just slap their own wrists. They are too young to know that slapping is a punishment, they have just thought it was part of the game (see question 10).

Although toddlers are able to do so many more things, they are not quite old enough to know about 'discipline'. If you are worried about losing them or them hurting themselves when they run off, simply put them on reins until you get to the park. They should be allowed to experience freedom. Of course, you will always need to try and keep them in sight, but let them do what they want and try to keep calm and relaxed about it. There should never be any need to tell a child off because he is 'naughty'. There is no such word in my vocabulary.

7 · *Don't you ever say 'No' to a child?*

Of course you have to say 'No' sometimes, but it is very important to mean 'No' when you say 'No' and mean 'Yes' when you say 'Yes' and it is a good idea to use both words sparingly.

When I want the children to do something I do not tell them what to do or what I am doing, I just simply get on with things, running the bath or laying the table, and they follow, they know what is happening. It gives them more of a feeling of freedom than having someone say 'Do this!' 'Do that!' or even '*Let's* do this or that'. If I call children it is always as part of the routine, rather than for something specific. When one of my girls was five and started school she slept in the top of the house and I still slept in the middle of the house with the baby. When she got up she would go to her parents and at 7.30 a.m. I would stand at the bottom of the stairs and simply call her name. She would come running down knowing it was getting dressed time, then breakfast and then school, but I would

just say her name, not 'Time to get dressed'. Let your behaviour be calm and consistent, then you never have to say 'No'.

Rather than saying 'No' I have always tried to offer an alternative to whatever I don't want a child to do because I think it is so important to be positive rather than negative. Instead of saying 'No' I always make a great point of distracting children, saying 'perhaps we better do this instead . . .' or 'Why don't we do so and so . . .?' With a young child I try to keep them out of the way of temptation in the first place, which is why I use a playpen and reins. Another way of saying 'No' is to ignore a child. If he is pulling open and shut a drawer which you would rather he did not touch and trying to attract your praise, or even just your attention, the best thing to do is just ignore it and he will soon get bored. If the drawer could be dangerous then stop him by simply removing him and calmly distracting him with something else.

Why not turn the waste-paper bin into a toy container if your child enjoys playing with it?

8 · But what if there is a serious danger? How do you stop a child doing something then?

Of course you must keep children out of danger but in their own space I think they should be allowed to do what they like, providing the space is child-proof – and you must make sure it is. There should not be anything in the room which could be a danger to them. But even if there are potentially dangerous items about, I always find it is best not to make a great song and dance about them. If there is a teapot on the table I never say to a child: 'Don't touch the teapot!' That will just draw their attention to it. If they want to touch it, let them. They will hurt their fingers, but they will not be seriously injured. If you forbid it, the moment your back is turned they will touch it and then they might tip it over and scald themselves. By letting them touch it gently they will have learnt by themselves not to touch it again. In the same way, if they want to try the hot English mustard that's on the table, give them a tiny, tiny bit – it won't hurt them. If you say 'It's too hot for you' they are likely to be even more curious about it and may help themselves to a large amount when you are not looking.

If you are out for tea in an adult room and your child starts playing with a really dangerous object you must just take him away from this as casually as possible. If you tell him not to touch saying, 'Electricity – HOT – Don't touch!' for example, you may just arouse his curiosity further and he will touch it when he knows you are not looking. I think it is so important when visiting an adult home to take some toys and books with you for your child to play with so you can distract him when he needs distracting. If you arrive empty handed, it does make it difficult to keep a young child amused when there is nothing for him to play with.

There are also dangers outside the home from which a child must be protected. If there is a real risk of his being injured of course you must do something about it. Always explain to the child what you are doing and why, though, once they are old enough to understand. I once held a little four-year-old friend's hand walking across the road and when we had reached the other side I released her hand and she hit me very hard in the tummy. I told her I had wanted to protect her, that I hadn't wanted a motor car to run over her, but she was right. I should have explained all that to her before grabbing her hand, out of politeness.

Punishing children

9 · Nanny, do you ever punish children?

In a way when you punish a child you are just getting rid of your own aggression; I don't think that it leaves any real mark on the child, it does momentarily, I suppose, make you feel better.

I do think that if a child is very exasperating, being rather provocative or extremely aggressive with their sibling, you do feel like saying 'Go to your room' just to get them out of the way. On several occasions I have sent a child off to his room (but not to bed, I would never do that because I don't think bed should ever be a punishment). I suppose it is a safety valve. You can get them off the scene and then you can keep calm. I remember the first time I sent one of my children up to her bedroom. She was about four and when I called her down an hour later for lunch, she walked down the stairs with her little nose in the air and said 'I did not like being sent to my room'. In a way she was quite right. I was really doing it for my own sake.

If a child is being extremely irritating, continuing to do something that he knows annoys you when you have repeatedly asked him to stop, it is tempting to say, 'If you do this, I will do that'. But if you do say this you need to be sure that you are in a position to do what you have said you will do, if he does go on. An unfulfilled threat is like a broken promise – the child feels he cannot trust your word. So never threaten a child with something you cannot or will not carry out.

10 · Would you ever smack a child?

I strongly disapprove of smacking children because it is hitting, which is hurting (see question 6). Why should you hurt a child because he has done something which you think he ought not to have done? Yet I could not truthfully say I have never smacked a child because I have, although only three or four times in fifty years. I remember one time very clearly because the child hit me back. Another time was when one of my children was lying in the road and refusing to get up and the third time was when two of my children were fighting each other. We were in the bathroom one day and one of them was beating the other rather hard with her head and I got so mad and smacked her bott very hard. I was defending the younger child and I was so exasperated, I was at the end of my tether. I should never have done it. I suppose it was the end of the day and I was tired. I certainly would never smack a child anywhere except on their bottom.

I think very often smacking is an automatic response. You can even see cats slapping their kittens with their paws. In the same way a busy mother with a demanding husband wanting his dinner, and children under her feet may well just lash out. It is the tension of the situation that makes you smack your child, it is often your frustration that causes your anger and sadly it is usually not the fault of the child. It is simply your patience snapping. Beating is cruelty, smacking is like a fuse blowing; it is a safety valve.

> *'There is no such word as "naughty" in my vocabulary'*

The 'aggressive' child

11 · My child starts fighting me and other people. What should I do?

If your child is aggressive, try and let him know at all times, even when he is taking it out on you, that he is safe and loved. If he wants to kick and scream then just leave him alone and let him go under the dining room table or wherever takes his fancy. I think children should be allowed to work out their aggressions. Once it is over I would try and keep it on a light note and never refer to it to anyone else in front of the child (see question 18 below).

I think dealing with aggression is very, very difficult. The child wants to attack another person, and quite often he will want to get this aggression out of his system and will not want to be cuddled and distracted. If you are looking after a child who is very aggressive you can see it coming and nine times out of ten you can steer it away, but often the aggression is against you, his keeper and he is so furious he wants to kick and punch you. I ignore it if a small child hits me, although if he is particularly aggressive then I do say 'That hurts. Could you please stop', but if I can, I do try and ignore it.

When an aggressive child is fairly small it is easier to ignore, but once they reach five or six I try and reason with them and say 'Please don't do that. It hurts. It really is most unfair. Why did you do that?' I would never say 'How would you like it being done to you?' because children are often not really in control of what they are doing. I would try and keep my admonishments as calm but as firm as possible. You often do not know what has made them want to lash out, seemingly unprovoked. You cannot see inside their heads or know what slight they have imagined and sometimes they feel they must let off steam. The last thing they want is to be cuddled and told to forget it.

A not particularly aggressive child often vents his frustration, by shouting 'I Hate You' to his keeper. A younger child is very honest; if he loves you he says so, if he hates you he says so. I remember a little girl saying 'I don't like you' to me once. I just smiled and said 'Well, I love you very much'. My answer took all the wind out of her sails. I think you have to reassure children in a very casual way.

Once children are a little older and say 'I don't like you' you can always smile and say 'Well, I don't like you very much either sometimes, but I'm not always saying it.' I think they are probably saying they do not like you to test you. You may well find that they often say it when they want to do something and cannot do it for some reason or another.

12 · What if my child attacks other children?

If a child starts hitting another child I would just scoop up the one that is being hit and cuddle him. I would never reprimand the aggressor, instead, if he did not have his keeper with him, I would cuddle him too and stop him hitting the other child, even if he then took it out on me. If the children are little (under five) I would never ask the hitter why he had hit the other child but if they were older I would. You may well find the child that was screaming louder was 'the guilty party' who most certainly needs to be talked to gently. I would try and understand what the aggressor was thinking and I would always be very much on his side. I would say 'Oh, I don't think he (the other child) is so bad. Why do you hate him? Why do you want to hurt him?' so we could have a discussion. It is important to let the aggressor try to talk and think it through. Cuddle them all the time though, and try to understand their point of view without encouraging it.

13 · What do you think about children fighting?

I do not like children fighting. None of my boys, or girls, were fighters. On the whole I do not think children 'pick fights' unless they have particularly aggressive parents or keepers from whom they learn. People say 'Oh well, they are boys' but I do not care if they are boys or girls. I cannot bear it when I hear people say 'A boy needs his father, because he needs to be tough.' I feel very strongly about this. People have their own characters and to make them tough (or aggressive) is something I do not think is very desirable.

I sometimes wonder whether mothers of bullies really do not care if their child is aggressive. I have met to my amazement people who really approve of and expect little boys to be 'tough'. A friend of mine's little boy was charming and I was horrified when I was once asked whether he had got out of his 'namby-pamby ways'. I do think people encourage toughness. When collecting children from school I have seen little boys fighting, shoving and pushing and their mothers just chatting to their friends and not doing anything about it. I do find it an extraordinary way to behave. I would never stand by and let my children fight.

14 · How do you stop children fighting?

When you have worked with children all your life you can soon spot a child who is going to be unruly. I would always jump on the 'problem' straight away before it got serious. I would never allow a child to shove or kick or push. I would stop it immediately. You can always see children getting all set to be a damned nuisance and you can stop it. Adults can always stop this sort of thing. Some people laugh it off but I do not think it is a laughing matter, an unruly child can ruin a whole party. I am known for wrenching fighters apart at parties and telling them that it was a party and they were to stop fighting.

If a child wants a fight I pull him off and make him and his opponent sit down,

'As long as you can fill a child full of confidence he will be able to cope all right in the end'

saying 'Stay there' quite fiercely. After a few minutes they can join in the fun again but it just gives them time to cool down, like fighting dogs. If a child is poking or pushing another child I would stop him at once, even if the other child is not being hurt. I would simply say 'Why are you poking Margaret? Don't do it any more'. One thing leads to another and it should be quite possible for a child to play without poking another child. If he cries when he is told off I would tell him to stop making that noise, but I would try not to tell him off in such an aggressive way that he cried. Of course I would not like it if anyone told my child off, but I would never let them get into such a state, I would tell them off myself before that.

Even the most gentle child will usually fight at some stage in his life but some children are more aggressive than others.

15 · My child seems to be getting bullied. What can I do about it?

Most boys never tell you at the time if they are being bullied, they only tell you afterwards. I stuck up for one of my girls because she actually told me, aged five or six, that she was being bullied by a particular girl. So when I went to collect my little girl from school one day I waited for this child (my girl wasn't there at that moment) and said to her 'How dare you be so unkind to my girl? You leave her alone at once, you wicked girl.' The child never bothered her again.

There is a school of thought that you should tell the teacher and she will cope with it, but very often they don't. They take the line that children will stand up for themselves but I think for a child to dread going to school because of a bully waiting is indefensible and I think it should be sorted out. It is terrible to be so unhappy. If the head does take action then this should also stop the bullying. The head did once give the child who had bullied one of my children a good hiding, which was probably the wrong thing to do, but he never bullied him again.

I think bullying happens all through a child's life and of course there is mental as well as physical bullying. John Betjeman told of his bullying at his London day school. It goes on all the time. Why do children bully other children? More often than not because the other children are different. It is frequently the sensitive, quiet child who is bullied or children who have unusual figures (small or large for their age), or very intelligent children. I think very often the bullies have met aggression at home. Children who push other children about probably do it because it is done to them, because they are bullied at home by their parents. One day I told a nanny I know that one of her children had bullied one of mine. She said 'Please don't talk to me about him, you don't know what his mother does to him'.

If one of my children was being bullied I would never say to a child 'You hit him back', or 'You must stick up for yourself'. I would actually speak to the bully

'I would tell him to stop bullying my child'

myself or if the bully belonged to somebody I knew I would ask the person to speak to him and tell him to stop bullying my child. And, if my child felt like it, I would suggest we invited the bully home for tea and see if the two children couldn't get along on a one-to-one.

16 · What do you do when small children bite and pull hair?

Around the age of a year to eighteen months children pull each other's hair, but that has nothing to do with aggression or insecurity. Hair is there to be pulled; it is intriguing and so they pull it. They smile as they do it – they don't know it hurts. They do not mean to be unkind, they are just being inquisitive and I would never scold a little child or pull his hair to show him how much it hurts, I would just remove the child's hair from his hands and move him away. Small children often pull your hair if you pick them up, they are just exploring, like feeling and touching and pulling and biting. If a small child bites you it is normally because he is excited and does not know how else to express himself, or possibly because he is teething, or even as a sign of affection – they sometimes slap you too as a sign of affection. I would just gently ask him not to do it again. I would never bite him back 'so he knows what it feels like'; children don't connect one situation with another so he wouldn't understand. It also means that you are then behaving like a one-year-old and what will he learn from that?

I did know a little boy who used to bite everybody – his nanny had to sit alone with him on one side of the park. He is now a very nice young man. It was a very interesting situation really, he had the best nanny you could ever have, so kind and gentle, so it wasn't that he was repressed. We never knew why, but he did bite lots of children, several times each, up to the age of four and then he stopped. Lots of children are biters. This little boy was very introverted, maybe he was born rather highly strung.

17 · What do you think about children and guns?

I never ever, ever, ever allowed guns in my nursery. Or, if it comes to that, soldiers. I didn't see an awful lot of play value in soldiers. The soldiers would all sit in a wooden fort and would kill each other and get knocked over. Rightly or wrongly, I didn't approve of them. If my children went to tea with somebody who had a gun, that wouldn't have anything to do with me because it wasn't my nursery. In fact, someone once gave one of my boys pretending revolvers with holsters and caps and he just sort of looked at them and gave them to me and I put them in the back of the cupboard. They were never mentioned again by either of us. I can't really see the point of introducing guns to children. There are so many interesting things to play with, so why give them guns or swords?

What does a three-year-old want with a plastic sword as big as himself?

All children meet older, possibly more violent children at school, if not before. I would discourage the friendship but often this is difficult. Certainly if a child came to my house who kept on talking about guns I would suggest various games to try and distract him and if he insisted on guns I would say 'We don't play with guns in my house' and hope for the best. When the 'undesirable' child goes home and your child starts pretend playing with guns I would ignore it as much as possible and it would pass. I would offer the child an alternative and I would say 'Please don't do that. I really don't think that killing people is a good game' or 'What a funny game to play'. As other more interesting things come along I think killing people would be forgotten.

The 'angry' child

18 · My child seems to have lots of temper tantrums. What should I do?

Unlike an aggressive child who is angry with another person, a child having a tantrum is angry with himself – often so angry that he will shout and kick his heels on the floor. The best thing to do if your child has a 'temper tantrum' is to just leave him alone to calm down. Most, though not all, children do have temper tantrums to a smaller or larger degree. Whatever happens do not let yourself be so ruled by your child that you begin to resent it. More often than not when a child is feeling angry and frustrated he will not do what you want him to, so just leave him alone. He will do it in his own time.

Most children feel angry at times. If you interrupt a child in the middle of a game he is enjoying to take him to a dental appointment of course the child will be very angry. He will feel frustrated and want to stay and you will have to be firm because you have to go to the dentist. Some children have frustrations which are more serious than this. They may be born with difficulties – what an adult might call a 'distorted point of view' – that you have to help them come to terms with. I knew a child who thought nobody liked him and it would make him so angry and frustrated he would have the most violent tantrums which started when he was two and lasted until he was quite old when, of course, he minded them so much.

When he was young and having one of his terrible rages I would cuddle him – unless he told me to go away – because I knew it was something he could not help and he needed reassuring. As he got older I would not take any notice unless he understood the reason for his rages and I felt it was possible to help. Once when he was about twelve, he was very sad about his inability to achieve anything in the holidays. That situation was easier to help with. We mended something together and he felt he had accomplished a task.

OPPOSITE *The cosy world of the nursery*

19 · My child screams and screams. What do you think this means?

One of my children did not so much have temper tantrums but rather screaming fits, again out of frustration. One of his first took place in the toy department of a large store. When I go shopping with children I seldom buy anything and they never think to ask me for anything either. We just look at all the toys. This boy was a different case. The first time we went to the toy department we looked at all the wonderful toys, as I usually did, but when it was time to go he started screaming because he did not want to leave. He had very powerful lungs and was a very strong child. I did not know what to do as we had to get home for lunch, so what I was driven to doing was locating something very small, like a small ball or a tiny animal from a farm and I said 'Shall we buy this?' Thank goodness, he stopped screaming and did not mind leaving when he had a little something. It meant that every time we went shopping I would quickly have to spot something cheap and cheerful to buy to lure him away from the shop.

This boy used to have the most terrible screaming fits. Sometimes we would go to the park via a drapers where he would scream and scream and scream. Or we would go into the Post Office and he would scream. He would scream in the park and do a lot of screaming on the way home. Once we were on a bus and he started screaming so much we eventually got off before our stop. I never ever scolded him because he was little and it was part of his make-up. Of course there was a reason, but I never really knew what it was. He began shouting when he was eighteen months old and still shouted when he was five. His father's theory was that it was generations of repression and he was the first member of the family to let it out. Once he screamed so much and looked so absolutely adorable with his little curls and his button-down shoes that a lady said to me 'Pick her up nurse, she's tired.' In the end we took a taxi.

With a screaming child you will just have to manage as best as you can. Do not get angry or punish the child, but do not hug him when he screams either. I would just stay with him and talk to him or take his hand and skip along if you are in the park. Try and lighten the atmosphere.

20 · If a child gets so angry is it because he is 'spoilt'?

When children are very angry and have temper tantrums or screaming fits people say they are 'spoilt' and that they are angry because they are not getting what they want. I still do not know what the word means. Do they mean that a perfect child has been spoilt? Are they really implying that you are ruining the little person who has come into your life? I often hear people say 'Don't pick up a crying baby, you'll spoil him'. How ridiculous. A baby wants to be comforted, he is not crying deliberately to be spiteful. Maybe you are indulging him, but you are not

'Just leave him alone to calm down'

spoiling him. Just remember the origin of the word. It is impossible to 'spoil' a baby.

However I do agree that over-indulging a child is a mistake. When people give their child everything he wants and more I do think it is wrong and very unkind to the child. It makes such a happy childhood for a child to look forward to his birthday or Christmas or someone coming from abroad who may bring a little gift home. A nanny friend of mine was with a little girl whose father brought her a present home every day. It seems such an unkind thing to do because to be given gifts all the time takes away your appreciation of things which is such an enjoyable thing to have. Somehow the excitement is lost if you are bombarded with presents all the time. It is such fun if you have not been used to getting things on a plate if you do suddenly get them. Once at the seaside with one of my girls I remember a lady with two little children, a baby and one about four, and we asked this lady to come and join us on the beach. The four-year-old had never ever been to the beach or played with a bucket or spade. She was in heaven. That is an extreme case but it did give her the most wonderful, wonderful joy. Of course it will probably not affect ('spoil') the child as an adult if he does get swamped with gifts because there will be so many new experiences in between now and then but I have observed that children who have very few treats really do turn out to be very nice people.

21 · How can I help my child overcome his shyness?

Although I always had lots of friends, when I was younger I always felt I was very shy. Looking back I think I first overcame my shyness when I was training and it made me realize that shyness was just when you feel as if you are less good than other people. But why should you? After all, you are jolly good.

For some reason it unsettles people seeing a shy child, they think there must be something wrong with him. It is so much easier to respect and encourage a child who is not shy that shy children often get denigrated. I think a shy child is often one who is thinking things over, who is not just going to do anything because everyone else does. I would rather describe such a child as 'sensitive' than shy.

It is possible to build up a shy child's confidence and at the same time try and retain his sensitivity. I think you can do an awful lot for a shy child. The great thing is not to scold or ridicule, but always be there with a hand or a word or whatever. When a child wants to hold my hand I would never ever say 'Oh, go on. You're a big boy'. If they want a hand I would hold it. I have heard people say in front of their child: 'He is so chatty at home but won't speak to new people'. Why should he accept people he does not know, especially as one day he will

> *'It is impossible to "spoil" a baby'*

The 'shy' child

be taught not to talk to strangers? I find that sort of behaviour is the sign of a very sensitive and intelligent child.

I also find the behaviour of many adults far too 'forward'. Why should a child want to be prodded and poked and tickled by a strange adult? So many adults take liberties with children. They would never walk up to a strange adult and start tickling him, so why a child? When I am with a group of people and a child is present who has never seen me before I simply smile at the child and then sit down and talk to my hostess. Usually after a short time the child will approach me, and if I have a small gift for him (or just a smile) I offer it and it will sometimes be accepted and sometimes not. A child, like an adult, should be accepted as he is and not ridiculed or criticized (see VIEW FROM THE PRAM).

One of my children was terribly shy until she was five. At parties she always held my hand, and if she left it for a moment I kept it by my side so if she wanted to hold it it was there. Now she is the most gregarious of my children. When she was almost five I took her to school for the first time and after I had changed her shoes and put on her pinafore, I stood her in a line with the other children and left her saying 'Bye, I'll see you at five'. When she came home she told me she had cried 'I want Nanny' and so they had let her sit by the fire. Nine months later she was invited to a party and when we got there she turned to me and said 'You can't stay. You weren't invited'. I was thrilled. From then on she never looked back.

22 · Do good manners matter?

Good manners are really thinking about other people; saying 'Excuse me' to get past people; passing your neighbour something they cannot reach during a meal and, of course, saying 'Thank you' to show the person you have noticed their kindness. But how can anyone expect a child under five to really think about anyone else?

I will never, ever forget a little three-year-old girl I once saw on the beach. She was running along the sand beaming with delight at her grandmother who was walking towards her carrying an ice-cream. As she got closer to her grandmother, her grandmother looked at her, holding the ice-cream firmly in her hand, and just said 'What do you say?' The child smiled. The grandmother repeated the question and the child became a bit confused. The grandmother repeated the question again quite aggressively and the child started crying. 'Right!' the grandmother said, 'You can't have the ice-cream'. The child was only about three, she was much too young to know about 'please' and 'thank you'. The smile should have shown how pleased and delighted the child was about her grandmother's thoughtful action, but the insecure grandmother needed her deed praised. In two years' time, when the child was five, she would have said 'Thank

Minding your manners

you' but she was too small. I felt so saddened by the grandmother's behaviour. I am very keen on good manners but I think a lot of it is greatly over-rated, especially with small children.

23 · *How do you think children learn manners?*

I do think that children learn by example. I always say 'Please' and 'Thank you' myself, whether someone is talking to me or to the child. On the other hand the mother who thinks that if she says 'Thank you' often enough the child will repeat it one day is probably a little too optimistic, or maybe too impatient. After all, until he understands *why* he is saying 'Thank you' you can't really expect him to remember to say it and he won't really understand until he is at least five. It annoys me when people say 'Yes. . . . and what else?' when they are asked by a small child whether they can have some bread, for example. I secretly quite admire the child if he answers 'Jam'. If I was the adult, I would just say 'Yes, certainly' and pass the child the bread without waiting for him to say 'Please' (see question 24).

24 · *When do you start teaching 'Please' and 'Thank You'?*

I only really start getting children to say 'Please' and 'Thank You' and 'Sorry' when they are five. Before that I make sure my manners are exemplary and if I am leaving a party with a child I will always say 'Thank you very much for the lovely party, Mary-Jane enjoyed it so much'. But that is enough until the child is five. I cannot bear it when people say 'Say thank you to Mrs So-and-So'. Why do they want their child to perform like a parrot? It is insulting to the child.

Once a child is five I remind him, out of earshot, before we leave the party to 'Hold out your hand, shake hands and say thank you'. I think most children do still have to be reminded about their manners at five and possibly even at six, but do it secretly. If you remind them gently beforehand they will remember to do it much better when you are not there the next time rather than saying it to them at the time. I think that good manners in a small child is very attractive, but I do not think it is attractive in a keeper to constantly be saying 'Say Please . . . say Thank You' all the time, because when the keeper is not there, the child will forget. If they do forget, I just say 'Thank you' to the hostess as I would normally and hope the child will notice me doing it.

I use the same technique when I introduce a child over the age of five to a new person. If there is someone in the drawing room I always say before we go in, 'When we go in, hold out your hand and say "How do you do, Mr Smith".' Once we are in the drawing room I never mention it again and if they forget, I just make sure they can learn from my example.

25 · Do you make a child write 'Thank you' letters?

After parties I always wrote a 'Thank you' postcard. Once the child was older and could read and write I would dictate the card, but when he was smaller I would write it myself and maybe he could put his name at the bottom. Once they had reached the age of five or six I would ask children to write their own cards. They always wrote thank you letters after a party but at Christmas and their birthday, when there were a lot of parcels, I would not expect a small child to do this. If you do want your child to write them then I think it is a very good idea to stagger the thank yous, but otherwise I or their mother would write them and they could sign them. Taking good manners too far can turn them into a bit of a chore which may put the child off when he is older.

Helping to write a 'thank you' letter. I make it fun so it will not put a child off when he is older

26 · What about saying 'Sorry'?

I would never make a child say 'Sorry' – it is only a word. When they are five or so they will understand about being upset and know what the word means, but up until then making a child apologize is a bit pointless. The child can say the word but it won't have any meaning for him. If a child breaks something precious, for example, I would show the child that I minded even though I am sure that they did not break the object on purpose. I would just pick the pieces up and say how sad I was because I did like it so much and perhaps it can be mended. If a child upsets an adult or another child they should know, but I wouldn't ask a small child to 'Say "Sorry"' – it won't mean anything to them. If the object could not be mended I would throw it away, but not in front of the child. If the object belonged to another grown-up, not me, I would apologize for the child; that way they can learn from my behaviour.

Golden rules

Help your child feel secure

1   Fill him with confidence. Be on his side.

2   Don't ask him to make decisions – freedom of choice will make a child confused and insecure.

3   Be consistent in your behaviour towards your child.

4   Never threaten a child with something you cannot carry out.

5   Avoid conflict by keeping to a routine and the child will follow.

Don't put your child down

1 Avoid saying 'No' to a child.

2 Encourage him to experiment – how else will he learn?

3 Allow him to develop his own personality.

4 Don't use discipline, encourage self-discipline.

5 Punishing a child is just a safety valve – for you.

Never encourage aggression

1 If your child is being bullied, don't expect him to stick up for himself. It is up to you to do something about it.

2 Stop all fighting as soon as possible.

3 Once children are old enough, talk to them about why they wanted to fight. Try to understand their point of view.

Don't expect perfect manners

1 Remember that children learn by example.

2 If you need to remind a child about saying 'Please' and 'Thank you', do it in private, not in front of others.

Index